Rolando Hinojosa's Klail City Death Trip Series

A Retrospective, New Directions

Edited by Stephen Miller and José Pablo Villalobos

Arte Público Press
Houston, Texas

Rolando Hinojosa's Klail City Death Trip Series: A Retrospective, New Directions is made possible through a grant from the City of Houston through the Houston Arts Alliance.

Recovering the past, creating the future

Arte Público Press
University of Houston
4902 Gulf Fwy, Bldg 19, Rm 100
Houston, Texas 77204-2004

Cover design by Mora Des¡gn
Photograph by Marsha Miller/UT Austin

Rolando Hinojosa's Klail City Death Trip Series : a Retrospective, New Directions / edited by Stephen Miller and José Pablo Villalobos.
p. cm.
ISBN 978-1-55885-767-4 (alk. paper)
1. Hinojosa, Rolando. Klail City death trip series. I. Miller, Stephen, 1946– editor of compilation. II. Villalobos, José Pablo, editor of compilation.
PQ7079.2.H5Z85 2013
863'.64—dc23

2013035095
CIP

∞ The paper used in this publication meets the requirements of the American National Standard for Information Sciences—Permanence of Paper for Printed Library Materials, ANSI Z39.48-1984.

11 12 13 14 15 16 17 18 10 9 8 7 6 5 4 3 2 1

Table of Contents

Appendix

Dedication

Rolando, many thanks for the trip.

Un "grand tour" para nuestros tiempos y espacios.

Acknowledgments

The co-editors of this volume wish to thank many entities and colleagues at Texas A&M University who made possible the publication of this volume. First among these are those which provided the funding for the February 2010 Symposium "Rolando Hinojosa's *Klail City Death Trip*: A Retrospective, New Directions": the Department of Sociology, the Melbern G. Glasscock Center for Humanities Research, the College of Liberal Arts, and most especially Larry Mitchell, then Interim Head of Hispanic Studies. The generous funding allowed for the gathering of a very distinguished group of established, mid-career and beginning scholars all united by their desire to discuss the work of Rolando Hinojosa, the Ellen Clayton Garwood Professor of Creative Writing at the University of Texas, and the recipient of an Honorary Doctor of Letters from Texas A&M University in 2007. From that very successful meeting, a smaller group of scholars, formed both of some of those who read at the Symposium, and others who did not, answered our request to submit essays for publication in this volume. More recently, sincere thanks are owed to Alberto Moreiras, the former Head of Hispanic Studies, and to Steven M. Oberhelman, Interim Head of the same Department, for organizing the funding for the subvention of this volume. Our gratitude also extends to Rolando Hinojosa: first for the *Klail City Death Trip* itself; and, second, for his participation in the Symposium and for other matters relating to the short interview that forms the appendix to this volume, as well as to prompt replies when we have queried him on matters relating to his biography and work. Finally, we thank the indispensable contributors to this collection of essays for their steadfast collaboration, and Nicolás Kanellos, the Director of Arte Público Press, and the staff of the Press for their encouragement and support.

S.M. and J.P.V.

Rolando Hinojosa and Contemporary U.S. Hispanic Literature

Stephen Miller and José Pablo Villalobos

> "It isn't true. The trip never ends. Only the travelers end. And even these can endure in memory, in stories. [. . .] It's necessary to return to the steps already taken in order to repeat them and to trace new paths beside them. It's necessary to begin the trip anew. The traveler returns to the way already travelled."
>
> —José Saramago, *Viaje a Portugal* (1981)

The present volume is meant as an homage to and continuation of *The Rolando Hinojosa Reader: Essays Historical and Critical* so ably coordinated and edited by José David Saldívar. That volume appeared first as a special number of the *Revista Chicano-Riqueña* 12.3-4 (1984), and then was published in book form by Arte Público Press in 1985. Since then the *Klail City Death Trip* Series (*KCDTS)* has gone from five volumes or "stops along the way" to fifteen, with the last volume to date—*We Happy Few* (2006)—being published a full generation after *The Rolando Hinojosa Reader*. The present collection of essays, always mindful of the scholarship and discussion of the field-shaping *Reader*, as well as subsequent scholarly work, is two things: a continuation of certain lines of research into the *KCDTS*; and a kind of "report" from the second decade of the 21st century on the new directions the *KCDTS* and critical conversation about it have taken since the early 1980s.

Rolando Hinojosa Smith's literary series the *Klail City Death Trip* may well be the most innovative and complex project of literary creation ever conceived and realized by a writer based in the United States. The *KCDT* consists to date of fifteen titles published between 1973 and 2006. While the starting point and time of the "trip" of the Series may be ultimately traced back to the 1749 arrival of the first Hinojosa to the Lower Río Grande Valley of South Texas, best known simply as "the Valley" or "*el Valle,*" the main actions of the *KCDT* are contemporary to the life of Hinojosa himself who was born in 1929. As sometimes happens in the roman-flueve series of other writers such as Benito Pérez Galdós, Emilia Pardo Bazán and William Faulkner, these actions and persons are centered in a fictional town and its surrounding area. Hinojosa's "Klail City," the county seat of the equally fictional "Belken County," is, like Orbajosa, Marianeda and Yoknapatawpha County, a composite which serves the writer to center "hir" own experience of the human and natural geography closest to "hir."

Hence, Klail City is not unlike Mercedes, Texas, the real Valley town where Rolando Hinojosa was born and where he spent much of his life before leaving the Valley; this happened after high school graduation in 1946 when he joined the U.S. Army in August of that year. After an eighteen-month hitch, which included training as an artillery man, he began studies at the University of Texas at Austin. Then, a little more than a year later, he was recalled to active duty and stationed in Japan as part of the Allied post-WWII occupation force. In June 1950, Hinojosa was incorporated into the hurriedly-formed Task Force Smith, the first U.S. response to the invasion of South Korea by the North. Hinojosa shares these life events with the two main characters of the *KCDT*: Rafa Buenrostro and Jehu Malacara. They, like him, come from a small town in the Valley, go into the Army following high school,[1] spend time in Japan, see much action in Korea, and become graduates of the University of Texas at Austin.

Neither of these two characters, however, is Hinojosa, especially in their years after Austin and Korea. While Hinojosa earned a Ph.D. in Spanish literature in 1969 and began a university-teaching career that continues even today as the Ellen Clayton Garwood Professor Creative Writing at Texas, Rafa Buenrostro received a law degree, but then began his adult career as a policeman and detective in Klail City in Belken County. For his part Jehu Malacara is first, more Hinojosa-like, a high school English teacher in Klail City, but then starts his career as a Klail City banker working for the mover-shaker Cooke-Blanchard-Klail family, a fictional creation which evokes the extended, real-life King Ranch family. The cousins Buenrostro and Malacara may, perhaps, be best viewed as the fictional vehicles through which Hinojosa portrays the generational experiences of many young Tejanos, i.e., the Texas Mexican Americans born in the Valley around the beginning of the Great Depression. A fundamental point to underscore: Buenrostro and Malacara are *not* immigrants. For like Hinojosa himself, the cousins are descendants of an eighteenth-century, southmost Rio Grande/Bravo Hispanic population which became an increasingly abused ethnic-linguistic minority following the Mexican-American War of 1846-48. For in many ways the treaty that ended the war, that of Guadalupe Hidalgo, left Hinojosa, Buenrostro and Malacara's people as despised foreigners in their own land. This means that four generations after Guadalupe Hidalgo, both the author and his characters have not only historical and folkloric knowledge of their ancestor's struggles, but also of their grandparents and parents generation's and of their own first-hand experience of some combination of ethnic prejudice, exploitation, oppression and violence. The contemporaneous time of the *KCDT* stands witness to this happening first at home in Texas, then in the upper Midwest of Mexican American migrant laborers, and then, while its protagonists serve in the U.S. Army, even in Japan and Korea. This said, Rafa and Jehu do have some good luck. Their early adulthood coincides with the ferment that began upon the return to the United States of WWII minority combat soldiers, accompanied by the G.I. Bill, and showed its greatest results beginning with the Civil Rights legislation of the 1960s and the wide-spread change of attitude toward minorities which that legislation marked and progressively implemented.

So it is that the *KCDT*, as seen and lived by Hinojosa and all his Valley Tejano and Anglo characters, portrays the transformation of that place and its peoples. It follows them as they go from living in a sleepy agricultural and ranching backwater of Mexican and American society and history, from where they must sometimes go north "to work the Welch grape vineyards near Lake Michigan,"[2] to our times. These are as the active NAFTA site of industry and commerce, and also the conflictive frontier of new immigration and drug wars. Hence, the *KCDT* traces the evolving relations between Anglos and Tejanos, Texans and Mexicans, and, not to be forgotten, the emergence of the Tejana as an independent person. Her experiences, especially in the 1960s and 1970s, are different from those of her recently enfranchised brothers, male cousins and friends, yet her gender has a diminishing social role as she pursues the same kinds of personal hopes, expectations and possibilities that her male cohort does. The *KCDT* reflects, then, how the professions and business are pursued with increasing success through to our day by way of the *KCDT*'s synthesis of Hinojosa, Buenrostro, Malacara and their Tejano and Tejana contemporaries.

The content and manner of Hinojosa's fictive portrayal of this great advance may be what most distinguishes the *KCDT* from other notable novelistic series in American literature. Tonally more like immigrant author Saul Bellow's Chicago on-the-make than, for example, like Faulkner's defeated South, Updike's increasingly gentrified Northeast, and McMurtry's dying southern Great Plains, Hinojosa's Valley is a place where his group finds an ever fuller present and more promising future as they become the majority population in Texas and, for that matter, across the American Southwest and (Alta) California. Moreover, while Hinojosa's Anglo author contemporaries center on those whose language of choice is English, Hinojosa's Tejanos and Anglos are often bilingual in Spanish and English and sometimes wholly bicultural. That said, the *KCDT* itself over time has become increasingly monolingual in English, and this fact has impacted the way Hinojosa has been perceived and read by critics. Some contextualization may help here.

The 1973 first edition of Hinojosa's first novel, *Estampas del Valle y otras obras*, is remarkable in many ways. It was the winner of the third annual Quinto Sol Prize for best Chicano creative work of the year, and was published as an illustrated bilingual edition with Hinojosa's Spanish being rendered into English by Gustavo Valadez under the title *Sketches of the Valley and Other Works*. Quinto Sol co-editor Herminio Ríos's untitled introduction in Spanish followed by his own version in English discussed the present and future readership of *Estampas* and other Chicano works, as well as the literary traditions to which such literature belongs.

Back in 1973 Ríos and his co-editor Octavio Romano had "two reading publics in mind."[3] The first was formed by "readers who are contemporary to the author, the work, and to the current efforts of the Chicanos" in literature and "all other disciplines of human knowledge" (7). The second group of readers, two generations later, is we now: we "of the future who will try to analyze and understand [the past Chicano] struggle" (7). Now, when one recalls that the first and second Quinto Sol Prizes were won by Tomás Rivera's Spanish language novel . . . *y no se lo tragó la tierra* (1971) and Rudolfo Anaya's English-language novel *Bless Me, Ultima* (1972), Hinojosa's Spanish-language *Estampas*, with accompanying English translation, reminds us that in the past that was the present of 1973, the Chicano literary movement was a mix of Spanish, English and Spanish/English bilingualism. But in our present, the Chicano movement in general has yielded to a more traditional form of American ethnic politics and today English is generally accepted as the public language of those interested in Hispanic/Latino issues in the United States. This evolution is reflected in the *KCDT* itself.

With the publication of the sixth title of the Series, *Rites and Witnesses* in 1982,[4] the *KCDT* signals definitively that English will also from then on be the primary language of the Series, while the second volume of the *KCDT*, *Korean Love Songs*, was written and published in English. This is because the first-person narrator Rafe Buenrostro tells of experiences in Japan and much more in Korea serving in an army in which English was virtually the only language of communication used among the officers and troops. Since the actions, characters and settings of the other early volumes of the *KCDT—Estampas del Valle y otras obras*, *Klail City y sus alrededores*, *Claros varones de Belken*—transpired mainly among the segregated, Anglo-subjected Tejano population and their primary language of communication was Spanish, it made perfect sense for Hinojosa to write about them in Spanish. For it was the language he and they used in talking with each other and remembering their common past. But with *Mi querido Rafa*, the fifth volume of the Series published in 1981, Hinojosa creates a totally bilingual Spanish-English set of letters from Jehu Malacara to Rafe Buenrostro. Ten years after Korea, Rafe is away from the Valley in a V.A. hospital because of persistent complications from the shrapnel wounds that required his hospitalization in Japan. The text is bilingual because the two cousins, living and working out of Klail City, are professionals whose primary language of business is English. Yet Jehu's bilingual letters to Rafe and, we assume, Rafe's to him, show the cousins sit uneasily astride the cultural-linguistic divide of the first decade of their professional careers: their early lives alienated them from the Anglo power structure, but both are now integrated into it. Meanwhile the bilingual, dying newspaperman P. Galindo, a generation older than the cousins and the third most important narrator of the *KCDT*, conducts the interviews which form the second part of *Mi querido Rafa* mostly in

Spanish. He uses English only when the interviewee is Anglo or is a Tejano who feels more comfortable speaking in English. Anticipating in fact part of the title of the next volume of the *KCDT*, *Rites and Witnesses*, Galindo is *the* witness of the linguistic and cultural evolution both of the Valley and of the earlier *KCDT* itself.

The final phase of this transition in the *KCDT* begins with the publication of *The Valley* in 1983. It is, to use Hinojosa's own term, a "recreation" from the original Spanish of *Estampas del Valle y otras obras* to a similarly idiomatic English.[5] Then followed recreations by Hinojosa into English of *Mi querido Rafa* (*Dear Rafe*-1985) and of *Klail City y sus alrededores* (*Klail City*-1987), and then of the Spanish-language recreation of the 1990 *Becky and Her Friends* into *Los amigos de Becky* a year later. Bilingual readers of the *KCDT* often comment that they prefer the Spanish originals to the English recreations, or, in the case of the Becky volumes, the original English to the Spanish-language recreation. While much can be said on this subject, important here is only that the four recreations in question are essential parts of the *KCDT* project. In light most especially of the bilingualism of *Mi querido Rafa* the recreations recall to mind Marshall McLuhan's dictum: "The medium is the message." Even without going so far as to affirm that the linguistic mediums of the *KCDT* are more important than the actions and characters of the Series, Hinojosa's linguistic registers—Spanish, English, bilingual in the two languages—require his readers to understand one thing above all: the experience of the "trip" that is the full *KCDT* stands the best chance of being completed only by the Spanish-English bilingual reader who can appreciate the differing cultural contextualizations that are part of his expression in each register. At the same time, and much as did the Chicano movement itself, Hinojosa came to terms with a fundamental reality. If he wanted to extend the potential audience for the *KCDT*, he had to make it more linguistically accessible. So while the editors of Quinto Sol and Bilingual Press, necessarily very cognizant of the need to sell books, published bilingual editions of *Estampas del Valle y otras obras*, *Generaciones y sem-*

blanzas,[6] and *Claros varones de Belken* which all included translations by others of Hinojosa's Spanish to English, it was a much more purposeful decision by Hinojosa to recreate linguistically and culturally his original texts. In a real sense, then, Hinojosa began with *The Valley* in 1983 to help actually create new works that would prosper with the second "reading public" hypothesized by Ríos ten years before, i.e., readers for whom the Chicano movement and *lucha* of the 1960s and 1970s would be the past, and who would be English-language dominant.

Another part of Ríos's introduction to the first edition of *Estampas del Valle y otras obras* concerns the traditions of Chicano literature, and, at the same time, is conceived of as a long term project. In large measure this is because, like Hinojosa himself, a Ph.D. in Spanish literature, many Chicano intellectuals from two generations ago who were interested in Hispanic literature and culture were steeped in the university-level study of literature written in Spanish, a tradition a thousand years long.[7] This fact contextualizes Ríos' assertion that "The fundamental issue before us is to establish the relationships that exist not only between Chicano literature and the rich Hispanic literary tradition," but also "within the scope of universal literature" ([7]).[8] To that end, Ríos asserts his position by making direct mention of not only Mexican and Spanish literary and cultural figures such as Julio Torri and Diego Torres Villarroel, but also U.S. and European authors like Norman Mailer and Thomas Mann ([7-8]). In combination with Ríos' view of there being two "reading publics" for Chicano literature and hence the *KCDT*, as early in its development as that body of literature then was, his point about tradition raises the following issue: to what extent did those early novels by Rivera, Anaya, Hinojosa and, it must be stressed, by their publishers, set the general course for all those authors male and female who would follow their early 1970s lead in the heyday of the Chicano Movement?

We know that with the passage of the decades since then, the original flowering of Chicano literature has spread to that of literature published almost solely in English by Hispanic/Latinos descended in their great numbers from immigrants to the United States from Mexico, the Caribbean and other parts of the Americas. One of the aims of the present volume is, therefore, to view the fifteen volumes of Hinojosa's *KCDT* as it travels through more than thirty years of a growing national and international panorama of the increasingly pronounced Hispanic presence in the United States and the world. Essays in this volume have a steady eye on the "death trip" itself as they contextualize the distances and areas travelled while bringing to bear the perspective our present time affords.

I: Broad Studies of the *Klail City Death Trip Series*

Joan Barrett's chapter, "A Cultural Journey: The Transformation of the Valley in the *Klail City Death Trip Series*," takes on the *KCDT* nearly in its entirety as it links the changes in Rafe Buenrostro and Jehu Malacara to those of the Valley. As these characters grow and evolve, so does the community to which they will forever belong. Barrett makes use of notions of hybridity and transculturation to counter arguments that may see in the transformation of the Valley a move away from its roots in the direction of complete assimilation to the mainstream. As this chapter argues rather, the constant push and pull that occurs when cultures come in contact provides evidence of an agency that results in the creation of a third space; a necessary location unique to itself that is a constantly negotiated product of both.

Nicolás Kanellos advances the thesis that both Rolando Hinojosa and the *KCDT* are products of the hybrid culture of the Texas-Mexican border. Different from readings rooted in Chicano narratives of resistance to or overcoming of Anglo dominance, Kanellos formulates and advances the case for reading the *KCDT* as the new creation of a Mexican-Anglo culture that is neither one nor the other, but which can only be experienced as a new and developing historical and cultural hybrid: the literary epic of what he calls "the Mestizo States of America."

In "The Polifacetic Individualism of Rolando Hinojosa's *Klail City Death Trip*," Mark McGraw also takes a panoramic approach to the Series. This chapter focuses specifically on the plight of the individual's needs in light of the communal exigencies placed upon him or her by both formal and informal institutions such as the church, the military, academia and patriarchy—all of which play an important role at various points throughout the *KCDT*. As McGraw calls it, "Hinojosan individualism" is mindful and respectful of institutions, but never to the point of allowing these the power to determine or limit one's aspirations. In the end, be it the Church, ethnicity, or their career, Rafa and Jehu—as Rolando Hinojosa himself and many of the characters that populate the *KCDT*—march to the beat of their own drum and look to improve themselves and their surroundings. Never succumbing to a determined role, the characters in the *Death Trip* that are most sympathetic to its readers are those who succeed in the face of adversity, even when these adversaries take the shape of social organizations.

After surveying the scholarship on the presence of Spanish Peninsular authors and work in the *KCDT*, Stephen Miller develops further the conversation on how Hinojosa dialogues with specific aspects of the Hispanic tradition as found in medieval, Golden Age and realist Spanish literature. Special, but by no means exclusive attention is given to the picaresque novel and the production of Benito Pérez Galdós, the subject of Hinojosa's 1969 Ph.D. dissertation directed by one of the most prominent Galdosian scholars of the twentieth century. Posited and explained is the overall thesis that during the nearly two decades of Hinojosa's B.A. through Ph.D. Spanish literary studies, Spanish Peninsular literature occupied a position of prominence that may have made it become a kind of literary "country" for a writer wanting to write in Spanish about his ethnic group while living in the Hispanic-phobic, Anglo-centric Valley and country of the period.[9]

In "The *Klail City Death Trip Series*: A Trovador's Eternal Space for an Enduring Transitory World," Alejandro Morales approaches the work of Rolando Hinojosa from a distinct perspective: that of the writer. As an accomplished bilingual novelist himself, Morales is the author of such titles as *Caras viejas y vino nuevo* (1975), *The Brick People* (1988) and, more recently, *The Captain of All These Men of Death* (2008). In his study of Hinojosa, Morales reflects on the historiographic metafiction that serves as history—the intra-history—of a place called Belken County, a place that, despite its clearly named protagonists, still functions in the order of a "micro-physics" that creates a network where everyone counts, where everyone, ordinary as he or she may be, has his or her space along that fictional continuum plotted by Hinojosa over space and time. Change as it may, this world is grounded firmly in the Mexican-American literary imaginary in such a way, Morales argues, that it serves as an archive which impedes it—along with the traditions and voices that compose it—from floating away.

II: Specialized Studies of the *Klail City Death Trip Series*

Eduardo Espina focuses on one aspect of *Estampas del Valle y otras obras*: the *estampa* itself as poetic subgenre in prose. In "Time That Remains in Time: The *Estampas* of Rolando Hinojosa-Smith," Espina traces the tradition of this subgenre in twentieth-century Spanish-language literature and notes how little noticed it has been despite having been cultivated by the likes of the Nobel Prize-winning Spanish poet Juan Ramón Jiménez and the Argentine novelist and short-story writer Julio Cortázar. The focus, though, of Espina's study is not historical. Rather, he probes how the *estampa* in itself and in Hinojosa most particularly portrays and otherwise forms a very particular experience of and meditation on the human time that is different from and beyond chronology and history.

In "The Wounds of War: Mapping Geographies of Trauma in Rolando Hinojosa's *Korean Love Songs*," María Herrera-Sobek is like Espina in treating a work by Hinojosa which has notable poetic dimensions. While the theory and thematics of Hinojosa's rendering of the psychological trauma suffered by American soldiers on the extremely fluid Korean battlefields dominates the study, Herrera-Sobek's exposition reflects the understated portrayals of true horror in the ironically-titled book. It is in her analyses of the actions, though, where Herrera-Sobek makes patent what Hinojosa's prose poem reveals in the quiet way of the narrator who records, more than comments on the life-changing events of intense, long periods under enemy fire.

Whereas Miller takes his comparativist approach across the Atlantic and through time as much as 600 years into the past, José E. Limón stays within the confines of Texas and the 20th-century Mexican-American and Anglo-American literary traditions in his chapter "Critical Regionalism and the Literature of Texas: The Comparative Case of Rolando Hinojosa and Larry McMurtry." Recognizing that despite sharing geographic space and time, and that both traditions are often displaced from one another, Limón makes the case for pairing both traditions to gain a better understanding of Texas writing as a whole. Approaching both McMurtry and Hinojosa through the lens of critical regionalism, this chapter addresses how both writers speak to how their particular version of Texas confronts and responds to the problems wrought by capitalist and post-capitalist modernity. Through a careful assessment of the work of each author, Limón concludes that Hinojosa's Texas offers a dialectical response to modernity whereas McMurtry's Texas offers less resistance and seems to be disappearing.

María Esther Quintana Millamoto's "Feminine Autonomy in *Becky and Her Friends* by Rolando Hinojosa" focuses specifically on the notion of feminine autonomy, a concept often deemed contradictory. In some way related to McGraw's overall look at individualism in the *Death Trip*, Quintana Millamoto specifically discusses the Mexican-American woman's quest for autonomy in the face of societal and familial tradition. Starting from theoretical readings that redefine autonomy in such a way that it incorporates attributes typically associated with femininity, this chapter highlights how Becky Escobar can be both female and autonomous in a world where these categories have been exclusive of each other.

Though in *Becky and Her Friends* a Mexican-American woman can achieve autonomy within a social group, rather than by separating herself from it as tradition implies, Quintana Millamoto concludes by critically displacing fiction into the realm of real life South Texas women such as Sonia Saldívar-Hull and Gloria Anzaldúa to establish the overall relativity that can emerge when considering the notion of feminine autonomy.

In "Rolando Hinojosa's Klail City: Sociological and Demographic Reflections of a Hometown," Rogelio Sáenz, a sociologist and demographer who hails from Mercedes, Texas, offers disciplinary perspectives on the hometown he shares with Hinojosa. In particular, this chapter overviews the social, political and demographic changes that Mercedes and the region have experienced over two periods in the last century. Furthermore, the analysis uses data from the American Community Survey to assess the demographic, social and economic variations that continue to exist today between Latinos and Anglos in the region. The chapter concludes with a discussion on the usefulness of drawing on social science and humanities approaches to situate Hinojosa's *KCDT*.

Much like Quintana Millamoto makes a leap from the fictional world of the *KCDT* to the real-life experience of women in the Valley, in "Rolando Hinojosa's Texas-Mexican Border: Writing the Landscape of Migrants, Mafias and Militarization" Klaus Zilles takes a similar approach. This multi-lingual, well-traveled German, who teaches in the Catalonian region of Spain, demonstrates Hinojosa's uncanny eye not just for social, but also historical and political developments of life along the U.S.-Mexico border. While this area has been partially explored by other critics in regard to Texas historiography, Zilles takes another route in his reading of *Ask a Policeman.* He details how the novel reflects and, at times, anticipates aspects of the so-called War on Drugs, the savagery of some of its battles, and the militarization of the border between the U.S. and Mexico. Reading *Ask a Policeman* primarily alongside Timothy Dunn's 1996 *The Militarization of the U.S.-Mexico Border, 1978-1992*, Zilles also connects Hinojosa's fictional rendition of migrants as criminally suspect to recent national events that have made people of Mexican descent suspicious in the eyes of nativists. As Zilles points out however, Hinojosa's view ends with a semblance of hope, something that often eludes life outside of fiction.

Finally, the Appendix to the present volume is an interview by Stephen Miller of Rolando Hinojosa on the subject of his doctoral-study years. There Hinojosa clarifies certain facts about that period which are not well-known to readers and critics, and tells what doctoral study in matters Hispanic meant in a leading Ph.D. program in the 1960s.

Notes

[1] There are significant differences between the military careers of Buenrostro and Malacara which are addressed in the article by Stephen Miller in this volume. The parallels with Hinojosa's Army life are closer to Buenrostro's.

[2] Hinojosa, *Klail City* (Houston: Arte Público Press, 1987), 62.

[3] No page number is printed in the first edition of *Estampas del Valle y otras obras* (Berkeley: Quinto Sol Publications, 1973) until p. 15. But collation of that page with the recto of the first leaf of the volume, which is the title page, establishes that the title page is p. 1, that the Spanish version of the untitled introduction occupies pp.[4-6], the English translation pp.[7-9] and so forth.

[4] This paragraph incorporates certain reasoned assumptions about the order of writing of the earlier volumes of the *KCDT* as well as presumes certain bibliographical knowledge about the complicated publication history of most especially the earlier volumes of the *KCDT*. These assumptions and publication history are explained in note 3 to Stephen Miller's contribution to this present volume.

[5] Note how the subtitle of the volume begins: "*A re-creation in narrative prose of* . . . ." (Tempe, AZ: Bilingual Press/Editorial Bilingüe, 1983, [3]).

[6] As with note 4 above, please see note 3 to the article by Stephen Miller for bibliographical comments on this title.

[7] The interview which is the Appendix to this volume supplies information in Hinojosa's own words about his university education in Spanish Peninsular literature.

[8] The term "fundamental issue" used here by Ríos is translated by him with the Spanish phrase "La cuestión palpitante" (*Estampas* [4]). Any reader familiar with the Hispanic tradition recognizes that phrase as the title of the 1881 book by the Spanish novelist Emilia Pardo Bazán, *La cuestión palpitante*, a study of the influence of French naturalism and Zola most especially in the Spanish Peninsular novel of the time. This "burning question" was so hot because of the contrast between what Spanish society viewed as French immorality challenging Spanish morality. Moreover, it was especially shocking to all that a woman, even though a countess fluent in French, would even have knowledge of such writers as Zola, let alone discuss them in print. Hence we can infer that for Ríos the issue of the place of Chicano literature in various traditions was very important.

[9] For more on this see the Appendix to this volume.

I. Broad Studies of the *Klail City Death Trip Series*

A Cultural Journey The Transformation of the Valley in the *Klail City Death Trip Series*

Joan Parmer Barrett
Baylor University

The *roman-fleuve* of *Klail City Death Trip* (*KCDT*) by Rolando Hinojosa traces the history of ten generations of a Texas Valley community from 1749, the date of the arrival of the José de Escandón (1700-1770) expedition, to the early 21st century. The fifteen volume chronicle, or *cronicón*, examines the cultural and historical trajectory of the culturally Mexican populace, *la raza*, in the lower Rio Grande Valley, but centers on its twentieth-century relations with Anglo society. Along the literary journey, the reader transitions from Spanish-only texts through a bilingual one to recreations and original tomes written directly in English. The coexistence of the two culture groups serves to shape and meld a new form of community throughout the Series. Although each subsequent text does not follow a rigid chronological sequence, the memories of places and people constantly color the present, and these works guide the reader through a process of the modernization of the Valley and its connection with other regions of Texas and the world.

The initial volumes of the Series portray the Anglos and Mexicans living in highly segregated communities, but over time, the interfacing of these two different groups and their world views creates an evolving, more integrated society. The preliminary conflicts of interest arise as a result of disputes over land ownership. The claims of *la raza* date from the eighteenth-century Spanish land grants while those of the Anglos arise mainly from the times of post-Civil War Reconstruction. Throughout the *KCDT*, the reader observes an increasingly dynamic interaction between the two cultures which eventually propels the Valley society toward post World War II and G.I. Bill hybrid structures that transform the collective perspective of *la raza* and move toward the *transculturation* of the Valley.

The philosophical conversation around the term *hybrid* has been an interdisciplinary debate and has been employed in discussions of identity, politics, religion, and social studies. In the anthropological and sociological fields, various critics have analyzed the cultural hybridization process through an investigation of literary discourse. The introduction of the term *transculturation* originated with the Cuban Fernando Ortiz in his book *Contrapunteo cubano del tabaco y del azúcar* (1940) where the anthropologist draws a distinction between the terms *acculturation* and *transculturation*.

> Entendemos que el vocablo **transculturación** expresa mayor las diferentes fases del proceso transitivo de una cultura a otra, porque éste no consiste solamente en adquirir una distinta cultura, que es lo que en rigor indica la voz anglo-americana **aculturación,** sino que el proceso implica también necesariamente la pérdida o desarraigo de una cultura precedente, lo que pudiera decirse una parcial **desculturación,** y, además, significa la consiguiente creación de nuevos fenómenos culturales que pudieran denominarse de **neoculturación**. . . . (96; my emphasis)

For Ortiz, acculturation is the process by which a dominated culture passively acquires and assimilates to the behavior and thought systems of a surrounding culture. By absorbing components of the dominant culture, the less assertive group acquires for itself a certain deculturation or partial loss of a prior composition. In contrast, transculturation is proposed to be the process by which a culture gains in a creative form certain elements of another culture through various phenomena of deculturation and others of neoculturation.

Ángel Rama adopted the term *transculturation* introduced by Fernando Ortiz to explore the hybrid nature of Hispanic discourse. In his work *Transculturación narrativa en América Latina* (1982), Rama investigates several novels in order to examine *la literatura transculturada* which reveals evidence of a rupture in the social order and is positioned in the conflictive intersection of societies and cultures. He proposes that the *mestizo* and his/her hybrid culture are situated in an environment where the key values of the dominated group are conserved. Rama's contribution to the theory of *transculturation* is to accentuate the active role of the dominated in the process (Sobrevilla 22-23). He contends that even though a dominated culture takes on elements of another more imposing societal presence, it does not participate in a process of *acculturation* to the dominant tradition rather "obligadamente, efectuará invenciones con un 'ars combinatorio' adecuado a la autonomía del propio sistema cultural" (Rama 38). The dominated culture is thus perceived as an active agent in its own transformation to a new third space.

According to the feminist writer Gloria Anzaldúa, the concept of the collision and subsequent coexistence of two antithetical groups rises above the extremes of truth and serves instead to fuse the two opposites into a unifying entity. She invokes the ancient Aztec goddess, Coatlicue, goddess of life and death, mother of fertility and savage devourer, as a comparable model for the synthesis of duality. That is to say that for Anzaldúa, the result of the fusion of the two groups will be the formation of a newly-generated third perspective. In chapter seven of *Borderlands/La Frontera* (1987), "La conciencia de la mestiza," Anzaldúa refers to José Vasconcelos' vision of a cosmic race, a fifth race that melds the four major races of the world, to be "una raza mestiza, una mezcla de razas afines, una raza de color—la primera raza síntesis del globo" (77). The writer, her soul existing between two contradictory worlds, considers the racial, ideological, cultural and biological fusion to be an "alien" consciousness in the making. "At the confluence of two or more genetic streams, with chromosomes constantly 'crossing over,' this mixture of races, rather than resulting in an inferior being, provides hybrid progeny" (77). The hybrid culture that results from the confrontation of two different social groups occupies a place where mutual cooperation enables the two factions to cooperate in the art of productive negotiating for mutual benefit (Ramírez 52).

The *transcultural* process of a society may be described as bidirectional like Janus, the Roman god of beginnings and endings, who is often depicted as a body with two heads back to back, facing opposite directions. One face views the past while the other looks toward the future. In a similar manner, the reader who follows the trajectory of Hinojosa's *KCDT* is a spectator on a literary voyage who witnesses the history of the early landowners, and eventually is able to visualize the future generations of the Valley society. The historical evolution of the Valley, its culture, and its people are the center of study. The struggle for survival and identity reveals passage through a transitional process to a new historic reality that leaves behind an earlier organic way of life. In the present work, we will trace the *transculturation* of the lower Rio Grande Valley of Texas—the Valley—through the life journey of its two most prominent characters, the cousins Rafe Buenrostro and Jehu Malacara (identified in the Spanish-language novels as Rafa and Jehú respectively), who were born into a segregated society around 1930.

Rafe and Jehu serve metaphorically as concrete examples of the social, political and economic evolution of the Valley's *raza* society. From a certain viewpoint that is not necessarily that of the *KCDT*, this process could be considered as leading to the realization of the American Dream. The influences and situations that guide their transformation are present in the dialogues and narrations of the characters themselves as well as in the narratives and conversations about them by other voices. The reader passes through three general time periods of the lives of Jehu and Rafe: the formative segregated years in the Valley, various life experiences away from the Valley, and the return to the Valley as professional adults in a still divided but more integrated society where socio-economic class and education level, not race, are the central markers. Rafe and Jehu are descendants of the old, land-based *raza* Hispanic society through whom deep roots of *claros varones/fair gentlemen* run.[1]

In the first few novels of the *KCDT*, racial and institutional segregation is the social reality in the Valley. Culturally Mexican adults sit outside chatting with family and neighbors after work, while children like Jehu and Rafe play chase through the Mexican American side of town. Inversely, the Anglos head directly home and go to bed soon after work. The Mexican children attend school in Spanish, and Don Manuel Guzmán, a U.S. born volunteer fighter in the Mexican Revolution of 1910, is the keeper of the peace in segregated Mexican town. By the later novels, the land-based *raza* Hispanic society is fading and the newer Mexican immigration influence has become more prominent. By the time that Jehu and Rafe return to the Valley as professionals, the racial division has diminished, Mexican and Anglo children attend the same schools, and, with the passage of more time, Mexican students have begun to seek educational opportunities at the relatively new, homegrown Belken State University.

A true citizen of the Mexican side of town, Jehu Malacara was also born into a situation of economic and social limitations. He had little association with the Anglo side until he started attending public school. But this was years after he was orphaned at age eight, briefly stayed with an harried aunt and her dysfunctional family, and generally bummed around until he was taken in by Don Víctor Peláez, a former horse trader and present-day circus owner. Jehu later attributes his desire to get a formal education to this disillusioned Mexican veteran of the 1910 Revolution who decided to make his life on the U.S. side of the Rio Grande. Don Víctor took Jehu under his wing and taught him practical skills such as how to change a tire while maintaining composure in the rain, hawk circus tickets, and how to read, beginning with medicine bottle labels. "It was because of him that I learned to read . . . my formal training and education, and what social manners I had come up with, were due, in no small part, to that man" (*The Valley* 27). The generosity shown by this Mexican "fair gentleman" to the orphaned Jehu is one of the happy chapters in the picaresque early life of the young man who survived by working odd jobs and by depending on the goodwill of others.

During the period when Jehu's cousin Rafe begins to attend public school, the narrative perspective begins to shift gradually from a closed Mexican culture toward a more integrated system with wider interaction with Anglo institutions. The first impressions of Rafe Buenrostro emerge in brief sketches of school memories and highlight the contrast between the Valley Anglo society and his own Mexican identity. He muses that Miss Moy, his first grade teacher, washes her hands with alcohol and uses a lot of Kleenex in class. Her sterile world differs from Rafe's own experience. Though only a child, Rafe recognizes that his reality is not the same as Miss Moy's, but he quickly gives her credit for having taught him to read. This valued skill eventually develops into a lifelong passion. In what serves as another example of these two worlds, Rafe also recalls a Mexican schoolmate who is ashamed to tell Miss Bunn that she ate a typical Mexican-style breakfast of a tortilla with peanut butter. Instead, she tells Miss Bunn what she expects to hear: she had eaten two scrambled eggs with toast and jelly and a glass of orange juice, a typical Anglo breakfast (*The Valley* 43). On the other hand there are some Mexican students who do not understand or refuse to adapt to new laws of conduct in the presence of the Anglo institutions. Leo Pumarejo, for example, is not taken with impressing the teacher and tells the truth about his breakfast: he had "one flour tortilla WITH PLENTY OF PEANUT BUTTER!" (*The Valley* 43; capitals in original text).

This new conscience of adapting contributes to the transformation of the Valley culture seemingly without compromising its roots or values. The eventual result is a new way of life for some Mexicans: a culture based on that which is *raza*-Mexican consolidating itself in its present situation within an Anglo framework. Even as early as junior high, Rafe, Jehu, and others initiate a boycott of the football team until they receive the same equipment as the Anglo players. They carry on the self-reliant, assertive tradition of *claros varones* like Don Manuel Guzmán when he says to men of his own time, " . . . the four of us here can still go out in the woods and live off the land . . . I don't know of too many things the four of us can't handle" (*The Valley* 112). Rafe's cohort has a similar sense of solidarity and pride.

Jehu and Rafe began associating with Anglos in an educational setting; however, they both continued to bartend off and on during their youth on the Mexican side of town. While behind the counter, they were privy to the conversations of the older generation as they downed *cervezas* and protested the changing society. Rafe heard about the discrimination that his people had suffered at the hands of *rinches* (the Texas Rangers) and the scorn of *la raza* when the Anglo from the water company came to cut off the neighbors' water because they had not paid. The tales passed on by the elders were contemplated and conserved by the two cousins who developed into depositories of the Valley past and simultaneously initiators of a new generation with hope for a different life experience.

Now it should be remembered that right after high school graduation Rafe, Jehu and other *raza* friends join the U.S. Army in August 1946. Following an initial year-long stint, Rafe leaves active service for the reserves and begins studies at the University of Texas in Austin. But he is recalled to service and winds up fighting during the first year and a half of the Korean War. Now it is, it seems, upon his first return to the Valley from his first stint in the Army, and finding perhaps too much unchanged, that Rafe finds a way of negotiating the problematic situations he re-encountered in Klail City and environs: "Leaving the Valley for a while; I've registered at the University up in Austin. It'll be a new town for me. Will it be a new life? We'll see" (*The Valley* 54). By hitting upon this plan, Rafe rejects putting himself in the same position as earlier *raza* generations while not rejecting his Mexican heritage.

While not discounting his first hitch in the Army, nor his first period as a university student, it appears that the young Rafe's most significant experience outside Belken County is the already-mentioned deployment to the Korean War. He and three of his friends from the North Ward School find themselves together in Korea where they encounter not only a foreign enemy, but also racial and social prejudice among the ranks of fellow soldiers. The official language spoken among military personnel is English, and the Valley soldiers are goaded for speaking the alien Spanish among themselves. "And . . . and, you speak Spanish? . . . Sure . . . (Laughs) . . . What's so funny? . . . I speak Spanish all the time when I'm home . . . " (*Rites and Witnesses* 16). Disaster, loss and racial discrimination reverberate from the Far East to the Valley in *Korean Love Songs* (1978). The verses are written in English in the tradition of British World War I poetry where surrealism and romanticism combine to portray Rafe's sometimes difficult, sometimes tragic experiences at the front with both literary and illustrative depictions. Many comrades, lifelong and new, are lost to bombs and bullets as well as to careless noncombat situations.

It is notable to mention that Rafe, during his second stint in the Army—as we learn in *The Useless Servants* (1993), the novel of Korea published fifteen years after the poems of *Korean Love Songs*—keeps a journal of daily activities with names and places where he also mentions the exchange of letters from home which keep him abreast of Valley life. In the texts that narrate Rafe's military career, the Valley soldier ponders the implications of fighting familiar racial prejudice in a foreign land. He considers the human factor in life and death issues such as foes against friends and war versus peace in the face of a world that has forever changed. While being mindful of the continued prevalence of racism in both worlds, Rafe's sights are on the Valley and taking advantage of the benefits of the G.I. Bill that will allow him to become a useful member of the new Valley that begins to develop after World War II.

Scattered throughout the depictions of war in *The Useless Servants*, the reader encounters titles of books that Rafe devours during his sporadic free time. The Valley soldier contextualizes the passages in his own life and military experiences and examines the state of Chicanos as a subaltern group in the mainstream military reality. During a respite from battle, Rafe traces a familiar historical connection:

> Finished a small book by a Greek soldier, Xenophon, who brought back his army across the Middle East . . . much like Cabeza de Vaca's trek through Texas and the Southwest. Started . . . *Histories* . . . Pretty fantastic stuff at times; some entries read like the stories Columbus' men brought over from the New World. Got two detective stories. . . . (*The Useless Servants* 171)

His attraction to reading about military adventures and detective stories serves to alert the reader to a future logical transformation from military service to a profession in law enforcement that Rafe will follow in the later novels of *KCDT.* The histories he devours evoke parallels between his two cultural realities: Korean victims of war and Valley victims of injustice. Through reading about prior historical struggles, Rafe comes to view his military position in Korea as part of the forces of oppression much like the invading conquistadores and the Anglo land grabbers of the Valley. His friends, however, recognize him to be a man who hated the war but also one who completed his duty (187). He recognizes the devastation that historical violence has caused and vows to return home to be a positive force to eradicate injustices within his realm of influence.

Rafe's love of reading naturally leads to a propensity to jot down thoughts and mundane daily activities, but his testimony surges from a deeper place. The details and lessons learned from battle are not lost on him. Just as Rafe has been able to survive the struggles encountered in the Valley during his youth and in the later pursuit of a higher education, he is also able to evaluate and clearly differentiate the behavior of soldiers in a foreign war situation. There are those who get the job done and those who abandoned the battle and "didn't pick up their carbines to fire . . . hid in their trucks . . . " (*The Useless Servants* 81). Rafe's personal journey from displaced orphan to soldier has led to a maturation of discerning abilities that help him make decisions that will serve him well in the future. He recalls Chaplain James P. Leary's quotation of Luke 17:10: "Well, will we then be like the useless servants who did nothing more than that which was commanded of us?" (184). Rafe accepts his duties as a soldier and goes beyond the minimum standards, which for him extend to returning home and consoling the families of his lost buddies: " . . . I'm the one who *will* make it back . . . I'm the one who'll talk to Charlie's sisters and dad. I'm the one who'll talk to the Vielma family. This is what we do" (*The Useless Servants* 168). Rafe notes in his journal that from his military experience, he has observed two kinds of behavior in the face of war: those who face adversity head on and those who retreat and are given to mere observation. Rafe is firm that he will be one who confronts challenges with dignity and strength unlike many he has known in the Valley and during his military tour.

Rafe contemplates his experiences of life and death in the war and compares them to his Valley home. He will not be the same again after the death and destruction he survives in Korea; yet, neither will he and those like him perceive the Valley to which they return in the same way as did earlier generations. At the end of *Korean Love Songs*, his tour of duty complete, Rafe writes: "It's back to Klail/ That slice of hell, heaven/ Purgatory and land of our Fathers" (53). His experiences of war and meeting many diverse comrades have given him new understanding and confidence. Just as the military was dominated by Anglo society and he won combat medals adapting to and mastering the rules of the U.S. Army, and the life-and-death challenges of combat itself, Rafe will similarly adapt and prosper in the Valley that for good or bad has been altered by the Anglo presence.

Upon his return home, Rafe observes that more young *raza* speak increasingly in English and that some have lost their ability or desire to speak Spanish. Rafe now becomes even more important as a vital bridge of cultural continuity and comprehension between the old and the new Valley. This development is underlined by a new element of *The Valley*, the 1983 English recreation by Hinojosa of the first volume of the *KCDT*, *Estampas del Valle*, published ten years earlier. There is an epigraph taken from Matthew Arnold inserted between the "Contents" page and the first page of the novel that aptly describes the new Valley *raza* youth: "Born between two worlds, one dead and one as yet unborn" (*The Valley* 9). This historic period of post-WWII and post-Korea marks a transition for Rafe and the Valley from a past segregated *raza* society toward a new, increasingly hybrid structure stemming from the continued synthesis of two distinct cultures.

In *Claros varones*, Esteban Echevarría, a prominent old veteran, "tiene la palabra" as he laments how the Valley has changed since his day: " . . . youngsters who no longer speak Spanish . . . the Valley's no longer the Valley, folks . . . Ranchers who don't ranch . . . Pharmacists with degrees but who don't even know who's who . . . the founding families are drying up . . . Where are those truckers who used to take people up North? . . . dead and gone . . . " (206).

Upon the return of Korean War veterans to the United States, there was a significant increase in enrollment in institutions of higher education. The G.I. Bill provided scholarships to returning veterans and opened universities to a wider socioeconomic group than in past years:

> Thousands of veterans used the GI Bill to go to school. Veterans made up 49 percent of U.S. college enrollment in 1947. Nationally, 7.8 million veterans trained at colleges, trade schools and in business and agriculture training programs. Later, the law was changed, in 1952, to help veterans of the Korean War . . . Some

> of the veterans went to college and never returned to the farm. (Reinhardt)

The presupposition that higher education was the privilege of the Anglo upper classes was changing in Texas. Like many veterans of all races and classes who previously would not have thought of college, the *KCDT* series places Rafe and Jehu as forerunners of the new generation of the Valley who took advantage of the G.I. Bill so that they could participate in a higher level of socio-economic life, and in so doing would become important players in the transformation of the Valley.

Nearly ten years after the rocket explosion that injured him in Korea, Rafe is receiving recurrent treatment for the shrapnel wounds near his eyes at the William Barrett, Texas, V.A. Hospital, and his cousin Jehu pens letters that keep him informed about Valley news. These letters and other documents are woven into a multi-perspective narrative, and the compiler of the book, the writer (the "wri"), details the contents of a "packet of letters addressed to and read originally by Rafe Buenrostro (Atty.-at-Law and currently a lieutenant of detectives in the District Attorney's office in Belken County) . . . [from] his cousin, Jehu Malacara, at that time, the chief loan officer at the Klail City First National Bank" (*Dear Rafe* 1).[2] Written in a style of select coded bilingual expression that could only be used among intimate friends, *Dear Rafe* explores the now essentially bilingual Valley from the perspective of the two cousins whose education and experience have won them important places among their first cohort of *raza* professionals integrating themselves into the power structure of Valley Anglo society. The reader becomes privy to the backroom negotiations of the controlling bank owned by the Klail-Blanchard-Cooke family and presided over by their in-law, Noddy Perkins, and his efforts to place his own selected political candidates, such as Ira Escobar, in office.

Much to Noddy's dismay, Jehu keeps at arm's length any offer to be involved in Belken County politics and his reluctance to participate is interestingly contrasted with Escobar's eagerness to be elected to public office and to be subsequently embraced by the Anglo elite. The reader learns that Jehu was hired by Noddy himself because of his banking skills. In sharp contrast, Escobar acquired his job because of banking connections and membership in the Leguizamón clan that came to the Valley around 1900 and made common cause with the Anglos against the *raza* represented by the land-holding old families dating back to the 18th century. While working at the bank, Jehu keenly observes that the Texas Mexicans, one of his English-language terms for *la raza*, are "learning a bit here and there" (*Dear Rafe* 25). He points out that in this upwardly mobilizing bilingual society of Belken County, there are presently four Mexican attorneys and two specialize in real estate. When Ibby Cooke declares, in reference to Jehu's hiring at the bank, that "we never needed Mexicans before," Noddy Perkins retorts, "We do now . . . " (*Rites and Witnesses* 7). The Mexicans are beginning to participate in the political and economic processes and are starting to take advantage of the loans and other financial aid available in order to recover land that had been lost to *la raza* for years. The Anglos still possess more wealth and influence, but economic prospects are improving for the Mexicans who are learning to maneuver in the Anglo legal and financial world.

In a bilingual Valley, the Anglo power brokers like Noddy Perkins visualize a great opportunity to gain the voting favor of the *raza*. A popular space for the Mexican community after hours is the city park; therefore, many candidates use the outdoor parks and events to reach potential voters. Rather than ignoring or avoiding the Mexican community, a new dynamic has emerged: the Anglo holders of power now need the Mexican vote. Jehu describes the political landscape as "Anglo politics, Mexican food, Texas beer" (*Dear Rafe* 28)—a seemingly true hybrid social structure. However, even though this new paradigm offers promise for a more mutually beneficial cooperation between Anglos and Mexicans, Jehu suggests that many Mexicans like Ira Escobar present themselves for office as mere puppets of wealthy Anglos like Noddy, and in turn, some Anglo candidates deceptively accentuate their even remote family connections to the Mexican culture only to garner the Mexican vote. Texas beer flows freely and Mexican food is the fare of election season, but the political spread is still not accessible for equal consumption.

Although the Mexicans have begun to activate their right to vote and present themselves as candidates in the public sphere, the political scene is not free from bias and scheming. Noddy Perkins continues to manipulate the elections behind and in front of the scenes, and the Mexicans are not unified in selecting their own nominees. Ninety-year old Esteban Echevarría, who represents the historical memory of the old Valley, laments that the Mexicans in Ruffing "side with *them* . . . " in the race for commissioner of Belken " . . . against our people. Bunch 'a sell-outs" (*Claros varones/Fair Gentlemen* 198). "We're doing the same thing that was done to us in the last century. When that happened, the few Mexican families with any land got taken by those Mexicanos who allied themselves with the Anglos" (*Claros varones/Fair Gentlemen* 202). The Leguizamóns, that family of latecomers to the Valley whose morals changed direction with the wind or with whatever proposition benefitted them economically, put forward one of their relatives against another Mexican candidate, and thus split the Mexican vote: "The division began at home and here's where it's got to be taken care of" (*Claros varones/Fair Gentlemen* 204). Echevarría places blame for the loss on la *raza* for not unifying against the Texas Anglos who always seem to come out ahead in these matters. Echevarría's authoritative voice, the collective memory of such events of historical significance in the Mexican community, serves to emphasize the painfully slow progress in the area of political parity in the Valley.

Some Valley Mexicans now occupy a seat at the table of politics, but are not drawn in by the persuasive and prominent Anglo institutions. At a Valley political rally, Jehu introduces his date, the pharmacist Olivia San Esteban, to Becky Escobar, the socially-striving wife of the much-manipulated elected official Ira Escobar. Becky's enthusiasm for inducting Olivia into the Women's Club stands out against Olivia's apparent lack of interest in such social pastimes. Olivia is a prime example of the new order of *raza* women and a marked deviation from traditional Hispanic female stereotypes. Like Jehu, the independent Olivia prefers to blaze her own trail and not allow political or social institutions to dictate her journey. In *Dear Rafe*, Olivia herself testifies that "I want to go to med school, and Jehu will help . . . he'd be a . . . support . . . " (77). He endorses her desire to go to medical school even when Olivia's own male family members object. Through Olivia's welcoming assessment of Jehu's open attitude toward her career, the reader notes a new order of Valley male that stands out against the traditional *latino* male philosophy that restricts women's participation in the public sphere.

Jehu is portrayed as an independent thinker in a long line of Mexican *caballeros* who is a solid citizen, much like Mexicantown constable Don Manuel, who helped in his day to take care of widows and orphans, and similar to Don Víctor Paláez, veteran of the Mexican Revolution, who took Jehu under his wing when he was orphaned. After working for a while as a loan officer in Noddy's bank, Jehu (no longer Jehú) unexpectedly disappears from Valley society along with his accented name. His sudden departure raises eyebrows among the Valley Mexicans and Anglos, and many disappearance theories are considered by citizens including theft, an illicit affair, and a personal conflict with the banker. The "wri," P. Galindo, interviews several dozen characters in *Mi querido Rafa* and *Dear Rafe* in an effort to highlight Jehu's importance in the community and to solve the mystery of his quick and unexplained exit. However, after the dust settles, the narrator explains that Jehu simply went to Austin to take advantage of the G.I. Bill, a perk from his military experience, and completed his degree in English. The narrator is convinced that Jehu will return to Klail City someday; " . . . he is, after all, a native son" (*Dear Rafe* 128). Many citizens, including Noddy Perkins, his boss at the bank, recognize the potential in Jehu and view him as someone to be trusted. "Jehu's got a job here whenever he wants it . . . if he wants his job back, it's his" (*Dear Rafe* 85).

When he goes back to the Valley as the first Texas Mexican to teach English in his old high school, Jehu's memories of the racial conflicts he suffered during his early school days echo in the hallways of his mind. During the twenty-second class homecoming reunion he sits with Elsinore Chapman with whom he has recently been a teaching colleague at Klail High. He is reminded of the fifteen year-old Elsinore who was authorized by a teacher to block his way to the school library because he had spoken in a loud voice in Spanish in the hallowed halls of books. Elsinore now waves at him with the same hand she used to deny him entry. Jehu carries out his role as the guardian of history of Belken County when he attends the reunion and in his mind reviews the events of prior school days that predict the future of each of the students along racial, economic, and political lines. Thinking back to graduation night in the novel *Klail City*, Jehu recalls "Diplomas in hand, and it'll be the Army for many of us. The Super's son had flat feet, but not so flat that he couldn't play ball up in Boulder . . . " (141). Even after attaining his superior education and returning as an authority figure in the long-integrated educational institution, Jehu still harbors memories of his turbulent childhood as the Other in an Anglo world and of the animosity and distance between the two cultural spheres of the Valley: the Anglo and the Mexican and those who served their country and those who found a way to defer—those who do and those who do not contribute.

Even though racism and social class distinction are still alive and well in the Valley in the later works of *KCDT*, the conflicts and alliances tend to be more political or professional. Many Anglos and Mexican Americans now compete on the same level politically, socially and economically. Both Mexican and Anglo Americans, including Rafe and Sam Dorson who are personal friends and have been partners for fifteen years in law enforcement, fight the violence of the international drug trade. Jehu is not just an employee needed to fill a racial quota at the bank, but rather has become a valued officer and Noddy's personal friend. Like many *bolillos* (a Valley term for Anglos) Noddy speaks Spanish to some degree and his central role in the business of the Klail Bank is due to his willingness to interact with the Mexicans since "Neither Ibby [Cooke] nor Junior [Klail] . . . would mix with the Mexicans" (*Rites and Witnesses* 35).

By the final novel of the *KCDT*, *We Happy Few*, both Jehu and Rafe are contributing members of Valley society and have been influential as the emerging exemplary models of *la raza*. Along with others of their generation, they have inspired and encouraged young people of the following generation to pursue higher education. With his bilingual skills, military experience and law degree, Rafe is named the Chief Inspector of Belken County Police while Jehu has traveled the path from orphan to odd jobs through the military to a university education. Jehu's journey has carried him from teacher to loan officer, Chief Loan Officer, to Cashier, and ultimately to President of the Klail City Bank.

The modern generation of university students in the Valley seems less defined by racial identity and more focused on achieving individual success. These students receive scholarships and sports equipment because of Jehu's position at the bank, which allows him to generously allocate community-service funds to support them. When a student named Eric Rodríguez wants to protest alleged racism by the Belken State University administration, and states that Belken students must be mindful of what their peers in California, New Mexico and Arizona will think and say, his fellow Valley Mexican students ultimately reject the sit-in Eric wants to lead. "I'm a jerk for listening to you, Eric," says Cindy Villareal; "I'm going to the dorm and write a letter of apology to the President and a letter of thanks, too" (*We Happy Few* 33). And, agreeing with Cindy, Thelma Lou Cantú tells Eric: "And don't call me a *vendida*" (34), later adding: "Belken isn't perfect, but it's home and it's ours" (35). Most Texas *raza* students are determined to gain a superior education at their university in the Valley.

In the modern Valley, fewer distinctions separate Anglos and Mexicans who occupy a variety of professions. Many Anglos and *la raza* speak Spanish and English equally well. There are—both good and bad—soldiers, teachers, bankers, pharmacists, politicians and laborers. There are still many who work for daily wages, and even though the middle class does not have a lot of money, there has been a boom in the number of banking institutions which serve to shelter illegal drug funds. Jehu is the trusted professional in whom two female bank officers confide facts of banking corruption in *Ask a Policeman* (1998). Rafe is a detective/policeman who is assigned to investigate crimes in the United States as well as across the Rio Grande. Violence, as in the day of the Mexican-town constable Don Manuel, is no longer centered in the local cantina or house of prostitution where arguments lead to drawn knives and *mano a mano* confrontations, but has escalated to active pursuit by plain-clothes and uniformed policemen of international criminals; uzis, cocaine trade, airplanes and even a military tank are now part of the equation.

To Belken State students and graduates, the quality of academic experience and the complexity of social networking are increasingly more important than the racial divisions of earlier years. Many Valley residents value higher education and serve as professors and regents of Belken State, the first accredited university in the Valley. In *We Happy Few*, a professor at Belken identified only by his first name, Beto, is pressing his colleagues to give him tenure, but they are holding his feet to the fire: " . . . your Ph.D. is six years old, and you haven't published a book . . . It's a vanity press publication . . . not . . . from a refereed journal . . . the community . . . expects us to work, just like they do" (60). The transition from a struggling local university to a more sophisticated, academic one is in progress and requires higher standards for professors who must merit promotions, not depend on personal or identity politics.

Belken State's search for a new president sheds light on a diverse board of regents, its transformation in the selection process, and its concept of race. Lalo Guerra, the only regent from Klail City, and one who has been appointed by two governors, in the past pushed for a Mexican American choice above all other criteria. A Valley high school dropout, Lalo is fifteen years later a self-made business owner and a pillar of the community. Lalo's Hispanic friend, Pete Morales, has a business degree from Sam Houston State University earned by the sweat of his own brow. Lalo, Pete, and a unified diverse professional regent body appreciate and admire outgoing President Nick Crowder, an honest, open (Anglo) man who has won the hearts of the Valley parents and other citizens because of his reputation for dealing fairly and effectively with all constituents. He has brought wonderful faculty to campus, including more Latinos, and has arranged financial support for many worthy students.

Now, after having been burned by two top Mexican American administrators who talked the game, but had not produced results, Lalo arrives at the conclusion that a candidate's race should not be the deciding factor for an administrative post. Lalo wants Belken State to improve and to focus on the best candidate, not on a racial quota. "We've a grown-up Board of Regents now" (*We Happy Few* 20). The regents also expand their vision to incorporate input from alums, some who now reside outside Texas. An out-of-state regent, Thomas Owen Wilson, is supportive when a woman is deemed to be the top candidate for Belken State's presidency. She is Dr. Merle Malone, a solid, single Catholic who is considered for her experience, innovation and ability to raise support, not rejected because of race or gender. Her experience working with all socioeconomic classes, her ideas on innovative teaching, and the proposal for implementation of an honors program have backing from the current board and faculty. Her credentials as a scientist who is consulted by NASA provide a strong credibility to her many talents. There is a brief interjection by Lalo Guerra regarding her marital status: " . . . There's always the fear of talk . . . she's a former nun . . . forty-nine years old [. . .] her life will reflect on the university, and we do have to think of the community" (*We Happy Few* 98).

The regents decide to sidestep the political maneuvering of the Governor's office and vote as an independent, egalitarian and unified voice for the good of Belken State and not let cronyism, gender, rumors of lesbianism or racial bias sway their important decision.

Returning to Jehu Malacara and Rafe Buenrostro, now both at the height of their careers and near the end of them in the present time of *We Happy Few*, the reader of the *KCDT* sees that as their transformational journey has progressed, they have turned out to be exemplary citizens and positive influences for the subsequent generation. This is the direct result of their accomplishments both inside and outside the borders of Belken County. Both have also achieved success in their personal lives: each has finally settled down with the love of his life. Although the cultural transformations the cousins Rafe and Jehu have witnessed have led to a shift from an agrarian society to an urban one along with other changes, one element of the *raza* story, as seen through the lives of the two cousins, remains constant: *los claros varones,* the fair gentlemen. Jehu, though not a perfect man, is one in a long line of *caballeros* beginning with Braulio Tapia, Esteban Echevarría, Manuel Guzmán and *El Quieto*, Rafe's father Jesús. Like his predecessors before him, Jehu visited sick people in the hospital, brought thieves to justice in banking corruption, was kind to the Old Revolutionaries in the bar, and is now a supportive father, giving his stepson the freedom to choose his own destiny at the university of his choice. For his part, Rafe is a decorated combat veteran and well-respected law enforcement professional who can work both sides of the border with equal efficacy. The inevitable comparisons between him and Don Manuel Guzmán, an Old Revolutionary and steady constable of Klail's Mexican town, show how far in Anglo society the *raza* through its *claros varones* has come. Whereas the first novels in the *KCDT* portray Mexican-American veterans as fringe figures who are not even recognized by the local VFW for their service in the U.S. Army of WWI and II, the later novels portray the Korean War veteran Rafe as a central, albeit local police figure in a new war, the international one on illegal narcotics. Who knows if Korean combat war veteran Hinojosa, always mindful that legally the Korean War was a United Nations-sponsored "police action," smiled over having his policeman Rafe fighting in still another war?

The Ángel Rama term *transculturation* aptly describes the rupture and gradual transformation of the social order of the Valley at the intersection of Anglo and Mexican cultures. The resultant hybrid society is situated in an environment where the key values of the dominated group, the Mexicans, are preserved by their active role in the process. Even though the descendants of the Escandón settlers adjusted to the educational, economic and political influences of the Anglo culture, they did not acculturate completely to that Anglo tradition. Instead, they became active agents in their own transformation to a third space much like Gloria Anzaldúa's "third element" (80), a new consciousness that breaks down existing paradigms of differing cultures. This process of cultural transformation in the Valley surges from individual creativity and initiative in the search to adapt and reinsert oneself in new conditions of productivity as the *KCDT* series moves forward in time.

The journey of Rafe and Jehu begins in the Mexican barrio where integrated schools eventually introduce them to a larger world. The two enter military service where they gain, as a benefit from the G. I. Bill, an opportunity to attain a superior education. Through various comings and goings, they eventually return to their departure point in the Valley to successfully reintegrate themselves in Anglo-dominated institutions as productive and eventually leading members in their community. In a simultaneous, almost reverse process, the reader sees the disappearance of the isolation of the Mexican *barrio* and its oral nature through a process of evolution to a more integrated bilingual society where the written word has certain power in the lives of the educated citizens. In the later novels of the *KCDT*, the ruling class of Belken County is portrayed as a combination of Mexican American and Anglo where some good and bad exist in all sectors of the hybrid society. Banker Noddy Perkins, although an in-law of the ruling KBC family, is eventually instrumental in making the opening for Jehu in his professional career. Rafe and Jehu are the model citizens who through their own initiative, along with their ability to adapt while still maintaining their own culture, are essential figures in the modernization of the Valley.

Even though Rafe and Jehu, men of flesh and blood, faced challenges during the journey to live successful lives in the Anglo-dominated society, their struggles did not cause them to succumb to intimidation or to settle for less that they wanted to achieve. They were not *los vendidos* of their own people as Echevarría described the Leguizamóns,[3] but rather developed into influential gentlemen, serious and genteel in their professional and personal lives. Echevarría warns Mexicans to steer clear of the sell-outs who "have been bought and sold so many times . . . They don't even know *what* they are . . . " (*Klail City* 19). The wise veteran advises the Mexicans at the community bar to not "wind up like those *vendidos*, those bought-and-sold-out lumps of caca-shit-mierda eaters . . . " (19).

The transformational journey of these two characters serves as a literary catalyst toward a better understanding of how those born into an environment of limitations can defy adversity by personal perseverance and higher education. The *claros varones* Jehu and Rafe, the symbolic representatives of *la raza* in the post WWII period leading to the Civil Rights Era, carry with them the code of the "fair gentlemen of Belken" and are resolved to not live like the unrefined residents of Flora. This place, it should be remembered, is named for the only daughter of its founder Rufus T. Klail and, according to some, its name "reflects the same barren aspect of its namesake (who never married): dry, insipid, meaner than the word mean, and with . . . a damned disinheriting countenance" (*Valley* 34). Instead, *la raza* of Klail City benefitted from interaction with elements of the Other, the Anglo population, by taking inventory, "despojando, desgranando, quitando paja" (Anzaldúa 82); and, through the collision of the two groups *la raza* helped create a new space where mutual cooperation, bilingualism, higher education, and a more egalitarian reciprocity transform the memories of the past into a new sense of a future identity, or a resultant negotiated existence. In the contemporary era of the Texas Valley, because of the triumph over racial, political and socio-economic adversity, a new generation achieved its American Dream.

Notes

[1] The term echoes the genre of literary *ejemplares* of the fifteenth century that serve to exalt the illustrious protagonists of the monarchy such as *Libro de los claros varones de Castilla* (1489) by Hernando de Pulgar. Present also is the implication of the subsequent satirical *Ingenioso hidalgo de Don Quixote de la Mancha* (1605, 1615) by Miguel de Cervantes Saavedra.

[2] While *Mi querido Rafa* (1981) is a bilingual text that relies heavily on an oral tradition and speaks from a polyphony of voices, narrators, generations and texts, *Dear Rafe* (1985), its English-language recreation is not a direct translation. Instead, it is a version that is rooted not so much in questions of language, but in translating the nuances of culture. The author reorganizes, subtracts from, or adds to the reworked text in order to communicate with a variety of readers. This recreation demonstrates the author's awareness that Chicano literature is read by a multicultural and multilingual public. The present work cites the English recreation.

[3] The term *vendidos* (sell-outs) reverberates with memories of the Treaty of Guadalupe (1848) where a large swath of the present-day southwest portion of what today is the United States was sold to the United States against the wishes of many Mexican citizens. The action of the Mexican head-of-state Santa Anna was viewed as a betrayal which contributed to the defeat of Mexico in land disputes rather than to allow early Mexican settlers to defend their land against the United States aggressors. See *Uncle Remus con chile* (1993), where Américo Paredes opines that as a result of the loss of land, the Mexicans called Mexican Americans *los vendidos* because they were lost with the territory (156). The reference to the Leguizamóns refers to the latecomers to the Valley of Spanish descent who, like Santa Anna, allied with the Anglos in land disputes and were in a constant land feud with the early landowning Buenrostro family at El Carmen Ranch.

Works Cited

Anzaldúa, Gloria. *Borderlands/La Frontera. The New Mestiza.* San Francisco: Aunt Lute Books, 1987. Print.

Hinojosa, Rolando. *Ask a Policeman. A Rafe Buenrostro Mystery.* Houston: Arte Público Press, 1998. Print.

___. *Claros varones de Belken/Fair Gentlemen of Belken.* Trans. Julia Cruz. Tempe: Bilingual Press/Editorial Bilingüe, 1986. Print.

___. *Dear Rafe/Mi querido Rafa.* Houston: Arte Público Press, 2005. Print.

___. *Estampas del valle y otras obras.* Tempe: Bilingual Press/Editorial Bilingüe, 1994. Print.

___. *Klail City.* Houston: Arte Público Press, 1987. Print.

___. *Korean Love Songs.* Berkeley: Editorial Justa Publications, Inc., 1978. Print.

___. *Rites and Witnesses.* Houston: Arte Público Press, 1982. Print.

___. *The Useless Servants.* Houston: Arte Público Press, 1993. Print.

___. *The Valley.* Tempe: Bilingual Press/Editorial Bilingüe, 1983. Print.

___. *We Happy Few.* Houston: Arte Público Press, 2006. Print.

Ortiz, Fernando. *Contrapunteo cubano del tabaco y el azúcar.* Carácas: Biblioteca Ayacucho, 1978. Print.

Rama, Ángel. *Transculturación narrativa en América Latina.* México: Siglo XXI, 1982. Print.

Ramírez, Liliana. "Hibridez y discurso en los estudios literarios latinoamericanos contemporáneos." *Revista de Estudios Sociales* 13 (2002): 47-55. Print.

Reinhardt, Claudia and Bill Ganzel. "Farming in the 1940s, The GI Bill." Wessel's Living History Farm, n.d. Web. 4 Aug. 2012.

Sobrevilla, David. "Transculturación y heterogeneidad: avatares de dos categorías literarias en América Latina." *Revista de Crítica Literaria Latinoamericana* 27.54 (2001): 21-33. Print.

Rolando Hinojosa-Smith Erasing Borders Cultural, Linguistic, Literary

Nicolás Kanellos
University of Houston

The *Klail City Death Trip* (*KCDT*), Rolando Hinojosa's continuing novel, traces generations of inhabitants and their stories in fictional Belken County in the Lower Rio Grande Valley of Texas. The *Death Trip* has often been compared to William Faulkner's Yoknapatawpha County and Gabriel García Márquez's Macondo,[1] but, as I hope to prove in this chapter, the organizing structure of generations, even celebrated in one of the novel titles, *Generaciones y semblanzas*, and the geographic determinism of a particular ethno-historic county,[2] are perhaps keys that are too obvious and too easy for understanding Hinojosa's complicated narrative project. The facile comparisons with the two Nobel laureates, whose works emerge from and sustain national canons, are far too limiting—and, needless to say, when Hinojosa's oeuvre is compared on this basis, it comes up short, precisely because he is not writing from within the American or the Latin American canon, but outside both and challenging both,[3] despite the fact that he more than any other writer draws broadly from *both* of these traditions and canons. The comparison with Faulkner and García Márquez is flawed,[4] in addition, because Hinojosa is writing out of hybrid culture, and hybridism characterizes all aspects of his creative project. This is marked by: 1) the use of the two languages, separately and in code-switching; 2) characters who are the product of Mexican and Anglo parents, as is Hinojosa; 3) literary genres and models, as well as references to authors and texts, from both Anglo and Hispanic traditions; and 4) the underlying and constant comparison of two worldviews and their knowledge bases, but a constant challenge to the truth and legitimacy of both, whereupon Hinojosa's satire is born.

We who write criticism and or publish literature—and I am referring to myself as a publisher, Rolando Hinojosa's publisher, in fact—from the margins of dominant societies, and like Hinojosa often serve as translators for both, probably understand best what Hinojosa is doing and where he is going with his ambitious, multiform, multi-generational, multi-genre, bilingual, bi-dialectal project. And we find his novels and his project just as worthy as those of the aforementioned Nobel laureates'; additionally, we find it more relevant to us in our multicultural and diversely linguistic lives at this juncture in the twenty-first century.

Rolando Hinojosa was born and raised in a region that was colonized by Spain in 1749 and later passed from Spanish administration to Mexican governance in 1821 for a period of 26 or 38 years, depending on how you understand Mexican and Texan claims to the area, and which side of the ongoing debate you support. Although not an historical novel in the common understanding of such, in which a narrative is constructed in a remote time period, *KCDT* evokes and recalls the foundational period of Valley culture. It also updates the irrevocable path towards extinction of the original cultural base, or, at least, extinction of the "old ways" on a path toward a new, hybrid culture. That said, Hinojosa's world focuses on the Anglo-Mexican binary and hardly ever considers the original Native American inhabitants, whom Hinojosa considers to have been "absorbed by the colonial population" ("The

Sense of Place" 21), in this chronicling of Hispanic and Anglo-American culture clash and then blending across the generations.

The oldest woman in Hinojosa's Valley, Reina Campoy, can trace her lineage back to the settlers of Nuevo Santander in 1749, and to

> Reina's grandmother, Doña Mauricia Puig, [who] was born a Spanish subject in 1814; at age ten she was a Mexican citizen; by the summer of 1836, she was a Texan. Later, in 1845, an American when Texas was annexed. . . . A citizen of the Confederacy in 1860, and an American citizen again after duly being Reconstructed. (*Becky and Her Friends* 107)

With such statements about Campoy and other old-timers, Hinojosa seems to indicate that national identity may change while the people themselves persist and endure. But these frequent passages also underline that for a little more than a quarter century the area was governed from the far off-capital of Mexico City and, later, as a spoil of war, was added as another star to the American flag. It was so far geographically and culturally from Washington, D. C. and even from the capital of the new state, Austin, that the Lower Rio Grande Valley only very slowly became incorporated into U.S. society, first only through the military presence and dominion, followed later by the imposition of new laws and a foreign educational system. But by and large, the majority of the population, of Hispanic-Mexican origin, continued daily life according to the social systems of parentage and *compadrazgo*, which extended beyond the imposed political border of the Rio Grande River, and still does today. In this manner in similar passages, Hinojosa emphasizes that it is the people and their culture not their "national" identity that occupies his attention and that is the core concern. Even in his essay, ironically entitled "The Sense of Place,"[5] he emphasizes that it is the inhabitants' world view, perspective on life and how they interpret particular events and life itself that is his subject; clearly, it is not the geographic location, per se. He further emphasizes that, "my stories are not held together by the *peripeteia* or plot as much as by *what* the people who populate the stories say and *how* they say it, how they look at the world out and the world in; and the works then become studies of perceptions and values and decisions reached by them" ("The Sense of Place" 21).

As for geography and politics, represented by the river border that has been imposed to divide two political entities, they too are malleable, subject to change; only the people endure. This is clear when the Buenrostros in *Rites and Witnesses* realign the border by dynamiting the Rio Grande to resume its original flow prior to Anglo intervention (110). Beyond the dynamite that many characters may have dreamed of igniting in the *KCDT* series, as in life, negating and obviating that border were many cultural systems, such as familial ties on both sides of the river, the common Catholic religion ministered by Spanish-speaking priests and an informal, at times formal, alternative Hispanic educational system not only in Catechism, but also in the type of little Mexican schools that Hinojosa himself attended as a child. Family and experience and culture, and Hinojosa's books themselves, all work to negate that imaginary line that authorities impose to divide people. And of course, in the later installments of *KCDT*, Mexican immigrants and smugglers continuously negate the border and irrevocably reinforce the Mexican/Hispanic culture of the Valley, which will remain predominantly Hispanic, with more than 90% of the population, into the far-off future.

Born in the small town of Mercedes to a Mexican-American police officer and an Anglo-American school teacher, Hinojosa was raised speaking and reading both Spanish and English. The bilingualism and biculturalism of his parents in this majority Hispanic/Mexican social environment, is nevertheless an environment resulting from conquest and marginalization—as far to the margin as can be imagined, being a border or frontier region. The bilingual/bicultural environment of Hinojosa's rearing would eventually incline Hinojosa towards a very clear vision of the world, one that would characterize his ideological and narrative stances for the rest of his life. That clarity of vision would allow him to assume the perspective of the observer of the human comedy, always slightly outside and slightly inside the two dominant groups in order to satirize the foibles of both in the microcosm for which he is so well known. That clarity of mind and vision would allow him to see beyond the constraints of one culture or the other, remove the social masks, and criticize the economic and political motivations and structures. These include the institutions of power in the Valley, especially in their imperative to construct and support an official history as a part of the process of integrating the Valley residents into a national American culture. Hinojosa's portrayal, in his texts and their linguistic heteroglossia, always reveals how successful or not that solidifying and homogenizing of the populace has been. This process ranges from the days of the first Spanish-speaking settlers through the coming ascendance of the Anglos, and then shows the later re-conquest of the Valley and its institutions. This reconquest or, at least, hybridization is seen in the police department in *Ask a Policeman*, the schools and the bank in a number of the *KCDT* volumes, and in the university of *We Happy Few*, where Mexican Americans are on the path of ascendance and control. It is the linguistic and ethno-cultural diversity represented in Hinojosa's texts that speaks to what early Chicano critics only saw as resistance,[6] but today under our examining eyes can only be understood, on the one hand as a synthesis and on the other as a breech between Anglo and Mexican pretensions of nationhood, an interstitial area that speaks and acts for itself and is a cradle of creativity and affirmation beyond national assignations.

Years after serving in the Army in Korea, and after studying Hispanic literature at the University of Texas and the University of Illinois, where he and Don Luis Leal had daily coffee together, Hinojosa commenced his career as an academic and a writer, producing more than fifteen volumes in English, Spanish and even in bilingual format. His first book, *Estampas del Valle y otros relatos* (1973), won the Premio Quinto Sol in 1973, and along with the first novels by Tomás Rivera and Rudolfo Anaya constituted what the Quinto Sol editors hoped would be the basis for a Chicano literary canon,[7] a bulwark for the creation of a Chicano cultural nationalism. Regardless of the canonicity or not of these marginal, minority group texts at Quinto Sol, they opened creative pathways and were emulated by literally thousands of writers in an effort to provide a language and literary corpus for what back then was cast as the "sleeping giant" of Mexican-American and Latino people in the United States. Hinojosa's mosaic of quirky and picturesque characters who, despite or because of their apparent isolation from a larger world, were stubborn and unashamed in their affirmation of place, tradition, dialect and worldview. Hinojosa's work even pointed to an apparent Golden Age, a time of cultural origins prior to the coming of the Anglo, when language was pure, traditions were established and a sense of identity and place were well-formed. According to Calderón, Hinojosa even invokes classical models and heroes[8] to be emulated, and this accounts in part for the selection of his title: *Claros varones de Belken*. In this volume, the ancient Esteban Echevarría even invokes an Edenic past:

> Me acuerdo, Rafa [. . .] árboles llenos de higos y de miel de abejas que chupaban la flor de naranjos . . . ruidos de animales que ya no se oyen ni se ven . . . bailes con gente invitada y ahora me cuentan que se tiene que pagar la entrada, pero ¿te das cuenta, Rafa? Y allí están las palmeras . . . Las palmeras que se daban en el Valle y que crecían como Dios quería hasta que la bolillada vino con sus hachas y las cortaron . . . (209)

This Edenic vision of Chicano origins was a perfect basis for early Chicano critics in their effort to build a cultural nationalism or fit Hinojosa's works into the internal colonial model popular among academics in the 1970s.[9] In addition to employing the memory of the old-timers such as Echevarría to recall and pass on the old ways and wisdom, Hinojosa himself has led credence to this Golden Age before borders were formed and capitalism was introduced in such essays as "The Sense of Place": "That river was not yet a jurisdictional barrier and was not to be until almost one hundred years later; but, by then, by then the border had its own history, its own culture, and its own sense of place" (19). At the same time Hinojosa affirms that "The Border wasn't a paradise, and it didn't have to be; but it was more than paradise, it was home" (20). Importantly, it "maintained the remains of a social democracy that cried out for independence, for a desire to be left alone, and for the continuance of a sense of community" (20). While this statement is not identical to Echevarría's invocation of a paradise,[10] it does privilege the culture that existed prior to Anglo immigration and imply that this original culture/nation was interrupted or destabilized—of course, it was. It is not only Echevarría's and the other old-timers' function[11] to recall those origins but also to mourn the loss of native identity and values and bemoan the transformation of life since the coming of the Anglo:

> Houses without porches, streets without lamp lights, friends who've died away, and the youngsters who no longer speak Spanish, who can't even say, "¿Cómo está?" . . . Hah! The Valley's no longer . . . The Anglos and their landed property, their banks, their legal contracts . . . What's the use of reaching eighty-three if everything's gone up in smoke? The Vilches? Dead. The Tueros? They're dead, too! The Buenrostros are almost gone and the founding families are drying up like leaves on a dying mesquite. (*Claros varones* 206)

However, as more and more texts in the *KCDT* series have been published, it becomes more apparent that the voices harkening back to a favored pre-Anglo past exist alongside many other voices and testimonies, from Anglo as well as Mexican residents, that document opposing views and/or synthesis. As Kaup has pointed out, there is a simultaneity of voices from different generations vying for the readers' attention:

> Significant change has occurred between the traditional, rural pre-Anglo Belken County of the older generation and the present urban, Anglo-controlled place, a master difference structuring the pattern of local native Chicano memory. I would suggest that *Hinojosa represents this historical sequence as spatial simultaneity, as separate worlds existing side-by-side in the voices of different generations.* As long as this simultaneous moment lasts (and the voices of the elders are still heard), it soft-

> ens the impact of one world being shattered by the invasion of another. (64)

Rafa Buenrostro and Jehú Malacara ascend and transform Anglo institutions on the socio-political plain as well as in their personal lives: the former marries Sammie Jo Perkins and into the ranching-banking power base; the latter weds Becky Escobar, who by her *mestizo* Anglo-Mexican heritage represents the hybrid present and future of the Valley. But, as I argue below, their hybridity does not make for a new synthetic life but one that is a culture of its own, born of the interstitial space that is the Valley; while wedding elements of both nations, it is neither of the two. The *mestizo* Hinojosa's overriding message, therefore, cannot be taken to be that of resistance to Anglo culture, as hoped for by Chicano cultural nationalists, nor an outpost of "greater Mexico," as Héctor Calderón has theorized.[12] As Hinojosa has stated in his essay "A Voice of One's Own," "All of us live within two cultures—in varying degrees, as I have said, and whatever the degree, the two cultures are inescapable" (In Saldívar, *Hinojosa Reader* 12).

The *KCDT* mosaic formed a firm base from which Hinojosa could focus his skeptical and removed vision, somewhat on the order of the *crónicas*, or local color, satirical columns that were still being published in the Valley and San Antonio newspapers during Hinojosa's youth.[13] *Estampas del Valle*, henceforth we came to understand, was nothing more than the first chapter of what Hinojosa's narrators would call *El cronicón de Belken* or *El cronicón del Valle*, that is, an ongoing, open-ended epic that would subtly trace the ascension of the Anglo-American population and culture in the Valley and the decline of the original Hispano/Mexican culture of the Valley. Yet today, Hinojosa's latest books are chronicling a resurgence of the ethnic Mexican/Mexican-American population, just as the old-timer Don Aureliano Mora would envision it in *Klail City*, like the Greeks recuperating their legacy from the Romans who had taken them as slaves (29): "the day will come when we'll see this ground as ours again. As sure as there's a God somewhere around here" (30).

Hinojosa's art is not just a simple chronicling of the ebb and flow of two cultures in contact, of farm and ranch and town real estate,[14] financial and legal[15] interests, of families and personalities, their conflicts, marriage lines and separations. Hinojosa's has been a highly literary experiment in which he not only gives artistic form to a life heretofore never represented adequately in literature and art, but his experiment also has involved, nay demanded, seeing how far he can adapt and mold the literary tools he inherited to capture that life at the crossroads of two cultures and two nations. His experimentation has led him to explore and recapitulate the complete history of literary genres, from oral lore and epic to *nueva narrativa latinoamericana*, from both the Spanish-language and English-language traditions, from his tipping his hat to *El Cid* and the *Quijote* to Ambrose Bierce, Faulkner and other American writers. Without characterizing each and every Hinojosa book, I will briefly summarize the trajectory of his conversation with the literary genres, which more often than not also can been seen as a satiric comment and/or deconstruction[16] of those same genres. The novel that won the Casa de las Américas Award in 1976, *Klail City y sus alrededores*, in addition to continuing the *crónica* genre, embeds a picaresque novel; Hinojosa would later recreate this work in English as *Klail City*, published much later, in 1987. *Korean Love Songs* (1978), written in verse, may be seen as Hinojosa's *corrido* or *epopeya*, documenting as a minstrel the Korean battlefield in the epic East-West struggle that would subsequently cool down to a Cold War during much of Hinojosa's adult life. Hinojosa never recreated *Korean Love Songs* in Spanish, but the war stories and reminiscences are woven into many of the novels that follow; it so obsessed him that it erupted into an entire novel, *The Useless Servants* (1993), which takes the form of a war diary, and although it found no outlet in Spanish, it has come to be the most autobiographical of his works, in which the satirist and distant observer of the human comedy for once, and only once, reveals the depth of his emotions and psychological reaction to pointless horror. Hinojosa's *Mi querido Rafa* (1981) and its recreation as *Dear Rafe* (1985) is partially an epistolary novel in the style of and with the narrative irony of Juan Valera's *Pepita Jiménez*, and partially reportage along the lines of García Márquez's *Crónica de una muerte anunciada*; however, the novel demands of the reader bilingualism and bi-dialectalism in order to derive the full value of the text which switches back and forth between Spanish and English. It is also the only text which pairs an extensive written document, i.e. letters, with monologs resulting from oral interviews. Following on the linguistic experiment of *Rafa*, the novel *Rites and Witnesses* (1982) is transitional, presenting mainly English dialogs and monologs continuing the dual structure of examining the political and economic machinations in Belken and taking the testimony of the "witnesses" in the form of monologs. *Partners in Crime* (1985) and *Ask a Policeman* (1998) are detective novels, in their police procedural manifestation, and well-suited to Hinojosa's search for ultimate truths in a world fragmented by vested interests, politics and social biases. Hinojosa's *Claros varones de Belken* (1986, with a side-by-side translation as *Fair Gentlemen of Belken*) takes us back to Spain's middle ages and the early Renaissance lives of noblemen, as cultivated by such authors as Hernán del Pulgar. *Becky and Her Friends* (1990) and its recreation in Spanish, *Los amigos de Becky* (1991) continues with a type of reportage but now with a new narrator because of the death of Hinojosa's former alter ego, P. Galindo (a satiric play on words in Spanish meaning something like "on target" or "shoots well," taken from a real newspaper *cronista* Pepe Díaz, read by the young Hinojosa). Hinojosa's most recent novel, *We Happy Few* (2006), is the only chapter in his *cronicón* situated in the environment that the mature Hinojosa knows best: academia, and his approach is vintage Hinojosa dry humor and laconic satire, as usual demanding an intelligent reader response.

The continuing novel known as the *Klail City Death Trip* is obviously of epic proportions, taking us back to the very origins of the novelistic genre. It documents the history, the language, the conflicts, the aspirations of a fictional community existing at the very point of contact of two nations, two nations in continuous evolution themselves. As Hinojosa compares the national projects of the United States and Mexico—not to mention the nationalistic aspirations of Texans themselves—he questions how history is narrated orally in every form, from gossip to political speech to the tales of old-timers and the *corridos*; and, how history is written[17]: from newspaper reports, to official depositions, battlefield reports, medical examiner reports and educational texts, not to mention novelistic representation of history in its relation to nation-building. It is frequent in these novels that three and four versions of an incident, not to mention the multiple opinions on the incident by Valley residents, are presented, none of them in total agreement with the others. In the more recent works, even television news stories, photos and videos are contrasted, for example with detective Rafe Buenrostro's examination of a crime scene. At the heart of Hinojosa's use of multiple, conflicting and unreliable narrators, even if they are alter egos of himself, such as Rafa, Jehú, P. Galindo and his unnamed successor, is his belief that perception is never pure nor unbiased. Even more so, his ambitious examination of texts, both oral and written, leads Hinojosa to question the empirical bases of knowledge, to doubt anything that can be considered ultimate knowledge, to doubt reportage and testimony and written accounts of any sort. In the earlier works, the *corridos* (See *Rites and Witnesses* 110) and the tales of the old-timers like Echevarría hold greater sway as an alternative history than the official history to be found in books and English-language newspapers. And in a more than symbolic act, old-timer Aureliano Mora smashes the historical marker commemorating those Klail soldiers who had lost their lives in World War II, two of his family members among them (*Klail City* 37). The official history, even engraved in metal, can never communicate the oppression and loss felt and expressed orally on other occasions by Mora. In another iconic comparison of orality and written culture, Brother Tomás Imás in *Klail City* imposes the poorly translated words of an Anglo-Protestant hymn on a well-known popular Spanish song in his effort to convert the

Valley Mexicans (95), thus exemplifying how the written word is imposed on and attempts to change the meaning and supplant the original and authentic oral expression and history. This process clearly emulates the overlaying of Anglo culture in the Valley. In *Rites and Witnesses*, P. Galindo emphasizes how old-timer Echevarría's handshake and *word* is good as gold (64) in this novel that details the fraudulent manipulation of contracts, deeds and laws by the bank and the powers that be in Klail. In the later detective novels, police procedurals, the incisive eyes and ears of the life-long student of the Valley, Detective Rafe Buenrostro, who is called in to solve the case, is far more valuable than all of the official federal and state agencies and all that has been documented in legal reports and the media (*Partners in Crime* 159).

Despite this great affirmation of oral culture in *KCDT*, which has been much commented upon[18] and, in fact, dominated much of the early criticism of Hinojosa texts, what Hinojosa has produced is a written document, one that, as I have mentioned above, recapitulates the generic history of literature and consistently transposes and compares written and oral sources. Whether the sources are written or oral, traditional or contemporary is not important; the importance lies in presenting the multiple resources and perspectives that the readers of his narrative—and we might add, human beings in society—need to consider in their search for meaning.

The multifaceted and fractured nature of perception that Hinojosa constructs imposes on his narrative a heteroglossia as P. Galindo listens to the testimony of scores of characters, and with a wink of the eye, asks his readers to supply what has not been said and for the reader to evaluate and complete the narratives.[19] Because the ultimate truth is beyond our reach, because knowledge is socially constructed, as is history, as is the nation. In *Mi querido Rafa*—which I believe is central to Hinojosa's epistemology—it becomes clear that only through a process of search and research and comparison of all written and oral testimonies, of all of the documents and sources, that we can begin to construct a history, a truth. But it will never be the ultimate truth, and it will always be a product of culture and not science, *scientia.* This is most clear in the Spanish original *Mi querido Rafa* when narrator P. Galindo reveals that what has been up to this point the driving force of the plot—that is, finding out what Jehú did and where he is—is only tangentially (*tangencialmente*) of interest: "Lo que más importaba era tratar de averiguar lo ocurrido y lo que de eso se pensaba en ambos lados de la ciudad" (90). In other words, the crux of the novel relies on attempting to ascertain the truth of an historical event and how people interpret it—interestingly, Hinojosa did not include this sentence in his English-language recreation of the novel. In this epistemological process in *Mi querido Rafa* and in *Dear Rafe*, the irony is thick, as P. Galindo announces in English and Spanish, respectively,

> As is usually the case, that which was thought to be a simple piece of research turns out not to be that at all. And, in spite of what has been said, by those who would know, and by the rest, those who know less but clamor the more, everything hinders and everything helps that which the wri would like to present and make known. A paradox, but here it is. (*Dear Rafe* 103)

> Como siempre, lo sencillo no resultó serlo. A pesar de lo que digan los que deben saber y los otros, los que saben menos y chillan más, *todo* impide y *todo* ayuda a esclarecer lo que se quiere traer a luz. Una paradoja, pero es así. (*Mi querido Rafa* 90; Hinojosa's emphasis)

And the Spanish-language testimony of P. Galindo ends with, "El esc. avisa que sigue estando de acuerdo con Roberto Arlt: 'En realidad, uno no sabe qué pensar de la gente'" (91). Hinojosa does not include the quote from Arlt in the English-language version. The reader has to wait until the end of *Becky and Her Friends* to get the following George Santayana quote from Galindo's successor: " . . . what a strange accident the truth is" (160). In an extra-literary text, an interview entitled "Crossing Literary Borders" with Barbara Strickland, Hinojosa confirms as much:

> "I'm saying that it's very difficult to ascertain what the truth is. I'm not talking about point of view." He sips his iced tea. "People use their imagination more than they use their intellect. And the reason is that the imagination is very active and inventive while the intellect is not. The intellect is very lazy. We prefer, really, not to use our intellect. So you use your imagination. So therefore the search for truth," he says, chuckling, "is ongoing. And you think you've uncovered it and it's like an onion. So I figure, well, the writer shouldn't know everything."

Hinojosa's novels, thus, represent a search for truth, a truth that may be out of reach, complex and multi-layered. When apprehension of the social and historical reality is further complicated by two cultures existing side-by-side, blending and/or competing, truth becomes even more illusive.

At the margins of the national cultures of the United States and Mexico, where even three national anthems are learned—the American, the Mexican and even "Texas Our Texas" (*Klail City* 76)—Hinojosa's Belken does not respect linguistic nor cultural limits, nor racial nor blood-line purity, nor geographic nor political borders, nor official truths. By questioning the official images and histories constructed and reinforced by both societies in contact and often in conflict (but there is also a middle ground of intermarriage, accommodation and hybridization in Belken), Hinojosa documents another way to be human and independent of the State and its nation construct. However, in so doing he produces a completely innovative oeuvre, completely original despite its dialog with so many genres from literary history and oral tradition. Hinojosa's experimentation, as can be appreciated from the foregoing, is separate and distinct from that of all the other authors with whom the critics have compared him.

In writing outside the canon—nay, destabilizing and undermining the canons by dominating and subverting the canonical genres—Hinojosa in the *Klail City Death Trip* series is operating as a translator and disseminator of texts across cultures, taking two series of national myths, re-writing them and generating a new imaginary, one just as fictitious and beautiful and outlandish as the two originals, and by the way, just as historical or a-historical as foundations for a people's identity. He creates this history and identity in that interstitial space we call the Borderlands, made from both nations but apart from both of them. In this process he seems to exercise what Homi K. Bhabha described as "a temporality of representation that moves between cultural formations and social processes without a 'centered' logic" (*DissemiNation* 293) and further explains, "The power of supplementarity is not the negation of the preconstituted social contradictions of the past and the present; its force lies [. . .] in the renegotiation of those times, terms, and traditions through which we turn our uncertain, passing contemporaneity into the signs of history" (*DissemiNation* 306). What Hinojosa accomplishes in his continuing narrative, to use Bhabha's phraseology once again, is that he

> contests genealogies of "origin" that lead to cultural supremacy and historical priority. Minority discourse acknowledges the status of national culture—and the people—as a contentious, performative space of the perplexity of the living in the midst of the pedagogical representations of fullness of life. Now there is no reason to believe that such marks of difference—the incommensurable time of the subject culture—cannot inscribe "history" of the people or become the gathering points of political solidarity. (*DissemiNation* 308)

Whereas old-timers like Echevarría and Mora may have provided an argument for the historical priority of Mexican culture, and *vendidos* like Ira Escobar may embody a negation of the prior culture in an effort to assimilate and be empowered by the Anglo interlopers, it is the contemporary generation, now mature, of Sammie Jo/Rafa Buenrostro and Becky/Jehú Malacara, that is responsible for generating the new and unique culture that is integrated and powerful and may represent a threat to both nations. I repeat, in deconstructing the literary genres and history of both nations, Hinojosa is disassembling the armature of myths that sustain nations. He does not travel the path of cultural nationalism in the process; instead, he posits a different history and literature, complete unto themselves.

Hinojosa not only subverts and replaces the U.S. national myths but treats the present as past: this is no longer an Anglo-European geo-political-cultural state. Mexico is no longer a Third-World backwater reacting to Anglo economic and cultural superiority. That was the past; the Mestizo States of America is the present and future, in *praxis*, not just in fiction and myth. The cultural transformations at the border represent the future evolution of the United States. The long predestined integration of the Americas is taking place, at least as far north as the Canadian border. Of course, Hinojosa's discourse is directed at readers who are familiar with the conflicting histories, myths and politics of the two peoples confronting each other at the border; these readers' initial disbelief is assuaged through irony and a subversive humor that allows him to propose what otherwise would be a preposterous mythopoesis; but it is made palatable, nay enjoyable, through the technique of reader response. Hinojosa's art has led the reader to greater truths and an insight into not only the reality of, to use Bhabha's words again, the "pagus—colonials, postcolonials, migrants, minorities," but also of "the *Heim* of the national culture and its unisonant discourse" (315).

Notes

[1] See Mark Busby, "Faulknerian Elements in Rolando Hinojosa's *The Valley*"; Héctor Calderón, *Narratives of Greater Mexico* (148); Hub Hermans, "Hacia una lectura deconstructivista de la narrativa de Rolando Hinojosa" (364); Guillermo E. Hernández, *Chicano Satire* (86); Manuel Martín-Rodríguez, *Life in Search if Readers* (30); José David Saldívar, "Rolando Hinojosa's *Klail City Death Trip*: A Critical Introduction" (48); among many others.

[2] See Neate, Wilson, "The Function of Belken County in the Fiction of Rolando Hinojosa: The Voicing of the Chicano Experience."

[3] Hinojosa himself has recognized this and, as he sees it, suffered from the marginalization of his work. He blames the important canonizing institutions, such as the Modern Language Association, *The New York*

Times Book Review, and major publishing houses for pigeon-holing his work as minority, regional and ethnic, like most Chicano and Latino writers. See his essay, "The Other American Literatures."

[4] Virtually the only critic to challenge this commonplace comparison with García Márquez has been José Limón in "Border Literary Histories," who refutes Saldívar's thesis in *The Dialectics of Our America* with the following: "[Saldívar] largely overlooks Hinojosa's rendering of the complex Mexican Anglo hybridity of the area and of the internal class divisions and exploitations within the Mexican-origin community" (163).

[5] He writes, "A place is merely that until it is populated, and once populated, the histories of the place and its people begin" (19).

[6] Even today, some critics continue to see an over-all resistance effort in the *KCDT*, especially in the use of oral cultural authority, as in Monika Kaup's *Rewriting North American Borders* (56-58), rather than seeing an irreversible evolution towards hybridism, as I shall emphasize later in this chapter. Likewise, Rosemary A. King, in *Border Confluences*, while not studying Hinojosa, per se, sees much of the literature produced by Native Americans and Chicanos as re-conquering at least a metaphoric space, "carving out and reclaiming sacred Chicano/a and Indian homelands in the U. S.-Mexico borderlands" (98). In Saldívar's *The Dialectics of Our America*, this resistance theory graduates to a new level, global, as this critic seeks to integrate Chicano and borderland literature within the context of Caribbean and Latin American literatures through resistance or opposition to the American Empire. I, of course, do not agree with this. Rather, I support Monika Kaup's observation that the testimony of such old-timers as Esteban Echevarría, Manuel Guzmán, Aureliano Mora and Braulio Tapia represents their effort to "salvage the memory of a disappearing local chronotope," but, like the *corrido* as an historical document in Hinojosa, their testimonies are presented as "one among many unrelated stories in the unending talk that composes Hinojosa's dialogic universe of Texas Mexican cultural conversation" (57).

[7] See Bruce-Novoa, "Canonical and Non-Canonical Texts."

[8] Calderón states, " . . . there is a sense of looking back at the turn of the century, and prior to the coming of Anglo settlers, as a classic period with Mexican models to emulate, claros varones, hombres rectos y cabales, 'complete gentlemen, just and real men.' As in Guzmán and Pulgar, Hinojosa's claros varones are dead" (159).

[9] See Salvador Rodríguez del Pino's *La novela chicana escrita en español.*

[10]But Hinojosa's words are close to another statement by Echevarría: "Tiempos malos fueron aquéllos también con sus rinches, la ley aprovechada, los terratenientes, las sequías y el engruesamiento de la vida misma . . . pero . . . al fin y al cabo era mi tiempo, mi gente, mi Valle querido . . . antes que hubiera tal cosa como el condado de Belken y Klail City y todo lo demás . . . había gente, Rafa, gente. . . . Labores y rancherías, y ese Río Grande que era para beber y no pa' detener gente los de un lado contra el otro . . . no . . . eso vino después con la bolillada y sus ingenieros y el papelaje todo en inglés" (*Claros varones* 207).

[11]Klaus Zilles, in "Cultura y memoria oral," states that Echevarría incarnates the collective oral culture of the Valley, with its pastoral heritage. He further states, "Esteban Echevarría, el más anciano de los cronistas, pertenece a la primera generación de tejanos que nacieron como ciudadanos estadounidenses después de la anexión de Tejas en 1845. En cierta manera, su nacimiento marca el nacimiento de una minoría, el comienzo de la paulatina extinción de una sociedad ranchera, la pérdida de sus tierras y la inminente anulación de su cultura y lengua. La muerte de Echevarría, que se narra en *Varones* (166), significaría . . . la muerte de la cultura chicana, si no fuera por las nuevas generaciones de cronistas como Rafa y Jehú" (8).

[12]See "'Mexicanos al Grito de Guerra': Rolando Hinojosa's *Cronicón del condado de Belken*," in *Narratives of Greater Mexico* (138-166).

[13]Calderón gives an excellent in-depth analysis of the genealogy of the *cronicón* and its use by Hinojosa in the previously cited "'Mexicanos al Grito de Guerra': Rolando Hinojosa's *Cronicón del condado de Belken*" (140-142).

[14]See Wolfgang Karrer, "Realism and Real Estate in Rolando Hinojosa's *Klail City Death Trip Series*."

[15]For a discussion of the law and Chicano narrative, see Carl Gutiérrez-Jones's chapter "Legal Rhetoric and Cultural Critique: An Institutional Context for Reading Chicano Narrative."

[16]Martín-Rodríguez identifies this process as "coherent deformation" and states that this is the means that Hinojosa uses to involve the reader "as major player" in the narration to "(re)construct reality from a literary point of view" (31).

[17]Many critics, such as Manuel Martín-Rodríguez (28), believe that Hinojosa is writing an alternative history, one that supplements and

contests official history, as written for example by such historians of the West as Walter Prescott Webb. But, as you can see from the arguments in my text, I believe Hinojosa's mission goes far beyond writing an alternative history.

[18]Which I, myself, have studied in "Orality and Hispanic Literature" (115-123). Nevertheless, I believe that critics who only interpret Hinojosa's texts as recovering, sustaining and making oral culture available to the reader are only partially correct; they also need to consider the written resources and perspectives in Hinojosa's toolkit and purpose. Thus I cannot accept such essentialist statements, for example, as the following in Guillermo Hernández's *Chicano Satire:* "Hinojosa does not aspire merely to transpose an oral into a writing mode but to attain an artistic re-elaboration of traditional culture" (104).

[19]Klaus Zilles, in "Cultura y memoria oral," refutes the idea that Hinojosa is presenting the fragmented nature of oral culture in which the truth is not apprehensible, as in many post-modern texts; rather, he emphasizes the role of the reader in completing the texts in order to arrive at his or her own conclusions: " . . . en lugar de una visión posmoderna de una cultura frontera fragmentada. El propósito es una representación mimética de una cultura oral mediante la inclusión del lector como jugador en un juego de descodificar las múltiples y enredadas interlocuciones" (14). In my opinion, Zilles is over-emphasizing the importance of oral text at the expense of the written documents that Hinojosa includes and counterposes throughout the *KCDT,* as can be appreciated in my arguments above.

Works Cited

Bhabha, Homi K. "DissemiNation: Time, Narrative, and the Margins of the Modern Nation." *Nation and Narration*. London: Routledge, 1990. 291-322. Print.

Bruce-Novoa, Juan. "Canonical and Non-Canonical Texts." *Retrospace: Collected Essays on Chicano Literature, Theory and History.* Houston: Arte Público Press, 1990. 132-145. Print.

Busby, Mark. "Faulknerian Elements in Rolando Hinojosa's *The Valley.*" *MELUS* 11.4 (Winter, 1984): 103-109. Print.

Calderón, Héctor. *Narratives of Greater Mexico: Essays on Chicano Literary History, Genre, and Borders*. Austin: University of Texas Press, 2004. Print.

Gutiérrez-Jones, Carl. "Legal Rhetoric and Cultural Critique: An Institutional Context for Reading Chicano Narrative." *Rethinking the Borderlands: Between Chicano Culture and Legal Discourse.* Berkeley: University of California Press, 1995. 9-49. Print.

Hermans, Hub. "Hacia una lectura deconstructivista de la narrativa de Rolando Hinojosa." *Actas Irvine-92. Asociación Internacional de Hispanistas.* Vol 5: "Lecturas y relecturas de textos españoles, latinoamericanos y US latinos." Ed. Juan Villegas. Irvine: University of California, 1994. 363-69. Print.

Hernández, Guillermo E. *Chicano Satire: A Study in Literary Culture.* Austin: University of Texas Press, 1991. Print.

Hinojosa, Rolando. *Becky and Her Friends.* Houston: Arte Público Press, 1990. Print.

___. *Claros varones de Belken/Fair Gentlemen of Belken.* Trans. Julia Cruz. Tempe, AZ: Bilingual Press/Editorial Bilingüe, 1986. Print.

___. *Dear Rafe.* Houston: Arte Público Press, 1985. Print.

___. *Klail City.* Houston: Arte Público Press, 1987. Print.

___. *Mi querido Rafa.* Houston: Arte Púbico Press, 1981. Print.

___. *Partners in Crime.* Houston: Arte Público Press, 1998. Print.

___. *Rites and Witnesses.* Houston: Arte Público Press, 1982. Print.

Hinojosa-Smith, Rolando. "The Other American Literatures." *Old Southwest / New Southwest: Essays on a Region and Its Literature.* Ed. Judy Nolte Lensink. Tucson: Tucson Public Library, 1987. 17-24. Print.

___. "The Sense of Place." *The Rolando Hinojosa Reader: Essays Historical and Critical.* Ed. José David Saldívar. Houston: Arte Público Press, 1985. 18-24. Print.

Kanellos, Nicolás. "Orality and Hispanic Literature of the United States." *Redefining American Literary History.* Eds. LaVonne Brown Ruoff, et al. : MLA, 1991. 115-123. Print.

Karrer, Wolfgang. "Realism and Real Estate in Rolando Hinojosa's *Klail City Death Trip Series.*" *Perspectivas transatlánticas en la literatura chicana: Ensayos y creatividad*. Málaga, Spain: Universidad de Málaga, 2002. 167-180. Print.

Kaup, Monika. *Rewriting North American Borders in Chicano and Chicana Narrative*. NY: Peter Lang, 2001. Print.

King, Rosemary A. *Border Confluences. Borderland Narratives from the Mexican War to the Present*. Tucson: The University of Arizona Press, 2004. Print.

Limón, José. "Border Literary Histories, Globalization, and Critical Regionalism." *American Literary History* 20.1-2 (208): 160-182. Print.

Martín-Rodríguez, Manuel. *Life in Search of Readers: Reading (in) Chicano/a Literature*. Albuquerque: University of New Mexico Press, 2003. Print.

Neate, Wilson. "The Function of Belken County in the Fiction of Rolando Hinojosa: The Voicing of the Chicano Experience." *The Americas Review* 18 (Spring 1990): 92-102. Print.

Rodríguez del Pino, Salvador. *La novela chicana escrita en español: cinco autores comprometidos*. Tempe: Bilingual Review Press, 1982. Print.

Saldívar, José David. *The Dialectics of Our America: Genealogy, Cultural Critique, and Literary History*. Durham: Duke University Press, 1991. Print.

___. "Rolando Hinojosa's *Klail City Death Trip*: A Critical Introduction." *The Rolando Hinojosa Reader: Essays Historical and Critical*. Ed. José David Saldívar. Houston: Arte Público Press, 1985. 44-63. Print.

Strickland, Barbara. "Crossing Literary Borders." *Weekly Wire Books*, 2 Sept. 1997. Web. 29 July 2010.

Zilles, Klaus. "Cultura y memoria oral en la comunidad chicana de Rolando Hinojosa." *Revista Aleph* 145 (2008). Web. 29 July 2010.

The Polifacetic Individualism of Rolando Hinojosa's *Klail City Death Trip*

Mark McGraw
Ouachita Baptist University

Few people can boast of a life of as much depth and variety of experience as Rolando Hinojosa Smith. In various stages of his life he has been a laborer, soldier, high school teacher, and academic administrator and he continues to flourish creatively as a professor and writer. His life experience has produced a personal philosophy that is reflected very clearly in his work. The key point of Hinojosa's philosophy has to do with individualism: that there exists in the human being a paradox of constancy and of inconsistency. "We are, at the same time, the same and different" ("Always Writing" 66). These individual similarities and differences go much further than race, gender, educational level or social class.

It is worth mentioning that the Rio Grande Valley of the *Klail City Death Trip* (*KCDT*) is not an environment that we would think of as lending itself to individualism. The gears of the social machinery in the *KCDT*'s Valley are very strong, the family ties are extremely deep and long-lasting, and many people are forced to live by the good will of powerful business interests like the bank and the ranch. The individual who dares to get out of step with community customs and expectations is punished with unjust gossip and salacious comments.

Nevertheless, Hinojosa's Valley is populated by people imbued with a remarkable spirit that gives them a tremendous individual dignity. *KCDT* gives us a unique opportunity to examine this individualism in the shadow of collectivity. This work studies the theme of individualism in the *KCDT* as it is developed within institutions such as the Catholic Church, the U.S. Army, the business world, patriarchic society, and the university environment.

There are various characters who reflect Hinojosa's brand of individualism, but the most notable are the two primary protagonists: Jehu Malacara and Rafa Buenrostro. These characters, together with Esteban Echevarría and P. Galindo, serve as the *KCDT*'s narrators. It is not accidental that three of these four raconteurs are orphans. The fact that they have no parents to guide and protect them from the world's vicissitudes causes them to have to navigate the world on their own, and so they face the cruel realities of the world's institutions very early in their lives. This underlines and brings into sharp relief the character's individualism. Additionally, there are dozens of secondary characters like Viola Barragán, Becky Escobar and Don Manuel Guzmán who demonstrate the same willingness to follow their own personal path instead of adhering to societal and institutional expectations.

Historically, one of the most important institutions in the collective life of the Valley has been the Catholic Church. Rolando Hinojosa was raised in a Catholic home and he continues to identify himself as a Catholic (Hinojosa 2009). But he saw in his adolescence the arrogance of the Spanish priests and he saw the Church slowly losing its influence over the Tejano population in the Valley ("Always Writing" 68).

In the first book of the *KCDT*, *Estampas del Valle*, the Church's hypocrisy is seen reflected in the local priest. Don Pedro abuses his power as a priest when he refuses to bury Bruno Cano for purely personal reasons, a decision doubly impactful due in grand part to the fact that Don Pedro's verbal provocation and refusal of assistance when Bruno was trapped in a deep hole were key contributing factors in Bruno Cano's death (*Estampas* 46). Although the entire scene was built around the comic episode of Bruno looking up at Don Pedro shouting insults about the priest's mother and demanding to be helped out of the hole, the religious context of this story is very strong, evoking the parable of the Good Samaritan in *Luke* 10 and the confrontation between Jesus and the Pharisees in *Luke* 14: 1-6. When his close friends manage to get approval for him to be buried in the parish cemetery, a great multitude attends the funeral in spite of the personal conflict between Bruno Cano and Don Pedro, a fact that reinforces the idea of the loss of the Church's influence and authority in the Valley.

The individualistic attitude toward the Church is symbolized by the personal voyage of Jehu, who starts as an altar boy, passes through a Protestant stage with Brother Imás, and takes a turn that includes service as an itinerant preacher (*Klail City* 80, 97). It is during this period of evangelization when Jehu confirms his rejection of Catholic doctrine (*Claros varones/Fair Gentlemen* 66). Later in his life, Jehu leaves the evangelizing field and separates himself once and for all from organized religion. Jehu maintains his individualistic attitude toward religion with a declaration that affirms the individualism of the Creator Himself: "God is great—and although I've quit preaching and other things—I can attest to His mysteries and His working alone, without a committee. God works on his own, then" (*Claros varones/Fair Gentlemen* 132). It is not a small point that Jehu, with his notable individualism, proclaims the individualism and sufficiency of God Himself.

The moral aspect of *Becky and Her Friends* presents a special opportunity to examine the theme of individualism since Becky makes a very public and well-known decision that violates both societal norms and Church law. The narrator of *Becky and Her Friends* interviews two local priests. Matías Soto, the Spanish priest, seems to be much more worried about the buildings and programs of the Church than the wellbeing of his parishioners.

Instead of considering the conditions that caused Becky's decision, he worries who will replace Charlie as an acolyte and who will take Sarita's place as a helper in the Dames of the Perpetual Candle Society (137). The other priest, Gualberto Ornelas, one of the few Tejano priests in the Valley, has a difference of opinion about the severity of Becky's offense and here we see a fundamental Church inconsistency. Ironically, Father Ornelas is exiled from his first parish in Houston to the Valley by Church authorities for attempting to help the socially marginalized (curiously the same ministry emphasized by Christ) (117). Another interesting note about the interviews with the priests is that they, in sharp contrast with the other people interviewed, fail to offer anything to eat or drink to the interviewer.

The *KCDT* is populated by Catholics who attend church only out of habit. In *Becky and Her Friends* Ursula Ortegón demonstrates her individualized faith when she says, "I attend Mass, still go to confession, and I'm a communicant, but it's become a pastime now. . . . So, I believe in Mary, in her Son, and in God; nothing easier. I just don't believe in the Church. I've seen too much, heard too much in this house on this porch, in my brother's old room" (70). Ursula's comments are especially impactful because of her status as a Church insider. The brother she mentions is a bishop of the Catholic Church (66).

Another important institution in the life and work of Hinojosa is the United States Army. Rolando Hinojosa develops his opinion of the Army through personal experience, having volunteered for service at the age of seventeen and serving in combat in Korea as part of Task Force Smith, the first U.S. response to the North Korean invasion of June, 1950 (Saldívar 45). Rafa Buenrostro, the literary reflection of Hinojosa in the Army, is a good soldier, brave in combat, faithful to his fellow soldiers, and dependable in his duties. Jehu Malacara also served in the Army and in Korea as a chaplain's assistant. For Rafa, Jehu and Rolando, the Army represented a way out of the Valley, an opportunity to see the world outside of the United States, and a chance to prove themselves in the crucible of combat.

Nevertheless, the Army in the *KCDT* is not a destination, but a path to Rafa's personal destiny. When Rafa's battery commander asks if he's going to make the military a career, Rafa emphatically but respectfully answers, "*No*, sir" (*Rites and Witnesses* 79). Rafa reiterates this idea in *Useless Servants* when he expresses a keen interest in learning all the workings and functions of the Army, but decides he will leave it to others as a way of life. So while Rafa shows himself to be a valuable soldier who gets along with his peers and his seniors, he is definitely on a different wavelength from the great majority of his fellow soldiers. Even in his chance moments of personal time in the Korean War, Rafa reads a book about the detailed history of the U.S. Navy while those around him read comic books (72). Rafa learns very early in his Army service that, like all soldiers, he is one more cog in the war machine and that his superiors will employ him as they wish in order to protect or advance their own careers. The same battery commander, Captain Bracken, who assures him, "you've got me . . . in your corner," when he visits the wounded Rafa in hospital, was also prepared to recommend him for a court martial for having opened fire on the enemy without permission, even though the lives of his fellow troops were saved (*Rites and Witnesses* 79, 83).

When Rafa learns that the institution has the tendency to sacrifice the individual on the altar of the organization's convenience, he does not think twice about lying to protect his friend against the Army's caprices. Rafa knows that his Valley friend Sonny Ruíz deserted the Army to live in Japan, but that is not what he tells the authorities in his "Starring role as 'a good man'" when he testifies falsely to the investigating board and swears that Ruíz was dead (*Korean Love Songs* 114). Rafa knows that a deserter's family would get no financial benefits and he reasons that Sonny's mother is "worth a howitzer or two" (114). To understand the complexities of Hinojosan individualism with respect to the Army, then, it is important to underline the fact that Rafa performs exceptionally well as a soldier: he is respectful to his seniors; he never shirks his duty, nor avoids the risks and dangers of the battlefield; numerous times he performs heroically in combat; and, he is decorated and promoted to sergeant. Yet, just as soon as his enlistment is over and he can go back to Texas, he does so.

The novel *Rites and Witnesses* juxtaposes two important institutions: the Army and business; and this gives us a good opportunity to examine the individual's role in the *KCDT*'s business sphere. Hinojosa explains his motives for including the business world in his work, stating, "I noticed, from elementary school through high school, that what we were taught regarding fair play and being Americans did not coincide when it came to equality in either the social sphere or the workplace. This too, formed part of what I was to include in my writing" ("Always Writing" 66).

Rites and Witnesses alternates two narratives from chapter to chapter: that of the Korean War and of Klail City Bank. The juxtaposition of these two narratives effectively shows the people of the Valley, with the Bank acting as higher command, as soldiers at war. The Bank cynically manages the region's politics, takes the best land from its owners, and hires and fires according to the caprices of the Bank's president, Noddy Perkins. The Bank's actions do not result in the immediate deaths of its victims, but the results are similar: those who do not fit the Bank's purposes are unflinchingly sacrificed; they are collateral damage in the Bank's fight for terrain and political leverage. Just as soldiers themselves are itemized weapons of the army, the likes of Ira Escobar and Polín Tapia are the political and racial tools of the bank.

The individualism of the employee in the *KCDT*, best represented by Jehu's role in the Bank, is complex because Jehu knows that he must participate, in certain measure, in the Bank's unethical arrangements. In fact, at one point, Jehu, at his wit's end with Noddy, leaves the Bank and the Valley and returns to the university for graduate studies. Jehu later returns to the Bank and continues in his previous job, eventually rising to the job of bank president (*We Happy Few* 72). Jehu knows that his value as an employee gives him a certain amount of influence over Noddy. He also understands that his job puts him in a position to help people: with time and patience he can be in a position to make the Bank a more positive influence in the Valley.

Patriarchy also acts as an unofficial, yet powerful institution in the Valley. Marta Castañeda and Jovita de Anda are typical Valley women who appear in the first stage of the *KCDT*. They turn up married and pregnant (not necessarily in that order) without any other resource than their own husbands. When Marta's husband goes to jail, she and her mother must depend on Marta's brother-in-law for financial support. When he dies, she and her mother become dependants of the state because they have no other independent options in the patriarchy (*The Valley* 65).

Parallel to the depiction of powerless and dependent women, however, is the participation of strong women like Viola Barragán. Her characterization in *The Valley,* the English-language recreation of *Estampas del Valle,* is noteworthy not just for her interesting role in the death of Pioquinto Reyes, but for her independence and sexual aggressiveness. Having accumulated a considerable inheritance from her multiple dead husbands, Viola fixes her gaze on a man she does not know and says to herself, "I'm claiming this one as my property, and I'm doing it 'cause I want to; I don't need the money for food, this time" (*The Valley* 76). Later in the *KCDT* we meet Ángela Vielma, a high school dropout who gets work as a law office secretary. She eventually becomes an attorney and an associate in the same office where she was first hired. Ángela never marries and remains prosperous and independent, unbowed by the gossip of the community about her sexual preference (*Claros varones/Fair Gentlemen* 122).

As the protagonist of a novel, *Becky and Her Friends,* as well as of its Spanish-language recreation *Los amigos de Becky*, Becky Escobar is the most obvious example of feminist individualism in the *KCDT* when she decides to divorce Ira, quit the social club of the Valley's governing elite, and start a new life with Jehu. Nearing forty years old with two small children, Becky breaks her mother's grip of control and goes against the Church and the social expectations of the Valley, knowing that she will be the subject of rancorous arguments, gossip and discussions. Becky emphasizes the importance of her decision, saying, "Let's just say I saved myself, and let it go at that" (159).

Viola Barragán returns in *Becky and Her Friends* as a personality much more important than the rich widow of the previous novels. She is seen as Becky's mentor and protector as she manages several businesses and gains the hard-won respect of a considerable part of the Valley's population, especially among the business community. Viola rejects the traditional role of patriarchy's chaste and submissive woman saying, "I like the bed and if I like the guy, let's go and no holds barred. I've loved, been loved, here and abroad" (28). Viola approves of Becky's decision to divorce Ira and says with admiration, "And good for Becky, says I" (34).

Rafa and Jehu's military service gave them the benefits of the G.I. Bill, which represented another way out of the Valley, this time to the university where they pursue educational opportunities that for them will result in new lives. It is obvious that these two characters enjoy the studies and the independence of university life. Both of them, as a result of their life experiences and military background, possess a level of maturity that equips them for success. Nevertheless, they both find themselves once again under the control of an impersonal and authoritarian institution. For having written a paper that offended the political sensitivities of his exiled Czech professor, Jehu has to take a C and "swallow it. There was no appeal: not to the chairman, not to the dean, nor to anyone else. Jehu said the prof was a sui generis son-of-a-bitch and one just had to let it go at that" (*Claros varones/Fair Gentlemen* 38). Rafa runs into problems with a Professor Arévalo who will not answer his question and does not let him talk. Rafa tells us, "I asked Arévalo why Lugones used the word *plinto*-plinth- in one of his poems, and he took off on *pingo*—for God's sake—and he talked on *gauchos*, *pingos*, the *pampa* . . . My God, what a way to earn a living!"

(*Claros varones/Fair Gentlemen* 44). Nonetheless, life at the university is attractive for Rafa and Jehu and both of them earn degrees and later return for graduate studies.

The final novel to date in the *KCDT*, *We Happy Few*, takes place at a university in the Valley, which, like Klail City itself, is a fictional composite. Here, we see some of the same politicking as we did in the Valley's business environment (8). This novel works on several storylines, the most notable being the selection of a new university president. The matter of the university presidency hangs on the question of whether the new president will be a man who is Anglo or Hispanic. As it turns out, neither is selected and the decision is made to hire an Anglo woman with superb qualifications. It is the individual's qualifications that matter most, not his or her social, gender or racial identity. *We Happy Few* also handles an episode where a handful of Chicano students attempt to stage a "sit-in" protest. The protest quickly loses steam when the students realize that they, in fact, constitute a numerical and power-holding majority and have no cause for protest (29). The lesson of Hinojosan individualism is that the individual should sink or swim on personal merit or the lack thereof.

The *KCDT* presents several propositions for the reader's consideration. The first is that we, as individuals, must learn to live with institutions. To flee from one institution is to put oneself under the shadow of another. It is best to be a valuable employee, distinguished soldier, excellent student and outstanding professor in order to influence positively the aspects of the institution that are within one's reach. Nevertheless, the individual's loyalty to the organization must be limited, understanding that the loyalty of the institution toward the individual is, in fact, very limited and short lived. Another point of the Hinojosan individualism is the respect for the individualism of others. Rafa does not condemn those who go to Mexico to avoid military service and he does not disapprove of Sonny Ruiz when he deserts in Japan.

The final hallmark of individualism in the *KCDT* is that the individual must be prepared to deal with the gossip, lies and condemnation of the tongue-waggers when one makes decisions that reflect his or her individualism. Another of the *KCDT*'s narrators, P. Galindo, concedes, for example, that the people of the Valley, being gossipy by nature, are going to speak badly of Jehu for having left the bank and they will consider him guilty of embezzlement without any proof whatsoever (*Dear Rafe* 128).

In addition to highlighting Hinojosan individualism in the *KCDT*, we should not fail to examine the work in the light of literary theory. The fragmented form of many of Hinojosa's novels and the combination of the oral and the literary are clearly post-modern (Zilles 78). His rejection of the Lyotard-defined *metanarrativas* and his lack of faith in the "received truths" of the institutions are also post-modern (Zilles 79). Nevertheless, an in-depth study of Hinojosa's work reveals a philosophy that defies theoretical classification. Hinojosa does not demonstrate an indifference that one would expect of a post-modern writer. At no time does Hinojosa the writer abandon the concept of justice. An important effect of *Rites and Witnesses* is created by the strong contrast between the young men fighting and dying in combat in Korea and the rampant immorality and cynical manipulations of the Valley's rich and powerful. This contrast deliberately and carefully underlines the gross injustice of the situation. Klaus Zilles points out this distinction saying, "In contrast to the exhilarating, liberating use of aleatory writing that has become a trademark of postmodernist fiction and that clearly shuns responsibility towards it subject, Hinojosa's work is informed by a genuine concern for the people and the culture he writes about" (81). Another aspect of the *KCDT* that does not neatly fit within a post-modern category is that the characters continue to live, work and function according to their individualist values within the institutions. Jehu's flight from the bank is temporary. Within a very short time Jehu makes peace with Noddy and returns to work in jobs of increasing responsibility in the Bank.

It is undeniable that the *KCDT* is Chicano literature and that Hinojosa is a Chicano writer, but those who view the work and writer strictly as products of an ethnic environment may be uncomfortable with the description of both as individualistic. Nothing comes from nothing, after all, and both the writer and the literature come from Chicano roots. But to stop the analysis of the *KCDT* at the ethnic or cultural level is to give it short shrift and ultimately, to harm it. Stephen Greenblatt would say that to view the *KCDT* only through the prism of ethnicity makes the same mistake as the already disqualified national narratives:

> The narratives that characterized national literary histories were subjected to withering critiques by feminism, deconstruction, and new historicism. These critiques are suspended, however, when the narratives are put in the service of an identity politics presumed to be worthy of admiration and support. But no coherent arguments are made to justify this presumption or to account for the suspension of skeptical analysis or to explain why claims of racial memory or ethnic solidarity that are anything but progressive in the real-world politics of, say, Serbia, Rwanda, or Sri Lanka, not to mention Israel, the Sudan, Ireland, or South Africa, should somehow be transformed when they are set in verse or canonized in literary history. An uncritical academic celebration of local knowledge runs the risk of repetition compulsion and political naïveté or, alternatively, of cynical opportunism and enforced parochialism. (58)

Greenblatt cites an exchange between Jorge Luis Borges and Argentine literary historians who criticized Borges for lacking a sufficiently robust "gaucho" component in his writing. Borges answered that his writing was not tied to ethnicity or nationalism, but had to do rather with a feeling of difference that gives these groups an unfettered access not just to an autochthonous culture but to a wider field: "nuestro patrimonio es el universo" (our patrimony is the universe) ("El escritor" 222-223). This statement does not advocate the achievement of some utopian vanilla sameness or universality, but reflects "a consequence of difference and the agent of a vital, ongoing creation of a particular literary identity" (Greenblatt 61). "Anything we Argentine writers can do successfully," Borges concludes, "will become part of our Argentine tradition, in the same way that the treatment of Italian themes belongs to the tradition of England through the efforts of Chaucer and Shakespeare" ("The Argentine Writer" 178-179).

The protagonists of the *KCDT* do not express Mexican-American or Tejano or Chicano attitudes as much as individual, human attitudes. Jehu and Rafa are not restricted to the Valley where they are condemned to live the same lives as their ancestors. They exercise their free will, travel the world over, study what they find interesting, obtain the education required for success as they define it and work in the professions that they like.

This strong current of Hinojosan free will in the *KCDT* runs contrary to the cultural determinism that would claim that the actions and attitudes of Jehu and Rafa are pure products of Rio Grande Valley *Chicanismo*. Determinism would dictate that Jehu, thrilled with the prospect of having a solid job at the bank, would never quit. But he did quit for a time. Determinism would tell us that Rafa, having returned to the Valley with a law degree, would open a law office and get in on the Bank's moneymaking bonanza legalizing real estate deals. But Rafa joins the police. Rafa and Jehu are driven toward something the crowd does not see. They obey an internal compass instead of following the social expectations of the Valley. Jehu captures this desire in a letter to Rafa, "Also, there must be something else other than that slow, winding road to Our Lady of Mercy cemetery. There must be" (*Dear Rafe* 54). The work of Rolando Hinojosa, like Hinojosa himself, respectfully resists our ethnic and literary taxonomies and categorizations. The work, like the man, is after all, individual.

Works Cited

Borges, Jorge Luis. "The Argentine Writer and Tradition." *Labyrinths*. Trans. James E. Irby. Ed. Donald A. Yates and Irby. New York: New Directions, 1962. 171-179. Print.

___. "El escritor argentino y la tradición." *Prosa completa*. Vol. 1. Barcelona: Bruguera, 1980. 215-223. Print.

Greenblatt, Stephen. "Racial Memory and Literary History." *PMLA* 116.1 (2001): 48-63. 20 August 2010. Web.

Hinojosa, Rolando. *Becky and Her Friends*. Houston: Arte Público Press, 1990. Print.

___. "A Chicano Life. Always Writing." *World Literature Today*. 75 (2001). 65-71. Print.

___. *Claros varones de Belken / Fair Gentlemen of Belken County*. Trans. Julia Cruz. Tempe: Bilingual Press / Editorial Bilingüe, 1986. Print.

___. *Dear Rafe / Mi querido Rafa*. Houston: Arte Público Press, 2005. Print.

___. *Estampas del valle*. Tempe: Bilingual Press / Editorial Bilingüe, 1994. Print.

___. *Klail City*. Houston: Arte Público Press, 1987. Print.

___. *Korean Love Songs*. Osnabruck: Osnabruck Bilingual, 1991. Print.

___. Lecture. Hispanic Studies 670. Texas A&M University. 5 May 2009.

___. *Rites and Witnesses*. Houston: Arte Público Press, 1982. Print.

___. *The Useless Servants*. Houston: Arte Público Press, 2005. Print.

___. *We Happy Few*. Houston: Arte Público Press, 2005. Print.

Saldívar, José David. "Rolando Hinojosa's Klail City Death Trip: A Critical Introduction." *The Rolando Hinojosa Reader: Essays Historical and Critical*. Ed. José David Saldívar. Houston: Arte Público Press, 1984. 44-63. Print.

Zilles, Klaus. *Rolando Hinojosa: A Reader's Guide*. Albuquerque: University of New Mexico Press, 2001. Print.

The *Klail City Death Trip* as Seen through Spanish Narrative: Authors, Themes and Techniques of the Hispanic Tradition, with Special Reference to Benito Pérez Galdós

Stephen Miller
Texas A&M University

Critics such as Ríos, Calderón, Martín-Rodríguez and Zilles, in their studies of the *Klail City Death Trip* (*KCDT*) by Rolando Hinojosa-Smith (RHS),[1] have mentioned or considered specific works and authors of the Spanish literary tradition. Starting with the medieval period especially, Calderón in 1985 and 2004 (154-59, 166) and Zilles (11, 12, 205) discuss the presence in the *KCDT* of the medieval Castilian court biographers Fernán Pérez de Guzmán (c. 1376-c. 1460) and Hernando del Pulgar (1436-c. 1492) through their respective word paintings of important historical personages attached to the court of central Spain: *Generaciones y semblanzas* (Generations and Portraits) and *Claros varones de Castilla* (Fair Gentlemen of Castile). These titles are nearly repeated in the titles of the second volume of the *KCDT*, *Generaciones y semblanzas* (*Generations and Portraits*),[2] and—in terms of writing date—the fourth, *Claros varones de Belken/Fair Gentlemen of Belken Country*.[3] Ríos also invokes a writer known today mostly to professional readers of Spanish literature only:

Diego Torres Villarroel (1694-1770), the author of an autobiography which sometimes resembles that of the *pícaro* or rogue, that literary type that came to life in Spanish-language literature with the anonymous *Lazarillo de Tormes* (1554). Finally, Calderón (2004: 156) and Martín-Rodríguez (75, 78) add the Spanish novelist, dramatist and newspaper columnist Benito Pérez Galdós (1843-1920) to the list. Among all these authors Galdós is unique because he alone was the subject of Hinojosa's 1969 Ph.D. dissertation at the University of Illinois.

While Galdós' complete works constitute a long and complex oeuvre that is of the order of magnitude of those of Balzac, Dickens, Twain and Zola, for our purposes most important are two things: 1) Galdós' mature preference for dialogue and monologue over narration as the best means of presenting characters;[4] and, 2) his abiding realism that constitutes one of those literary "mirrors" in which the author's society then and, mutatis mutandis, now can see itself faithfully recreated in its daily, best, and worst aspects. Like the Shakespeare of the histories, the Scott of the Waverley Novels, and all the major nineteenth-century realists, Galdós placed the persons of his work in their historical place and time, and then created scenarios wherein his invented and historical characters revealed the situations, problems and conflicts of their very specific lives and times. Important for Hinojosa, who was also an undergraduate and master's level major in Spanish literature, was that his near contemporary Galdós, as in the case of other writers of the tradition in question, wrote in Spanish.

Therefore, given that Spanish was the first language both of Hinojosa and of four of the first five titles of the fifteen-volume *KCDT*, the following thesis suggests itself. When RHS began experimenting with what would become the *KCDT*, the Spanish-language novels of Galdós were his most immediate and closest model. In them Hinojosa, holder of three university degrees in Spanish language, literature and culture, found warrant and, perhaps, inspiration for writing about the *raza*, the default *KCDT* term used to denominate the traditional Spanish-language people of the

Valley. Just how different, from the viewpoint of majority Anglo culture (that of the *bolillada* or *bolillos)*, were, on one hand, the Spain of the Black Legend and Yellow Journalism of the Spanish-American War, and, on the other, Hinojosa's native and plundered Spanish-speaking southmost Texas homeland? Moreover, in Galdós RHS could see two things: the considered study of the socio-linguistic group with which the author identified; and, extensive recreations in dialogue of the particular speech registers unique to members of each strata. By extension, according to this reasoning, RHS could also feel confident in taking seriously his own socio-linguistic group just as did Galdós did his, and in rendering his group through its oral traditions in the very words of the characters he would create.

The fullest range of speech in Spanish among characters of the *KCDT* is recorded by those who have the most commonalities with RHS himself. These are his alter ego protagonists, Rafe Buenrostro and Jehu Malacara, who are in frequent contact with the many different speakers of their group. This means author and characters share upbringing in the Valley of the lower Rio Grande where they, all born around 1930, were members of a culturally-Mexican and Spanish-speaking minority. As RHS portrays and the informed reader knows, both the fictional characters and author share membership in a group whose hereditary lands, dating from the mid-eighteenth century, wound up in Anglo hands as the result of armed violence and legal chicanery (*The Valley* 78-81). Also, like RHS himself, when Rafe, Jehu and their Valley ethnic cohort fight in the Korean War,[5] they meet prejudice. For example, while the cousins Rafe and Jehu are bilingual in English and Spanish at a university level,[6] and most definitely use English in dealing with superiors and Anglo peers, they find themselves on the battlefields of Korea under some suspicion. This is because they sometimes fall into their first-language Spanish when talking with Valley friends. Even the general officer under whom they serve, an Anglo Texan from the center of the state as a matter of historical fact, wonders in public about their patriotism because he thinks of them as Mexicans.[7]

Given this unattractive panorama of the experience of RHS's minority group "at home" in the United States and abroad fighting its wars, it is most relevant to bear in mind a quote by the Spanish dramatist and screen writer Alfonso Sastre (b. 1926), an anti-Francoist militant in the Spanish communist party who was sometimes jailed for his activities. When asked about his nationalistic identification in the post-Franco Spain of the increasingly prominent and sometimes separatist regional autonomies movement, Sastre, who for some years was identified as a supporter of separatist Basque Country politics, responded: "I am neither Basque nor Spanish [. . .]. My country is the Castilian language for which I have a true love. Hence I am not an ex-patriot because I have the Castilian language which is my country. For me the Castilian language is my true country!" ("Ni soy vasco ni soy español. [. . .] Mi patria es la lengua castellana, por la que tengo un verdadero amor. Así que no soy un apátrida porque tengo a la lengua castellana, que es mi patria. ¡A la lengua castellana la considero como mi verdadera patria!").[8] Is it too much to suggest, in view of this perspective offered by Sastre, that the younger Hinojosa who, to my knowledge, never expressed any notion about being Spanish,[9] did nonetheless find in Spanish-language literature something like his "country" and without doubt part of his tradition?

It will be remembered that during the period of RHS's 1952 B.A. in Spanish through his course work and thesis for his 1962 M.A. (related to *Don Quixote;* see Saldívar 45), and, seven years later, Ph.D., Latin American literature was just beginning to assert its rightful place in the curriculum of university programs centered around Spanish language and Ibero-American culture. For its part, literature in Spanish or English by U.S. Hispanics had no standing whatsoever. These personal and generational facts of RHS's pre-professorial university career lead me to form an hypothesis: that in the literature of Spain the bilingual Hinojosa, who had been born into a culturally-Mexican, discriminated-against native population within the United States, found at the very least his first linguistic-literary country; and that some of the most influential leading "citizens" for him were medieval chroniclers of Castile and included Cervantes, other Golden Age authors and Galdós among others. It is in this context that the work of Benito Pérez Galdós achieved the particular standing of being his dissertation subject. But before specifically discussing Galdós and Hinojosa, let us consider certain details of the Spanish literary tradition as it relates to RHS and the *KCDT*.

I: The Identification of Cultural-Literary Protagonists

Taking as our starting point, then, the theory that the literature of Spain was an important literary "country" for RHS, it seems he probably saw several things in Pérez de Guzmán's *Generaciones y semblanzas* and Del Pulgar's *Claros varones de Castilla*. First were parallels between members of his group and those whose Castilian biographies he was reading. Yet, unlike the author of a mock epic, for example, who signals the gravitas difference between greats of the past and the contemporary figures he satirizes by revealing the smallness of the latter when compared with the history-spanning former, Hinojosa's implicit invocations of the Castilian chroniclers are positive. It is not that there is the claim that there are literal parallels between, on one hand, the historical Castilians on the verge of creating the greatest empire the world had seen to date, and, on the other, some of the leading *raza* figures through two centuries in that semi-forgotten corner of the world known as the Valley. Rather, as a combat-veteran of one of America's non-epic, "forgotten wars," the one in Korea, RHS saw an underlying common ground. He knew that greatness, even if removed from public view and witnessed by few, was serious, real and needed to be chronicled. Whether among the Anglo-spurned *raza* of the remote—above all in the early *KCDT* volumes—Valley, or in the anonymous ranks of young soldiers, NCOs and junior officers in Korea, RHS needed to create characters as *estimable for their time, place and struggle* as were for theirs the distinguished members of the fifteenth-century Castilian court.

Beginning with *Estampas del Valle y otras obras* and his English-language recreation of it titled *The Valley*, and extending through other early volumes of the *KCDT*, RHS created the fictional equivalent of the real-life, *raza* generational cohort he first calls the "Los revolucionarios" ("The Revolutionaries"; *Estampas* 91-95)[10], and later "The Old Revolutionaries" (*The Valley* 78). Just as the Rafe Buenrostro journal entries, which constitute *Useless Servants* in the *KCDT*, make no exaggerated claims for the "Old Guys"—old China hands by the time WWII made them into veteran sergeants—who later must both train artillery recruits to hold the line in Korea and then lead by example,[11] there is no unseemly praise for the Valley's "Old Revolutionaries" generation in their time and place. Both groups of veterans did something of inestimable worth: each stood fast where their lot had determined, i.e., respectively in South Korea against the North and China, and in the Valley against Anglo depredations. And just as the Old Guys trained and prepared the artillery recruits for Korea, which included Rafe and his military cohort, the Old Revolutionaries prepared the 1930s birth cohort of Buenrostros and Malacaras for their role in Valley confrontations between the *raza* and the *bolillada*.

The Old Revolutionaries generation consisted of men like Don Braulio Tapia, Don Evaristo Garrido, Don Manuel Guzmán and Don Esteban Echevarría. In the late 1860s through early 1880s they "were all born here, in the United States, but they too fought in the 1910 Revolution as did the Mexican mexicanos" (*The Valley* 78; cf. *Estampas* 91) and for truly American ideals: the freedom of Mexican peasants from the Mexican government-protected exploitation by foreigners and the Mexican land-holding class. Stressed also is the *American* pedigree of the Old Revolutionaries. It dates from Spanish royal land-grant times among people who lived in what became the United States nearly two generations before the country came into being, nearly four generations before Mexico did, and more than four before Texas did: "The parents of these men were also born in this country, as were their grandparents; this goes back to 1765 and earlier, 1749" (*The* Valley 91; cf. *Estampas* 78). Further clarifications about these early Americans come in the next paragraph: "Other relatives stayed here, in their native Texas, during the [Mexican] Revolution, and some formed part of the Liberating Texas-Mexican Army—the seditious ones they were called" (*The Valley* 79; cf. *Estampas* 91). To be noted in this quote is the fact that these native-born Texans had to fight for their freedom from depredations by Anglos who often were not even born in Texas.

Without going into extensive detail, suffice it to say that the Old Revolutionaries ceased active participation in the Mexican Revolution when they saw its ideals being negated by the self-interested fight for power among corrupt generals.[12] Unfortunately, as can be understood from the quote towards the end of the previous paragraph, more violence awaited the Old Revolutionaries on their return to the Valley around 1915, and they did not hesitate to join their generational cohort of the Texas mexicanos who did not go to Mexico around 1910. These, instead, were the vanguard of those who found themselves in armed conflict on their native ground to retain what Anglo law and violence had left of their hereditary lands. This fight for freedom coincided with or was occasioned by the Anglo movement to "repatriate" to Mexico *raza* citizens of the United States, particularly in Southwestern states such as Texas.[13] In the *KCDT* there is no extended treatment of this violence, yet it is a theme periodically invoked by the Old Revolutionaries and understood by the youth of the Rafe/Jehu cohort. Hence, this history always lies close to the surface in *raza-bolillada* relations throughout the entire *KCDT*, albeit with time their historical bitterness and violence begin to recede.[14] Finally, while it can only be noted here, in the *KCDT*, as in the chronicles of Castile, fundamental to the formation of their respective *claros varones* or "fair gentlemen" is the experience of war, be it in Mexico, the United States, Europe, the Pacific or Korea.[15]

II: Orphans and the Picaresque in Spanish Narrative and the *KCDT*

Perhaps not so surprising in a literary series titled the *Klail City Death Trip*, there are a lot of deaths in its fifteen volumes. All the same it is striking when in *Useless Servants*, the narrator Rafe Buenrostro notes, during a mail call in Korea that he shares with two good Valley friends and members of his artillery unit—Charlie Villalón and Joey Vielma—, that only one of these three twenty-year olds has both parents living (81). Furthermore, all three are veterans of the poorly-equipped Task Force Smith, the first troops shoved into action against the invading North Koreans in the first days of July 1950. Explaining their status to Rafe and other new guys like him, a veteran NCO refers to their unit as "orphans" because the hastily-formed, "makeshift" Task Force was not a regular army unit with all the structure and support such units have built into their organization (*Useless Servants* 28, 18). Implicit in the NCO's observation is a need to belong to something bigger than only to their "small unit, the battery" (18). As his time in Korea continues, Rafe indicates that within the ranks of American soldiers the Old Guys (the old China hands and WWII battle-made sergeants) form among themselves their own kind of family and that the growing number of combat deaths among them are like deaths in their blood families. This fact is enhanced as Rafe comes to realize that some of these thirty-something year old men have already been in the Army for twenty years in 1950. For example: his mentor and, eventually, friend Sgt. Hatalski "lied about his age" when he "enlisted in 1930" (*Useless Servants* 30). Among the recruits who are Rafe's age, there are, if they survive, future Hatalskis, products all, it must be assumed, of families broken by some combination of Depression-era poverty and deaths. One of these "young guys" is Skinner. He was adopted in very early childhood, but has been on his own since eighth grade. Following some time as a commercial fisherman in Louisiana, the throw-away child that was Skinner enlisted at sixteen and, otherwise without family, states now: "I plan to make the Army my home: I like it here" (54). Three months later, following horrific casualties and more makeshift reassignments of personnel, Rafe sees himself and his battery as "Orphans all over again" (77). Finally, when his something like seventeen months under fire come to end, just about everyone Rafe served with and under, including the spotter Lt. Brodkey, Sgt. Hatalski and other Old Guys, as well his life-long Valley friends Charlie and Joey, was dead, and he again a kind of orphan (*Korean Love Songs* 53). The first thing Rafe does upon return to the Valley is go to Joey and Charlie's surviving parents to tell them of the exploding shell that hospitalized him, but left them "orphaned" of their sons.

Orphanhood, as indicated literally in the mail-call reference above, is an implicit theme of the *KCDT*. Jehu Malacara, the first identifiable narrator/protagonist of the series, is also the most-orphaned of all characters. He is introduced in the fourth *estampa* or sketch of *Estampas/The Valley*. The section is narrated retrospectively by Jehu and titled very expressively in Spanish: "Huérfano y al pairo" (29); and in the 1973 Valadez translation: "Orphaned and Looking Forward" (*Estampas*, 1973 ed., 58). Jehu, an only child, was seven when his worn-out mother died; then, at nine, his drunkard father passed away, and no family member came forward to care for him. Moreover, about three years later, Jehu was figuratively orphaned again when Don Víctor Peláez dies. This man was a Mexican who had left the Mexican Revolution and Mexico for the same reasons explained above as the *raza* Old Revolutionaries. In Texas he made his living with his travelling carnival, and, taking pity on the nine-year-old Jehu, became more of a father and family to him than his biological equivalents ever had been (*Estampas* 29-39/*The Valley* 21-27).

For his part, a very young Rafe Buenrostro witnessed his father shoot and kill a man who had come at him with a knife (*Estampas* 116/*The Valley* 45), and when Rafe was twelve, his father died because of the Leguizamón-organized assassination by hired killers (119/49; also see note 14). Rafe's mother's death may have occurred when he was too young to remember her (*Claros varones/Fair Gentlemen* 188-89), but that information is a bit obscured because he sometimes refers to a paternal aunt as his mother (188-89). To be noted is that despite all the parallels between the first twenty-four years or so of RHS's life with those of Jehu and Rafe,[16] the young RHS's family life in the Valley was a happy one, not the violence-filled and/or sorrowful orphanhood of Jehu and Rafe.[17] This very specific break between creation and biography may signal a conscious artistic decision. And the fact that the third most important narrator of the *KCDT*, P. Galindo, is also an orphan underlines this assertion.

In the chronological order of the writing of the *KCDT*, P. Galindo first appears briefly in *El condado de Belken. Klail City* (97-106)/*Klail City* (7, 54-70). Then he has greater importance in *Claros varones de Belken/Fair Gentlemen of Belken* (67-131). He subsequently authors more than half the pages of *Mi querido Rafa* (54-112)/*Dear Rafe* (61-134) where his interviews of many characters are accompanied by side-comments on his own impending death from some combination of a bad liver, lung and skin cancer (*Mi querido Rafa* 7/*Dear Rafe* 7). Finally, in *Becky and Her Friends* (9, 27, 31)/*Los amigos de Becky* (22) his probity and knowledge of the *raza* is recalled. Born around 1910,[18] the relatively short-lived Galindo soon learned of death first hand. It happened as a result of the ur-death-trip event of the *KCDT* when in the town of Flora "a train struck and killed some twenty to thirty people in a farm truck on their way to work in the fields" (*Estampas* 45/*The Valley* 34;[19] *El condado de Belken* 103/*Klail City* 61). Among the dead were the relatives of many figures in the *KCDT*, and, in the present context, most particularly both of Galindo's parents. Later it seems he may have fought in WWII in the Pacific (*El condado de Belken* 101/*Klail City* 59).

Especially poignant, then, for the careful reader is a short conversation between Galindo and Arturo Leyva. Both men are the same age, have known each other their whole lives, and have been aware of and then been friendly with Jehu most of his life. At one point and quoting the deceased, venerable Old Revolutionary Esteban Echevarría in defense of Jehu against all who would find fault with him, Leyva says: "Leave that boy be! What can any of you teach him that he hasn't already seen or lived? Being an orphan's a bitch, and it gives but one lesson: if you quit, you die! Leave him be, I say" (*Dear Rafe* 120; cf. *Mi querido Rafa* 104).

Such a direct apologia for Jehu resonates through the reader's whole experience of the first half of the *KCDT*. At varying ages and degrees in their lives the three principal, identifiable narrators—Jehu, Rafe, Galindo—have known what it means to be deprived of the support and shelter which the functioning nuclear and extended family gives to its children. After his father's funeral Jehu naturally goes to an aunt's house, but soon understands his aunt has all she can handle with her own dysfunctional family and feels no responsibility for him. At that point Jehu begins his series of positions as servant/errand boy for strangers. Among these, who in classical picaresque fashion become his masters, figure: the good man and mentor Víctor Peláez who for three years gives Jehu shelter and occupation while helping him learn to read; some time in service to the Anglo-friendly Javier Leguizamón, a detail that shows how much on his own he was when it is remembered that there was great enmity between the Leguizamóns and the Buenrostro part of Jehu's extended family; time as the local Catholic priest's acolyte and boy-for-everything, but then a much more satisfactory period serving as guide and translator to Brother Imás, a Pentecostal evangelizer with broken Spanish; then some work in an uncle's gambling parlor that probably coincides with his high school years; and, finally post high-school graduation enlistment in the U.S. Army. All these periods have accompanying anecdotes, and, as Echevarría was quoted to say, taught him much about life.

Moreover, at this point in the *KCDT* these narrators have no significant other in their lives: Jehu is a ladies-man-about-town; Rafe's first very young wife and her parents drowned in the Rio Grande before he went to Korea (*Claros varones/Fair Gentlemen* 182-85; *Rites and Witnesses* 37); Galindo has been widowed twice, divorced presently and has no children (*Dear Rafe* 103; cf. *Mi querido Rafa* 90). Even old Echevarría, who is the oral-culture repository of so much knowledge of the late 19th- and early 20th-century Valley, is widowed with no children, and no relatives who merit mention. Moreover, the orphanhood/aloneness theme in the *KCDT* is further underlined when it is remembered that Viola Barragán, the most dominating female presence in the *KCDT*, has lost her parents by the present time of the Series and, what is more, has been widowed three times (*Becky and Her Friends* 26). Also, between her second and third husband, this widow who never had children had her married lover Pio Quinto Reyes die during love making in the motel they were using (*Estampas* 87/*The Valley* 74). And, Lt. Rafe Buenrostro's friend, the gunned-down, assistant Belken County district attorney Dutch Elder, was an orphan at age eight who married a woman who entered the same orphanage at age six and married him when she was seventeen (*Partners in Crime* 103).

Now there is a literary subgenre particularly associated with the Hispanic tradition in Spanish that is linked with orphans and their attempts to make their way in the world. It is the picaresque novel, and its protagonist, the *pícaro* or rogue, is as original and essential to Hispanic culture and literature as are Don Quixote and Don Juan. Yet, whereas Don Quixote and Don Juan have well-known literary progenitors—Miguel de Cervantes (1547-1616) and the friar Gabriel Téllez (1579-1648), who wrote under the pseudonym Tirso de Molina—, the *pícaro* has no literary father. Fittingly for Lazarillo, the original starving Salamancan throw-a-away child who first incarnated the *pícaro*, his story titled *Lazarillo de Tormes* (1554), was published anonymously and to this day remains a literary "bastard" whose "mother" is Hispanic literature and culture, and for which the Tormes River flowing through Salamanca serves as patronymic.

At its initial and simplest level, the picaresque novel narrates episodically the adventures of a young person, who is an orphan, from a very early age like Lazarillo and Jehu Malacara, or somewhat later in life as occurs with Rafe Buenrostro and his fellow soldier Skinner. The young orphan must secure food and otherwise make his way through the world by serving a succession of masters and, in today's world, foster-parents. There is a succession because the masters themselves are characteristically impoverished and not infrequently cruel. With increasing age and experience the *pícaro* becomes less adaptable to the present master and needful of a new one who offers, in exchange for the naturally age-increased ability of the *pícaro*, the prospect of a better situation in life. The young serving person becomes a rogue or knave when and because s/he is obliged, every time with more wit, to cheat "hir" current unscrupulous master in the struggle to survive. When the *pícaro* reaches a certain age and the issues of subsistence are less central in "hir" life, different fates await.

Importantly within the free-will doctrines of traditional Hispanic culture, from the beginning of the subgenre and the ur-*pícaro* Lazarillo, there are moral choices to be made. An example is in the last episode of his narration where Lazarillo tells of his life, when as an adult he is at the peak of his socio-economic success. Yet, his success has a price. The condition of continuing to enjoy it is that he must look the other way as his wife and his patron, a high-ranking priest, carry on together. Another classic Spanish rouge, Francisco de Quevedo's 1626 *Paul the Sharper* (*Historia de la vida del Buscón, llamado Don Pablos*), lives a dicey street life on his way to becoming a wanted criminal who flees Spain for the Americas in order to avoid jail or life as a galley slave. At the conclusion of his autobiographical narrative, a product it should be remembered of Counter Reformation Spain, Paul the Sharper admits that nothing changed by going to America because he, of his own free will, continued to make poor choices in his life. The importance of this orthodox Catholic assumption of responsibility can best be understood, in our era of the doctrines of socio-economic determination and its specific version of victimization, by returning to critic Ríos in his editor's introduction to the first edition of Hinojosa's *Estampas del Valle y otras obras/Sketches of the Valley and Other Works*.

As part of his contextualization of Hinojosa and Chicano literature in general, Ríos observed that Chicano writers "entered the literary scene during the last stages of the period known as literary modernism" ([8]). For Ríos, keying off the Lionel Trilling of *Beyond Culture* (1965) and the Irving Howe of *Literary Modernism* (1967), this meant that contemporary mainstream American literature published in English was largely a product of a pervading cultural pessimism and exhaustion which, from Ríos' viewpoint, was totally foreign to Chicano peoples and writers. Inherently, still according to Ríos, Chicanos live by a "determination and hope" which "spring from a feeling of being completely free and capable of forging one's own destiny" ([9]).

Now, independent of the reader's personal position on deterministic philosophy, it is certain that Hinojosa's *KCDT*, beginning most decidedly in *Estampas/The Valley*, records how the main characters of the "trip," the orphaned cousins Jehu and Rafe, as well as many of their generation do forge, as much as is humanly possible, their own destiny. At the same time the *KCDT* makes it implicitly clear that luck is always a factor in life. While Rafe and Jehu survive Korea, Charlie Villalón and Joey Vielma do not. The same exploding shell that killed Charlie and Joey, as well as the Old Guy Sgt. Hatalski, only hospitalized Rafe who in due time fully recovered from his wounds.

It seems, in light of the foregoing, that the a hallmark of the *KCDT* is the non-autobiographically related decision by RHS to have his main narrators, as well as numerous other characters, be orphaned literally or practically in their lives. They then find themselves lacking a familial support system. As a result they are obliged and become accustomed to fending for themselves from as early in life as must the classic young rogues or *pícaros* of Spanish literature. All the same RHS's narrators do not become *pícaros*, but, as happens with some of the older and younger artillerymen Rafe meets in Korea, they are able to find and/or create circumstances for themselves which make them into anti-*pícaros*, i.e., into young people who are successful in finding the means to take charge of their lives and to avoid the immorality and, often, criminality that characterizes the life of the classic *pícaro*.

III: The Galdosian Anti-Picaresque, War and the *KCDT*

The first of the several major Galdosian creative projects was the series of historical novels known as the *National Episodes* (*Episodios nacionales*). Even though these novels came to consist of forty-six volumes, divided into four complete series of ten volumes each and of one incomplete series of only six volumes, published between 1873 and 1912, our interest is with the First Series written and published between 1873 and 1875. It has a global narrator/protagonist named Gabriel Araceli who in old age writes the story of his early life from its beginnings as a street child and potential *pícaro* in the southern port city of Cádiz. His single mother is wretchedly poor, has other smaller children at home, and hence Gabriel as the eldest must learn to earn his own bread the best way he can.[20] On the first page of his retrospective narration Araceli compares his early situation to that of the protagonist of Quevedo's *Paul the Sharper.* Yet he does this to establish from the outset a fundamental difference between him and Paul: even though his lack of birthright might have led him to turn out as did Paul, Gabriel made better choices and did not. It is important that we can use Ríos' already-quoted words describing the Chicanos to characterize Gabriel's life: this is always oriented by a "feeling of being completely free and capable of forging [his] own destiny" (9). This does not mean he does not suffer adversity or receive timely help in his life. Rather that he is always disposed to fight for his honorable place in the sun. Why Galdós orders his character's life in this manner is a complicated matter, but one Hispanic cultural factor behind this ordering is clear. Independent of the extent and depth of their relations to formal religion, Ríos' Chicanos—including Hinojosa's Buenrostro and Malacara—and Galdós' Araceli share a fundamental characteristic: they are culturally Catholic. They believe in free will and that their lives are fundamentally the product of the decisions they make, not of the situations into which they were born. Even Paul the Sharper recognizes, at the end of his narrative, that he was always the one making the bad decisions that obliged him to flee from the law in Spain to the New World and, once there, to continue in his errant ways. For his part Lazarillo makes his reader understand that he has made an aberrant moral choice in the present of his narrative: to assure his finally comfortable situation in life, he has entered into a marriage whose only purpose is to provide social cover for the illicit relationship between his nominal spouse and his priest benefactor.

In their books, Galdós and Hinojosa do not shy away from the portrayal of the difficult world of the young person who must survive by his intelligence and wits. Yet, at the same time, they do not portray deterministic hells of egoism and evil everywhere. Both authors populate their fictions with many good people, and their young men on their own find more good masters than bad. Jehu's Víctor Peláez is matched by the experienced Old Guy NCOs who teach young Rafe how to survive on the battlefield. And this last point is especially important because it marks another commonality authors Galdós and Hinojosa share: their portrayal of violence and combat deaths as a significant rite of passage for youths who could have been *pícaros* as they transition to manhood.

While, as we saw above, Rafe spends about seventeen months under fire in Korea, Jehu's Korea time was no vacation. As a chaplain's assistant in that exceptionally dynamic war zone, he must have seen much destruction and suffering, and almost necessarily found himself at one time or another under fire. For his part Gabriel's life as soldier is much longer than that of Jehu and Rafe, dates from earlier in his life, and, to be sure, has an epic dimension. It begins when Gabriel is perhaps twelve years of age, at nothing less than the world-historical Battle of Trafalgar in 1805, and then stretches from May 2nd, 1808 to 1814, time of the Peninsular Wars, i.e., the period of the Spanish War of Independence from the French.

Gabriel found himself at Trafalgar because he accompanied his elderly first master, a former naval captain onto a Spanish ship-of-the-line going into battle. When the casualties aboard the ship mounted on that storied day, the twelve-year old Gabriel stepped into the breach by helping man a cannon whose first crew were mostly dead, and, so most interesting from our *KCDT*/Hinojosa perspective, became an artilleryman firing 32 pounders instead of a howitzer! Following that experience, Gabriel decided to leave his first master who was responsible, in anticipation of Jehu's Víctor Paláez, for him learning to read and write. He walked and, as he could, rode the 300 miles north to Madrid. There he finds new masters, but more decisively for our purposes finds himself obliged to enter into the May 2nd, 1808 street fighting immortalized by Goya. This and the full development of the Spanish rebellion leads to Gabriel's military career as soldier, guerrilla liaison, officer and secret-agent acting for Spain. In this latter role he serves/receives direct orders from no less a historical personage than Arthur Wellesley, the 1st Duke of Wellington. And, despite having been a street boy, Araceli's rise is so pronounced by this time that a fictional English Lord, who plots to abscond with a young, innocent Spanish woman, accepts an honor challenge from Araceli to duel to the death by sword. When Araceli's skill is too great for the nobleman, the lord dies by the one-time street boy's hand.

Now, clearly, Galdós' Gabriel Araceli, the creation of a writer who was never a soldier in any form, has an epic/heroic/fictive dimension which Hinojosa shuns in treating Rafe and Jehu. After all, just as Korea, whatever its dangers and importance for the soldiers who fought there, did not approach WWII in its scope and geo-political impact, the combat veteran Hinojosa invokes no comparison between Gabriel's novelesque military career and those of the cousins Buenrostro and Malacara. As with the 15th-century Spanish court chronicles *Generaciones y semblanzas* and *Claros varones de Castilla* in their relation to the *KCDT*, Hinojosa suggests a structural, not an historical level of significant parallelism. His orphaned, potential-*pícaros* Rafe and Jehu share with the orphaned street urchin, potential *pícaro* Gabriel the refusal to be determined by circumstance. In the case of Rafe, particularly his experience of war in Korea, does for him what Gabriel's involvement in the Peninsular Wars effects for him: these experiences, much longer in the case of Araceli, more compacted, more intense in the case of Buenrostro, become the last stop in their young lives on the way to the men they will become. Notable, it bears mention to say again, is the role both Galdós and Hinojosa assign to war in forming their young protagonists.

About the time Galdós was finishing the First Series of *National Episodes,* he began his second major literary project, the contemporary novel of manners (i.e., his series of *novelas contemporáneas*). In a group of three of these titles (in four volumes published between 1878 and 1884[21]), the pre-teen Felipe Centeno, inspired by a specific series of chance events to want to become a physician, migrates from his poor mining town and poorer family in northern Spain to Madrid. Once there and having no luck, he one day falls unconscious in a park from hunger. By luck he is found by a kind, if quixotic, university law student and aspiring dramatist. Sometimes as a secondary character, sometimes as protagonist, Centeno, as with Araceli, becomes the prism through which some of the best and worst of contemporary Spanish life comes into focus. Like Araceli, Centeno does not meet the classic *pícaro*'s fate of bad masters. Rather, at one point as did Lazarillo before him with one of his masters, Centeno goes from being cared for by the law student to caring for him. How to interpret this modification of the picaresque pattern? It appears that Galdós' Araceli and Centeno and Hinojosa's Malacara and Buenrostro are the exemplars of the new men each writer offers to their respective societies, the new men for whom the times call. Yet while the structuring of the process is similar in both writers, the specifics are those proper to their respective times and societies.

Galdós invents Araceli in 1873. That year is toward the end of the period following the 1868 expulsion of Queen Isabel II from her throne and country and the series of democratic experiments which culminated in the unsuccessful First Spanish Republic which lasted from February, 1873 to December, 1874. Unlike the historical period of the triumphing Civil Rights movement in the United States which is reflected in the midway installments of the *KCDT*, the increasingly undemocratic Spain of the mid 1870s and early 1880s seems to have made Galdós' Centeno, the author's second anti-*pícaro*, very different from his first and from Hinojosa's Buenrostro and Malacara. While the elderly Araceli narrates his War of Independence era story from a position of accomplishment and ease towards his life's end, Centeno does not tell his own story. It is a third-person omniscient narrator who paints for the reader Centeno's warm spirit, modest intelligence, and, so different from the first-person narrators Araceli, Malacara and Buenrostro, low degree of self-awareness. Moreover, the reader learns of nearly the full spans of Gabriel, Jehu and Rafe's lives. The first goes from orphaned street boy to military officer to a true love marriage with the daughter of a countess and socio-economic success. In *We Happy Few* (2006), the last volume of the *KCDT*, we see Rafe and Jehu happily married and at the highest rung of their chosen professions of chief of detectives and bank president respectively.

By contrast, the reader never learns the full span of Centeno's life. When he, around age fifteen, leaves the main stage of Galdós' series of contemporary novels, it seems clear that Centeno's future, as that of Spain, will not be especially bright. The Restoration of the Bourbon monarchy ends the Republican dream, and Centeno no longer has hopes to be a doctor. Even as the reader admires him and feels concern for him, the literary character Centeno, as with so many tens of thousands of his decent real-life counterparts, simply disappears into the Galdosian rendering of the vast and growing urban landscape of Madrid.[22] In this Centeno prefigures so many of the good people of the *KCDT*: the salt of the earth types who play their numerous, albeit anonymous roles in the life of any society.

What the picaresque elements in Galdós and Hinojosa share, then, is the attention and care they demonstrate for even the most disadvantaged members—the initially defenseless orphans—of the literary versions of the real societies they recreate. And in common with the Chicano era of the Hispanic culture described by Ríos, both the Hinojosian and Galdosian portrayals demonstrate a confidence that the individual can make his own life, not be determined by his poor start in life. In so doing Galdós, Hinojosa and Ríos all agree with other authors of the Hispanic picaresque tradition, beginning with the anonymous creator of *Lazarillo de Tormes*, in attributing to the individual the strength needed to take the primary responsibility for his life. Almost as in nature, the protagonists of the Hispanic picaresque and anti-picaresque tradition fight and survive, or cease. There is no plot against them, simply the hard and sometimes extremely hard struggle for life.

IV: Commonalities of Technique in Galdós and Hinojosa

Over a long lunch with Rolando Hinojosa on Monday, August 25, 2003 in south Austin, he and the author of this study discussed among many other things the writing of Galdós. At the time of our first long one-on-one conversation, I simply wanted to discuss with a living writer that I admired the work of another writer I knew him to favor, and about whom I had written much over more than twenty years. In these days of specialization in the sub-fields of Hispanic Studies, and Herminio Ríos' broad vision notwithstanding, it is not easy to find contemporary writers in Spanish on this side of the Atlantic who know Spanish Peninsular literature well. Such is the power of the contemporary and such is the scorn many writers in Spanish feel today for their tradition.[23] But, returning to that 2003 August afternoon in Austin, it became especially clear that RHS knew the Hispanic tradition and, more to the point, Galdós.

The Galdosian-oriented part of the conversation began, then, with a question about William H. Shoemaker, Hinojosa's dissertation director and a man who evoked strong opinion in everyone who knew him. Rolando smiled, and said that "Bill Shoemaker was difficult and mean," that he had a real vision for the Department at Illinois, but that he was dictatorial in implementing it. When I asked specifically about Rolando's dissertation, "Money in the Novels of Galdós," part of Shoemaker's all-encompassing Galdosian project, RHS, still smiling, commented that if I read it, "perdemos las amistades" ("we're no longer friends"). He then elaborated that the dissertation covered Galdós' aforementioned *novelas contemporáneas* as distinct from the historical novels in which Gabriel Araceli, as we saw above, bulks so large.

In the context of a question about which part of Galdós most attracted him as author of the volumes of the *KCDT*, Rolando did not hesitate. He affirmed that it was constituted by *La incógnita (The Unknown)*, an 1888 epistolary novel in which Galdós broke from the dominate third-person narratives of his masterworks of the earlier 1880s, and a second Galdosian experiment, the 1889 novel *Realidad (Reality)*, written completely in dialogue, with some scenic indications, and published in the same format as would be the printed version of a dramatic work. What impressed Rolando, author of the epistolary novels *Mi querido Rafa* and *Dear Rafe*, was that the letters of *La incógnita* read like real letters, and that the dialogues of *Realidad* sound like the words of real people talking.

Now these two titles are neither normally cited nor studied as Galdosian masterpieces at the level of such narratives as *La desheredada* (1881; *The Disinherited Lady*), *Fortunata y Jacinta* (1886-87; *Fortunata and Jacinta*) and *Misericordia* (1897; *Misericordia*). So I asked Rolando if he was familiar with the 1897 Galdosian prologue to his third dialogue novel *El abuelo* (*The Grandfather*), to which he answered, "por supuesto" ("of course"). This is important because that is where Galdós gives a succinct, retrospective justification for changing from his dominant-until-then third-person, omniscient narrative to the epistolary novel and dialogued novels of 1888 and 1889.[24] At least two complementary factors were at play in the Galdós of that time: a profound change in the thematic center of gravity of his work and the need to develop requisite new means of artistic expression.

Toward the end of the 1880s Galdós is moving towards a predominately modernist literary aesthetic. Because he has come to doubt the social efficacy of the realist portrayal of the problems of contemporary society, he shifts his focus to the exploration of individuals who are problematic because, having found their nominally Catholic and democratic society's norms to be hypocritical mouthings signifying nothing, they no longer look to society to remedy its ills. The highly atypical priest Nazarín incarnates the new kind of Galdosian protagonist. He turns his back on the Church which fails to minister in a Christ-like way to the least of society, and begins by himself just such a ministry that serves directly the physical and spiritual needs of underdogs and outcasts who have nothing. This initiative causes scandal in a Church and society used to viewing its priests as part of the upper reaches of the social hierarchy, not as ministers to the poor. So, with the full force of hypocritical logic the Church and society persecute and eventually prosecute Nazarín for—in effect—so directly imitating Christ's own public life, thereby offering an unflattering contrast with the way the Church and society relate to the poor.[25]

Based even only on what was stated above, it should be clear that Galdós lost faith in the project which created Gabriel Araceli as the exemplar of a new middle class in Spain: that which created the second constitution of the Hispanic world (that of Cádiz, written in 1812); and that which foreshadowed a new, democratic Spain led by those who rose up, in the absence of their king held under "palace arrest" in France, and fought successfully for their independence from Napoleonic France. Yet as we saw above, in the 1883 *El doctor Centeno* the implicit contrast between Felipe Centeno and Araceli pointed to an increasingly less optimistic Galdosian view of his national society. Then, several years later in the late 1880s, it demonstrably made no sense to Galdós to chronicle the society presided over by a middle class which had forgotten its origins and whose richer echelons became a high bourgeoisie interested only in maintaining and bettering its privileged socioeconomic position. Having taken over many of the prerogatives and much of the wealth of the decaying or ruined landed aristocracy, the members of this group and the directions they set for society were no longer the novelistic themes about which Galdós cared. But before centering on the few extraordinary, atypical individuals in society, Galdós, precisely in the novels identified by RHS—*La incógnita* and *Realidad*—began to experiment with how best to present atypical, problematic characters. And this meant, as RHS observed about the novels, that Galdós would let the characters speak in their own words, whether epistolary or dialogue, and diminish almost completely the role of a narrator. But only some years later in the 1897 prologue to *El abuelo* did Galdós explain the technique: the characters "were made, were composed, imitating more easily . . . living people" as "they manifest their moral fiber with their own words and, through them, as in life, give, more or less, the key to what underlies their actions" (see the Appendix).

In the *KCDT* there is a different interface between techniques of representation and the social sign of the content. In the by now oft-mentioned introduction to the first edition of *Estampas del Valle y otras obras*, Herminio Ríos stressed in modernist Irving Howe's thesis that "A major impulse in modernist literature is a shocking nausea before the idea of culture" and the resultant "extremely pessimistic vision of man and society" (9). But, whereas Galdós was a leader in the first European manifestations of modernism, Ríos understands well that the work of Hinojosa and his generational companions comes when the exhaustion of the modernist period is evident: "Chicano literature arrives on this literary scene with a challenge and a great determination" (9). And he explains that Chicano "determination and hope spring from a feeling of being completely free and capable of forging one's destiny" (9). What Rios saw, then, in *Estampas* was the revelation "in a wide panoramic view" of "the vital strength of a people" (9). Needless to say, this was the Galdosian vision behind the creation of Gabriel Araceli, but which was already waning by the mid-1880s when he lets Felipe Centeno, his second anti-*pícaro*-protagonist, simply melt away into the anonymity of Madrid. Centeno will probably always be a good person, but never the medical doctor or person of consideration he had proposed for himself. The

Spain of that time did not let Galdós create such an ending. It was not verisimilar.

Hence, while the poles of the relation between favored techniques and socially-signed content reverse in key sections of the respective Galdós-Hinojosa creative trajectories, forming a kind of technique-content chiasmus, the following is certain: both Galdós and Hinojosa begin as keen, sympathetic observers of their societies and their typical people. This can be seen in how their anti-*pícaro*, *first* person narrators (Araceli in the First Series of *Episodios nacionales*, Jehu Malacara and Rafe Buenrostro beginning in *Estampas*) move through and document their hard-luck societies. Yet, in the end, the Galdosian and Hinojosian narrator/protagonists find more good than bad crossing their paths, and then as maturing individuals go on to be positive and public forces, respectively, in Spain and in the Valley. Moreover, Hinojosa chooses to follow the mature Galdós' discovery of how to best reveal character. Let the characters speak directly. And although Hinojosa writes no completely dialogued novel, he does have: 1) a prevalence of characters who without introduction simply speak in their own voice as in *Estampas del Valle*; 2) others whose interviews are recorded in their own words with quasi stage-direction interventions by the interviewer Galindo and, later, his nameless successor in such works as *Becky and Her Friends* and *Los amigos de Becky*; 3) the letter-writer Jehu to his cousin Rafe in *Mi querido Rafa* and *Dear Rafe*; and, 4) the lyric I of the prose poems of *Korean Love Songs* and the first-person singular narrator of the journal entries of *Useless Servants*.

In conclusion, then, I think we have seen in specific terms the justification for Herminio Ríos' large claims for Hinojosa, Chicanos and their culture in 1973, now two generations and fourteen volumes of the *KCDT* ago. We have seen also how Hinojosa may have found his linguistic-literary country in Spanish Peninsular literature from the medieval period through Benito Pérez Galdós. And the how and something of the why that by the second volume of the *KCDT* in 1976, no less a major figure of Spanish-language literature than the Uruguayan Juan Carlos Onetti joined others in greeting in Hinojosa's work "the rise of a singular Latin American literature: the Chicano" ("del surgimiento de una literatura singular: la chicana").[26]

Notes

[1] Many authors refer to the *Klail City Death Trip Series* as opposed to the *Klail City Death Trip*. While this is not the place to discuss at length the relative virtues of each denomination, I prefer *KCDT* because it puts the accent on "trip," a more dynamic word for me than "series." The books that compose the *Death Trip* are, to be sure, a literary series. What I wish to emphasize: the development of the *KCDT* characters is a journey or "trip" through different places and times.

[2] Archetypical of the checkered history of the publication of book-length narratives by Rolando Hinojosa, and indicative of the problems of publishing original works in Spanish by a U.S. writer, is the case of the second volume of the *KCDT*: its first edition was printed in Cuba, after winning the Casa de las Américas prize as the best Latin American [sic] novel of the year, under the provisional title *Klail City y sus alrededores* (1976); the second edition was published under the title that is important here to us: *Generaciones y semblanzas/*[Generations and Portraits] (1977); and, the third, definitive edition to date was published as *El condado de Belken. Klail City* (1994; see the Works Cited below for more detailed bibliographical information). For this second volume of the *KCDT* the author is listed either as "Rolando Hinojosa" or "Rolando R. Hinojosa-S"; this "S" stands for "Smith" and dates back to a mid-twentieth-century Mexican convention, since abandoned, of abbreviating the second or maternal first last name of person with only the capitalized first letter of it. The first, 1973 edition of *Estampas del Valle y otras obras* is also attributed to "Rolando R. Hinojosa-S".

[3] In an e-mail of August 2, 2012, RHS gives many details about the publication of *Claros varones de Belken/Fair Gentlemen of Belken*. These include his extensive editing of the Cruz translation from Spanish to English. He also writes that his copy of this translation work "will go to the Stanford library when the acquisition comes by (third trip) to pick up what's available." At the same time RHS says that he is by now uncertain of the date of composition of the novel in Spanish. My reasoning for considering it the fourth title of the *KCDT* in terms

of composition is a matter of language and content. The early volumes of the *KCDT* are written mostly in Spanish and thereby reflect the base language of its protagonists. While *Korean Love Songs*, the third volume in terms of writing and publishing of the *KCDT*, is written in English, this reflects the fact that its narrator, Rafe, is in a military society where *all* communication among the troops and officers is in English. Moreover *Claros varones* is the chronicle of the post-Korea return to the Valley of Rafe and Jehu, and to their Spanish-dominant society. *Mi querido Rafa*, the fifth volume of the *KCDT* is a totally bilingual volume and reflects the linguistic-social reality of Jehu and Rafe around 1962: they are both professionals whose life makes them natural linguistic and social bridges between their Spanish-speaking ethnic group and the still economically dominant Anglos. After *Mi querido Rafa* my contention is that no first edition volume of the *KCDT* has any primary Spanish-language dimension. For *Claros varones* to be the exception, an assumption which I reject, it would be necessary to posit that RHS decided to compose a new novel about the early 1950s written in Spanish, but at a time when the *KCDT* was centering on Rafe and Jehu as established professionals of the 1960s, not as recently-returned, young Korean War vets.

[4] For the primary theoretic statement by Galdós on the advantages of having characters present themselves in their own words, see the Appendix to this chapter.

[5] Not stressed in the *KCDT*, as in the case of Rafe, is that Jehu Malacara is also a Korean War vet. He served as a chaplain's aide (*Becky and Her Friends* 98,152/*Los amigos de Becky* 107), but the *KCDT* makes clear that all manner of support-role, non-line soldiers and officers, including chaplains, could, because of the rapidly changing front lines and consequent over-running of positions, find themselves in life-and-death situations on the front (*Korean Love Songs* 10, 13, 53; *Useless Servants* 56, 83, 108, 187).

[6] Interesting because of the parallels between RHS and his characters Jehu and Rafe is the following information about the intertwined military-university careers of RHS. According to an e-mail communication of February 20, 2011 from RHS to the author of this chapter, his first stint in the U.S. Army immediately followed graduation from high school as was the case for Rafe and Jehu. This was from August 46 to December 47. RHS then did a total of three semesters and four summer terms at the University of Texas at Austin between January 1948 and July 1949. He returned to the U.S. Army in September 1949 and was in Japan until his June 1950 deployment to Korea; there he stayed until

December 1951. After being in Japan from December 1951 until March 1952, RHS returned to the U.S., and completed his B.A. between June 1952 and August 1953.

[7] See esp. RHS's *Korean Love Songs* 10-11, 16, and *Useless Servants* 87, 116; Lt. Gen. Walton Harris "Johnnie" Walker, the historical figure referred to in these works, was born in Belton, TX in 1889 and died in Korea in December, 1950.

[8] See Caudet 149. The translation to the English is mine. I would like to thank Martha Montejo-Pizarro, a Ph.D. student in the doctoral program of Hispanic Studies at Texas A&M, for giving me access to this quote.

[9] In fact in *Useless Servants* the narrator mocks a Coloradan who "called himself Donald Trujillo. Says his people came from Spain," and then the *raza* friends of the narrator asked Donald "if those were the Spaniards that landed in Virginia and then trekked across the South until delivered safely and soundly to the Promised Land" (41). After remarking the same experience with two other Coloradan "Spaniards," the narrator concludes: "Well, that's the first Mexican of any kind I've ever met named Donald" (41). We can assume that such a circumspect author as RHS would not be guilty of ridiculing such snobbish ignorance and then fall into the same fault himself.

[10] Unless otherwise noted, in this study all citations from *Estampas del Valle y otras obras* are taken from the easily-available, 1994 Bilingual Press edition which is titled simply: *Estampas del Valle*.

[11] See *Useless Servants* 15-17, 29-30.

[12] For information on this, see *Estampas* 39-43, and *The Valley* 27-32.

[13] An helpful introduction to the "repatriation" is found in McKay.

[14] An interrelated sub-theme can only be mentioned here. The Leguizamón family arrives in the Valley from Mexico after the U.S. Civil War. From the beginning it works, albeit in a subservient position, with the Anglos against the traditional *raza* and its current Spanish-speaking allies. The Leguizamón part in the Anglo land-grab ultimately leads to a blood-feud between them and the Buenrostros, with the assassination of Rafe's father and his being fully avenged on both sides of the Rio Grande by his brother/Rafe's uncle Julian. See: *Estampas* 99-101 and *The Valley* 86-88; and, *El condado de Belken* 40-44 and *Klail City* 25-30. A favorable view of the Leguizamóns, infrequent in the *KCDT* and as seen by an Anglo, is found in *Rites and Witnesses* 67-68.

[15] Indirectly this point reminds us that the role of women in the early and middle *KCDT* is limited as it was in the Castile of the early and mid 15th century. While the financially independent and successful Viola Barragán is in a position to recommend Jehu Malacara to the preemi-

nent banker Noddy Perkins (see *Rites and Witnesses* 7), it is only with *Becky and Her Friends* (1990), which is set in the late 1960s, that the fact of and reasons for the liberation of women—and hence their active or, better said, public role in society—become prominent in the *KCDT*. By the time the *KCDT* arrives at its last "stop" to date, i.e., *We Happy Few* (2006), women are protagonists and the experience of war is not made formative of any main character's life.

[16]The specific large parallels between the life of RHS shares with his alter ego protagonists Rafe and Jehu begin with being a member of a *raza* family whose Valley roots go back to the 18th century; and, having a family memory and personal experience of living in the Valley as a discriminated-against minority. Further parallels, those commencing with a Valley high school graduation in 1946, may be found in note 6. They show Hinojosa and his alter ego characters in lock step as regards their alternating between service in the U.S. Army and attendance at the University of Texas at Austin between August 1946 and August 1953. After that last date the literal parallels are fewer.

[17]While this is not the place to elaborate on a matter tangential to this chapter, but lest there be any equivocation, in numerous places over the years RHS has expostulated on the secure and nurturing family of readers which his parents created for him and his four siblings. Most recently he touches on this subject in his interview with Raab.

[18]In *Mi querido Rafa* 90/*Dear Rafe* 103, where the contemporary action appears to occur in summer and fall of 1962 (because, in part, it is a U.S. Congressional election year, but not a presidential one), Galindo says he is 52; on the same page of *Dear Rafe* he adds that he has been married three times, widowed twice and divorced from his last wife. No children are mentioned by him who calls himself "writer, poet, journalist" (103). He is of the same age as the old-school politician Polín Tapia (*Mi querido Rafa* 55/*Dear Rafe* 63). For information on the real life inspiration for P. Galindo's name and activities, see Calderón 142.

[19]Numbers, ages, dates and, sometimes as we have seen, even events are often not exact and/or subject to modification in the *KCDT*, particularly in the earlier, more orally-based volumes. For example: in *Estampas* reference is made to "unas veinte," while in *The Valley*, its English "re-creation" by RHS, the reference is to "some thirty" people who were killed in the accident. This is not the place to consider these variations which assuredly merit study.

[20]During his Mexican period, the legendary film maker Luis Buñuel wrote and directed his 1950, award-winning film *Los olvidados* (*The Forgotten*) in which he tells the story of Pedro, a Mexico City youth,

whose family life is exactly that of Gabriel's. Unfortunately young Pedro, unlike Gabriel, is unable to escape the disadvantages of his situation, becomes a *pícaro*, and is killed by another boy also born into poverty and on his own. Buñuel wrote and directed three more movies based on novels by Galdós: *Nazarín* (1959), adapted to Mexico City and its environs; *Viridiana* (1961); and *Tristana* (1970). His negative views on the Catholic Church and the doctrines of established religion are well-recognized.

[21]The Galdosian novels are: *Marianela* (1878), *El doctor Centeno* (1883; in two volumes), and *Tormento* (1884).

[22]For more details on Centeno and the contrast with Araceli, see Miller, "Iriartian Intertexts."

[23]This cannot be documented or discussed here, but my experience of decades has shown that as a group U.S. writers in English know the British tradition infinitely better than western-hemisphere writers in Spanish know the Spanish Peninsular tradition. That said, I have never met a younger or even middle-age Spanish feminist who knows the writings of the truly great Spanish novelist, short-story writer, essayist and pioneering feminist Emilia Pardo Bazán (1851-1921) anywhere near as well as s/he knows those of the English woman Virginia Woolf (1882-1941).

[24]See the translation to English by me of the whole prologue in the appendix to this study.

[25]In *El mundo de Galdós* 124-27 and *Del realismo/naturalism al modernismo* 153-62, I document and discuss exhaustively the statements of this paragraph and section of this chapter. In his film version of *Nazarín*, Buñuel's interpretation agrees with that given in the text.

[26]The quote comes from a statement signed by Onetti and other members of the 1976 Casa de las Américas Prize panel. It was reprinted in the first American edition of what is now most commonly referred to as *El condado de Belken* under the title "A guisa de prólogo"; see note 2 for bibliographic explanations concerning the second volume of the *KCDT*, and for the quote itself see Hinojosa-S., *Generaciones y semblanzas*, the recto of the third unnumbered leaf.

Works Cited

Calderón, Héctor. "'Mexicanos al grito de guerra': Rolando Hinojosa's Cronicón del Condado de Belken." *Narratives of Greater Mexico. Essays on Chicano Literary History, Genre and Borders*. Austin: U of Texas Press, 2004. 138-166. Print.

___. "On the Uses of Chronicle, Biography and Sketch in Rolando Hinojosa's *Generaciones y semblanzas*." *The Rolando Hinojosa Reader. Essays Historical and Critical*. Ed. José David Saldívar. Houston: Arte Público Press, 1985. 133-42. Print.

Caudet, Francisco. *Crónica de una marginación. Conversaciones con Alfonso Sastre*. Madrid: Ediciones de la Torre, 1984. Print.

Hinojosa, Rolando. *Claros varones de Belken/Fair Gentlemen of Belken County*. Trans. Julia Cruz. Tempe: Bilingual Press/Editorial Bilingüe, 1986. Print.

___. *El condado de Belken. Klail City*. Tempe: Bilingual Press/Editorial Bilingüe, 1994. Print.

___. *Dear Rafe*. Houston: Arte Público Press, 1985. Print.

___. *Estampas del Valle*. Tempe, AZ: Bilingual Press/Editorial Bilingüe, 1994. Print.

___. *Estampas del Valle y otras obras/Sketches of the Valley and Other Works*. Trans. Gustavo Valadez and José Reyna. Berkeley: Editorial Justa Publications, 1977. Print.

___. *Klail City y sus alrededores*. La Habana: Casa de las Américas, 1976. Print.

___. *Korean Love Songs. From "Klail City Death Trip."* Berkeley: Editorial Justa Publications, 1978. Print.

___. *Mi querido Rafa*. Houston: Arte Público Press, 1981. Print.

___. *Rites and Witnesses*. Houston: Arte Público Press, 1982. Print.

___. *The Valley*. Tempe: Bilingual Press/Editorial Bilingüe, 1983. Print.

Hinojosa-S., Rolando. *Estampas del Valle y otras obras/Sketches of the Valley and Other Works*. Trans. Gustavo Valadez. Berkeley: Quinto Sol Publications, 1973. Print.

___. *Generaciones y semblanzas*/[*Generations and Portraits*]. Trans. Rosaura Sánchez. Berkeley: Justa Publications, 1977. Print.

Martín-Rodríguez, Manuel M. *Rolando Hinojosa y su cronicón chicano: una novela del lector*. Seville: Universidad de Sevilla, 1993. Print.

McKay, Robert R. "Mexican Americans and Repatriation." *The Handbook of Texas Online*. Denton: Texas State Historical Association, 2012. Web. 27 July 2012.

Miller, Stephen. "Iriartian Intertexts to Gabriel Araceli and Comments on the Relation to Felipe Centeno." *A Sesquicentennial Tribute to*

Galdós 1843/1993. Ed. Linda M. Willem. Newark, DE: Juan de la Cuesta Press, 1993. 190-203. Print.

___. *Del realismo/naturalismo al modernismo: Galdós, Zola, Revilla y Clarín (1870-1901)*. Las Palmas: Ediciones del Excmo. Cabildo de Gran Canaria/Biblioteca Galdosiana, 1993. Print.

___. *El mundo de Galdós: teoría, tradición y evolución creativa del pensamiento socio-literario galdosiano*. Santander: Sociedad Menéndez Pelayo, 1983. Print.

Pérez de Guzmán, Fernán. *Generaciones y semblanzas*. Ed. J. Domínguez Bardona. Madrid: Espasa Calpe/Clásicos Castellanos T. 61, 1941. Print.

Pérez Galdós, Benito. Prólogo [to *El abuelo*]. *Novelas y miscelánea*. By Pérez Galdós. Madrid: Aguilar, 1971. 800-801. Print.

Pulgar, Fernando del. *Claros varones de Castilla*. Ed. J. Domínguez Bardona. Madrid: Espasa Calpe/Clásicos Castellanos T. 49, 1954. Print.

Raab, Josef. "At Home in the Borderlands. An Interview with Rolando Hinojosa." *American Studies Journal* 57 (2012): n. pag. Web. 2 August 2012.

Ríos C., Herminio. [Introduction]. *Estampas del Valle y otras obras*. By Rolando R. Hinojosa-S[mith]. Berkeley: Quinto Sol Books, 1973. [7-9]. Print.

Saldívar, José David. "Rolando Hinojosa's *Klail City Death Trip*: A Critical Introduction." *The Rolando Hinojosa Reader. Essays Historical and Critical*. Ed. José David Saldívar. Houston: Arte Público Press, 1985. 44-63. Print.

Zilles, Klaus. *Rolando Hinojosa. A Reader's Guide*. Albuquerque: University of New Mexico Press, 2001. Print.

Appendix

Benito Pérez Galdós' "Author's Prologue" to
The Grandfather. Novel in Five Acts (1897)
Translation from the Spanish by Stephen Miller

To the readers whose repeated indulgence has favored me, I wish to reveal that I have wanted to please myself and them in creating *The*

Grandfather by giving this time the greatest possible development to the use of dialogue and the least possible to description and narration. My readers certainly believe as I do that all is possible in art, and that we should raise our brow only before that which is foolish, useless or bothersome. Clearly were I, in this or any other occasion, guilty of the sins of stupidity or commonness, I would suffer with resignation the disdain of those who read me; but, at the same time I cursed my lack of ability, I would not believe that the path was bad, rather that it was I who did not know how to follow it.

The dialogue system, which I first adopted in *Reality*, is like the veritable smithy of the characters. They make themselves, compose themselves, imitate more easily, let us say, living beings, when they manifest their moral fiber with their own words and with them, as in life, give us the more or less deep and firm relief of their actions. The author's words, narrating and describing, do not have, in general terms, so much efficacy, nor do they give so directly the impression of spiritual truth. They are always a reference, something like History, that tells us of events and that sketches portraits and scenes. Yet by the mysterious virtue of dialogue it seems that we see and we hear, without third parties, the action and its protagonists, and we forget more easily the hidden artist who offers us an ingenious imitation of Nature. No matter what may be said, the artist will be more or less hidden; but he never disappears, nor does the scenery of the sets completely hide him, no matter how well they are constructed. The impersonality of the author, hailed today by some as an artistic system, is nothing more than a vain emblem of literary flags, which, if they wave triumphantly, is because of the vigorous personality of those captains who carry them.

The one who composes a matter and gives poetic life to it, both in the Novel and in the Theater, is always present: present in the raptures of poetry, present in the telling of passion or of analysis; present in the Theater itself. His spirit is the indispensable spark which causes the imagined beings that mimic the palpitation of life to enter into the artistic framework.

Even though by its structure and its division into acts and scenes *The Grandfather* appears to be a theatrical work, I have not hesitated to call it a novel, while not conceding an absolute value to the terms. In this, as in all that which belongs to the infinite reign of Art, it is most prudent to flee from the cataloguing pigeon holes of genres and forms. In all novels in which the personages speak, there lies a dramatic work. The Theater is nothing but the condensation and joining of all that which constitutes action and character in the modern novel.

Because of mistakes or the public's fatigue, and even for social and economic reasons that would constitute the matter of a long study, scenic art properly speaking has limited itself in our time to a range so narrow and poor that the capital works of the great dramatists appear to us to be *spoken novels*. Jumping from our smallness to the example of the greats, I ask: could Shakespeare's *Richard III*, colossal canvas of life and human passions, be considered today a *stageable* piece of theater? A century ago Garrick played whole the work, and there was a public capable of understanding it, feeling it and assimilating its intense poetic essence. Today that and other immortal works belong to the theater of the ideal, read without *staging*. They are art, which because of the quantity and variety of its inflections, and the degree of its passionate intensity, what we call the public (a thousand ladies and a thousand gentlemen seated in a hall) does not withstand. They are art which in our time does not find a suitable intermediary between the creative genius and the readerly genius, even when both the creator and the reader must be geniuses for the emotion and fine taste for beauty to be perceived.

Moreover, may he who knows tell me if *La Celestina* [*Tragicomedy of Calisto and Melibea*; 1499] is a novel or a drama. *Tragicomedy* it was called by its author; *drama for reading* is what it really is, and is without doubt the greatest and most beautiful of the spoken novels. It is the case that the names which are used for the genres signify nothing, and in literature the variety of forms will always overwhelm the nomenclatures which the rhetoricians capriciously make. Without bothering, then, about *how to name* this work, a humble essay of a form which I believe very appropriate to our time, so enamored of the contrived and busy, it remains only for me to ask my good friends to receive benevolently this work.

B[enito].P[érez].G[Galdós].

The *Klail City Death Trip* Series
A Trovador's Eternal Space for an Enduring Transitory World

Alejandro Morales
University of California, Irvine

I have been fortunate to have spent time in conversation with Rolando Hinojosa at conferences, literary events, at his home and often separated from the literary fray at a bar in Mexico, the United States or some place in Europe. Conversations with Hinojosa are always humorous, engaging, challenging and at times unpredictable. I recall a recent exchange about where writers write. I told him that I write wherever I can but most of the time I write in my office at home. "I prefer a freighter, a huge freighter crossing the Atlantic headed for Spain. In the crossing I would write a novel," he responded. Hinojosa has a gift of language. With a phrase or two he charms audiences big or small. I have listened carefully to his lectures and readings and seen how he enthralls his listeners.

From these conversations, the advice "Write, Alejandro, write" that the late Tomás Rivera, Hinojosa's close and dear friend, gave me many years past became more imperative. I learned from Hinojosa's unconventional examples. His writing spirit and calling I have found in the Bible in a passage that says:

> Write down, therefore, what you have seen,
> and what is happening,
> and what will happen afterwards.
>
> *Revelation* 2:19

This passage conveys what Hinojosa has done in his oeuvre. He has written about the past, present and future. The passage has become a kind of literary motto or axiom that frames my work. It also illustrates the literary and social mission that produces Hinojosa's early publications during the turbulent decades of the 1960s and 1970s. This period is considered a literary renaissance for Chicano literature. Theorists have claimed that in the 1950s and 1960s there occurred in the United States an epistemic change that announced the possibility of a new social order. This time has been described as the Postmodern moment. Frederic Jameson discusses Postmodernism and situates it during the second half of the twentieth century:

> It is also, at least in my use, a periodizing concept whose function is to correlate the emergence of new formal features in culture with the emergence of a new type of social life and a new economic order—what is often euphemistically called modernization, postindustrial or consumer society, the society of media or the spectacle, or multinational capitalism. This new moment of capitalism can be dated from the postwar boom in the United States in the late 1940s and early '50s . . . The 1960s are in many ways the transitional period, a period in which the new international order (neocolonialism, the Green Revolution, computerization and electronic information) is at one and the same time set in place and is swept and shaken by its own internal contradictions and by external resistance. (112-113)

This particular description of Postmodernism locates the contextual moments of its rise to the public scene of Chicano literature. Jameson's use of Postmodernism as a "periodizing concept whose function is to correlate the emergence of new formal features in culture. . ." identifies the space where Chicano fiction, one of the "new formal features in culture," emerges as an intellectual, aesthetic, literary, oral and social resistance expression.

Andreas Huyssen identifies minority literature as a Postmodern artistic expression of the 1970s and 1980s:

> It was especially the art, writing, film-making and criticism of women and minority artists with their recuperation of buried and mutilated traditions, their emphasis on exploring forms of gender- and race-based subjectivity in aesthetic productions and experiences, and their refusal to be limited to standard canonizations, which added a whole new dimension to the critique of high modernism and to the emergence of alternative forms of culture. . . .
>
> Actually, the suspicion is in order that the conservative turn of these past years has indeed something to do with the sociologically significant emergence of various forms of "otherness" in the cultural sphere, all of which are perceived as a threat to the stability and sanctity of canon and tradition. (198-199)

Into this social, cultural and literary opening enters Quinto Sol Publications founded in 1967 by Octavio I. Romano, Herminio Ríos and Nick C. Vaca. In 1972, Quinto Sol awarded the Premio Quinto Sol to Rolando Hinojosa for his novel *Estampas del Valle y otras obras* (*Sketches of the Valley and Other Works*) the first of the *Klail City Death Trip Series* (*KCDT*). Upon winning the Quinto Sol Prize Hinojosa became one of the major national Chicano literary voices. During these early years of the Chicano literary movement, I attended graduate school at Rutgers University where I studied Latin American and Chicano writers. Also during this time I finished my first novel and prepared to submit the book to a publisher.

I was excited by the Premio Quinto Sol and the subsequent publications of the winning manuscripts and the introduction at a national level of Chicano writers including of course, Hinojosa. I did not know any of the winning writers. All I knew about Hinojosa was that he lived in some place called Belken County, Texas.

And frankly, I was unaware of whether this place existed or not. Yet his winning the Premio inspired me to submit my novel. I was sure I had a chance at the Premio. Quinto Sol had not published any west coast writers and it was a Chicano press, how could I miss! Finally, I submitted the novel and soon after I began to get accustomed to rejection. Nonetheless, I was still inspired by Hinojosa and the other Quinto Sol Prize winners that included Tomás Rivera in 1970, Rudolfo Anaya in 1971 and Estella Portillo Trambley in 1973.

Hinojosa's Premio novel *Estampas del Valle y otras obras* is a fragmented text consisting of portraiture sketches of the principal characters developed throughout the *KCDT*. The novel is also an example of Linda Hutcheon's historiographic metafiction, a concept that is employed and expanded in the development of the *KCDT* narrative. Historiographic metafiction requires the author to have a direct or indirect knowledge or awareness of theory, history and literature as human constructs and as mechanisms for housing the contents of the past. Historiographic metafiction is where history and literature and their forms are consistently challenged, reconsidered and reworked.

History has been taught focusing on the great men, women and events that formed nations and empires. In the United States presidents, generals, athletes, entrepreneurs and so forth represent success, wealth, power, knowledge and are common information. However, in the world that Hinojosa creates it is not these kinds of individuals that stand out. His historiographic metafictional narratives focus on the intra-history of the Rio Grande Valley and aspire to document the intra-history of the people and their language in the border region where he was born and raised. He writes about what he knows intimately, about a world that he loves. He affirms that the physical and spiritual life of the Rio Grande Valley offer a strong sense of place that fulfills a need of belonging and provides a strong bond to the Valley. Yet, he selects not to write directly about this world that is most dear to him. Instead he creates Belken County, an alternative world, a parody that "recasts" the real world of the Rio Grande Valley. The alternative world of Belken County is a kind of "recreation" or "rendition" juxtaposed to the constantly changing world beyond its imagined borders. Belken County signifies an emphasis on an exploration away from "the problems of *knowing* to the problems of *modes of being*—from an *epistemological* dominant to an *ontological* one" (McHale 10). Brian McHale describes postmodern fiction precisely as ontological:

> That is, postmodernist fiction deploys strategies which engage and foreground questions . . . "post-cognitive": "Which world is this? What is to be done in it? Which of my selves is to do it?" Other typical postmodernist questions bear either on the ontology of the literary text itself or on the ontology of the world which it projects, for instance: What is a world? What kinds of worlds are there, how are they constituted, and how do they differ? What happens when different kinds of worlds are placed in confrontation, or when boundaries between worlds are violated? What is the mode of existence of a text, and what is the mode of existence of the world (or worlds) it projects? How is a projected world structured? And so on. (10)

The problems of modes of being and the other ontological questions above apply to the present day Chicano experience in the rural and urban border zones where Chicanos live. The fast changing world of the 21st century demands of the Chicano the constant negotiation of identity, space, time and personal and public behaviors and roles. Life and space are not fixed but change and float away. Hinojosa's work reveals him to be a conjurer and conscious myth maker and chronicler of the images of the ephemeral way of life of the Rio Grande Valley. His journey is a constant battle against the inevitable and he strikes back with his pen by creating a fixed written space, the world of Belken County where he has complete control over natural and supernatural events. Here he is comfortable. In the construction of this world the notions of intrahistory, the micro-physics of power, the collective unconscious, orality, the floating world and recreations/recastings/renditions are central guides to its possible meaning(s).

Intra-History

Intra-history, a theory of history developed by Miguel de Unamuno, emphasizes the daily life, knowledge and power of ordinary people from ordinary places, who are the backbone of history and whose contributions remain unnoticed. Intra-history is the fundamentally important ordinary experience of common humanity that fills in the spaces between the "great moments" or "news worthy" events of history and makes them possible but most often goes unrecognized.

> Todo lo que cuentan a diario los periódicos, la historia toda del "presente momento histórico", no es sino la superficie del mar, una superficie que se hiela y cristaliza en los libros y registros, y, una vez cristalizada así, una capa dura, no mayor con respecto a la vida intra-histórica que esta pobre corteza en que vivimos con relación al inmenso foco ardiente que lleva dentro. Los periódicos nada dicen de la vida silenciosa de los millones de hombres sin historia que a todas horas del día y en todos los países del globo se levantan a una orden del sol y van a sus campos a proseguir la oscura y silenciosa labor cotidiana y eterna, esa labor que como la de las madréporas suboceánicas echa las bases sobre que se alzan los islotes de la Historia. Sobre el silencio augusto, decía, se apoya y vive el sonido; sobre la inmensa Humanidad silenciosa se levantan los que meten bulla en la Historia. Esa vida intra-histórica, silenciosa continúa como el fondo mismo del mar, es la sustancia del progreso, la verdadera tradición, la tradición eterna, no la tradición mentida que se suele ir a buscar al pasado enterrado en libros y papeles, y monumentos, y piedras. (41-42)

The *KCDT* archives the intra-history of Jehu Malacara, Rafa Buenrostro and others, chronicling the past and the present, and points to the future of the Rio Grande Valley. Jehu's transformation to a successful employee of the Klail City First National Bank and Rafa's earning a law degree and becoming a police officer announces the inevitable cultural changes that will leave the Rio Grande Valley radically different from Hinojosa's place of origin.

The original old world sense of place is fast disappearing. Hinojosa's characters seem to distance themselves from a Chicano identity and move toward an American identity. In analyzing these changes, Joyce Glover Lee states "The often wrenching transformation of the minority into a being who is, for all practical purposes, one of the majority is the central issue for Hinojosa and his fictional world" (203).

The Micro-Physics of Power

Hinojosa's characters reside in and are better understood in the field of intra-history. The principal protagonists of the *KCDT*, Jehu Malacara, Rafa Buenrostro, Esteban Echevarría and P. Galindo bring with them hundreds of unheard voices, related directly and indirectly to them and to each other. "Besides Jehu and Rafa and their families, friends and enemies, Hinojosa populates his Belken County with a cast of over a thousand characters that appear, disappear and reappear in disjointed episodes that may or may not have a bearing on the central plots" (Zilles xiii). Each of Hinojosa's main protagonists operates rhizomically creating relations that extend and proliferate through time and space. The network of relations created by these characters living in Belken County parodies the structure of power outside in the world of the Valley. Power does not necessarily operate hierarchically or vertically; instead it exists horizontally, rhizomically circulating through these characters and throughout Belken County and comparatively the Valley. Each individual, no matter how insignificant they or their role might seem, is a relay of power in an invisible network. Michel Foucault describes these networks as a kind of microphysics of power:

> . . . power is not something that is divided between those who have it and hold it exclusively, and those who do not have it and are subject to it. Power must, . . . be analyzed as something that circulates, or rather as something that functions only when it is part of a chain. It is never localized here or there, it is never in the hands of some, and it is never appropriated in the way that

> wealth or a commodity can be appropriated. Power functions. Power is exercised through networks, and individuals do not simply circulate in those networks: they are in a position to both submit to and exercise this power. They are never the inert or consenting targets of power; they are always its relays. In other words power passes through individuals. It is not applied to them. (29)

Unamuno's intra-history and Foucault's micro-physics of power describe ancient, previously unrecognized mechanisms of survival ingrained in the Chicanos of the Rio Grande Valley. These practices might be invisible yet they are eternal and passed down from generation to generation. Unamuno refers to these strategies, that represent a way of life that is today in danger of disappearing and under constant attack by the fast changing postmodern world, as "la verdadera tradición," "la tradición eterna" (42). Intra-history and the notion of the micro-physics of power in Hinojosa's work draw from his experience as a native of the Borderlands and from his study of world literature, in particular from Spanish and American literature and his awareness of the ordinary daily praxis of literary and cultural theory. However, there is an underlying tradition that gives the series its engaging and marvelous literary and folk quality. The *KCDT* is a combination of two methods of recording the human condition: Literacy—what is written and read—and Orality—what is memorized, sung and heard.

Orality

At the start of this essay I referred to Hinojosa's wonderful literary readings. I mentioned how with a phrase or two he charms audiences big or small. I have been enthralled by his style of presentation and have always left with the feeling that I have learned. His ability to entertain and to make his listeners experience a moment of enlightenment, of discovery, is a result of the strong oral tradition that is part of the Chicano intra-historical micro-physics of power that sustains the survival of the people of the Rio

Grande Valley. Hinojosa refers to the didactic importance of the oral tradition in his formation as a writer.

> The history one learned there was an oral one and somewhat akin to the oral religion brought by the original colonials. Many of my generation were raised with the music written and composed by Valley people, and we learned the ballads of the Border little knowing that it was a true native art form. And one was also raised and steeped in the stories and exploits . . . ("A Sense of Place" 20)

The oral tradition is manifested in Hinojosa's readings and in his written texts. His reading style is that of a master "trovador." Hinojosa naturally follows the narrative structure of a trovador's ritualistic performance. He enters a town, announces his presence, gives an invocation thanking those who made his presence possible and asks permission of the authorities present to begin his song. He makes an introductory statement outlining the general content of his oral composition; before he starts he might make a humorous comment or say hello to someone in the audience and after, when everyone is charmed and comfortable, he begins his first narrative sketch. The stitching together of oral narratives continues until he graciously ends with a coalescing statement. The performance and the readings of the narratives are never the same but follow this general design. The diversity of performance is expressed in the epigraph included in the original of *Estampas del Valle y otras obras*: "Estas estampas son y están como las greñas de Mencho Saldaña: unas cortas, otras largas y todas embadurnadas con esa grasa humana que las junta y las separa sin permiso de nadie" (15).

The trovador's artistic freedom is revealed in the performances and in the readings never being the same and is demonstrated in Hinojosa's self-translations, that he calls "renditions" or "recastings." He considers his "renditions" or "recastings" new novels. Hinojosa writes double texts, two versions of the same book: one in Spanish and the other in English. Klaus Zilles points to the translations of *Estampas del valle y otras obras* as the examples where Hinojosa takes liberties with his texts to create new novels

(Zilles 4). His double texts are uniquely Hinojosa and challenge traditional thinking about what constitutes a novel and its translation. Hinojosa writes against canonical hegemonic tradition and continuously test the limits of culture and society. This literary posture speaks to the engaged role of the writer in contemporary society, a role that Hinojosa practices and teaches by example. In his self-translations he complies with the role of the trovador by giving the audience different ways of understanding the world.

The Collective Unconscious

Intra-history, the micro-physics of power and orality are strategies of recognizing and of recording humanity's daily experience. Carl Jung's concept of the collective unconscious is also a mechanism by which Hinojosa's work perseveres, lives on to tell the tale of the people of the Rio Grande Valley. In Hinojosa's novels the collective unconscious reveals itself in flashes of the past, in human relationships and modern life structures of a people in an ancient land. As Gayana Jurkevich has pointed out, there is a correlation between Unamuno's intra-history and Jung's collective unconscious. Both men were mystics who argued the existence of transpersonal experiences not entirely explicable by science. Unamuno's concept of intra-history and Jung's collective unconscious are manifestations of human experience at a transpersonal, collective level. Jung explains the idea of collective unconscious as:

> The other part of the unconscious is what I call the impersonal or collective unconscious. As the name indicates, its contents are not personal but collective; that is, they do not belong to one individual alone but to a whole group of individuals, and generally to a whole nation, or even to the whole of mankind. These contents are not acquired during the individual's lifetime but are products of innate forms and instincts. Although the child possesses no inborn ideas, it nevertheless has a highly developed brain which functions in a quite definite way. This brain is inherited from its ancestors; it is a deposit of the psychic functioning of the whole human race. The child therefore brings with it an

> organ ready to function in the same way that it has functioned throughout human history. In the brain the instincts are preformed, and so are the primordial images which have always been the basis of man's thinking . . . (310-311)

Jung believed that all collective human actions were deposited in the collective unconscious including universal symbols and archetypes. The mind is like the storehouse of consciousness. It is a kind of inner force that connects all humanity through a shared collective unconscious. Similarly, Unamuno's intra-history is also applicable to all humanity and is transmitted by heredity from generation to generation. These psychic sites, humanity's intra-history and collective unconscious, are Hinojosa's primary sources of symbols and archetypes of the ephemeral world of the Rio Grande Valley.

The symbols and archetypes in *KCDT* are a kind of collective knowledge and behavior that through human evolution have gone through changes and modifications. The same bedrock symbols and social structures held in common by humankind are expressed or celebrated differently by diverse human groups throughout the world. In the Rio Grande Valley they appear distinctive from how they are manifested in other parts of the United States. The archetypes and symbols in Hinojosa's Belken County are not the classical figures of Greek and Roman mythologies but the grass roots deep cultural images of ordinary human beings battling to survive at a particular time and place. A list of these archetypical images and social structures include 1) the coming together of people, gatherings of family, friends; 2) gatherings of elders; 3) the process of social ordering of private and public space; 4) the constant struggle to resist change that will destroy a way of life; 5) the individual's personal desire to improve their overall human condition; 6) the individual's desire for immortality; 7) the celebration of birth, marriage and death; and 8) the recognition of the coming of age reaching manhood and womanhood and so forth. It is these basic human behaviors and desires that are warehoused in the collective unconscious that are recognized by and convey meaning to Hinojosa's diverse readership.

The Floating World

For some time now I have been working on a biography or a biographical novel titled *A Rainbow of Colors*. The book deals with the lives of Paul Jacoulet and Stewart Josiah Teaze. Jacoulet was a Frenchman taken in 1904 to Japan by his parents who were affiliated with the French Embassy in Tokyo. Jacoulet lived all his life in Tokyo and became a master of Ukiyo-e painting and wood block print. Teaze lived in Japan for about twenty-five years up to 1941 and became a collector of Jacoulet's prints and also wrote a short biography and study of the artist's paintings.

Among the possible themes of Ukiyo-e is the depiction of the popular pleasures of town life. "Ukiyo-e carries the nuance colored by a Buddhist world-view that such pleasures bring pain because people are unable to disentangle themselves emotionally from this their transitory, or literally, 'floating world,' of human existence" (Kanada 11).

Jacoulet considered the art form of Ukiyo-e prints a way to preserve the floating world. He painted portraits of people involved in their daily routines, their customs and traditions and their work. By the late 1930s, the different ways of life that Jacoulet experienced in Japan and in the islands of the South Seas were in danger of vanishing from time and memory. Jacoulet's efforts to conserve the traditional ways of life by reviving Ukiyo-e painting contrasts against the modernization, technology and the great violence of the time.

> Japan, Korea, China, the South Seas—no longer isolated, no longer able to retain intact their age-long customs! It is almost as if Jacoulet has been unconsciously seized with a premonition that these modes of living are truly floating away, and he must grasp them and record them before they are lost in oblivion. It is small wonder that in his pictures there is something of sadness, a hint of that which lies below the surface of life, which he says, is true art. Perhaps that is why one is irresistibly drawn to look again and again at his prints, coming little by little to understand that underlying idea. (Wells 24)

The same applies to Hinojosa and his work. Hinojosa is motivated in a similar way to save the traditional ways of life of the Rio Grande Valley. Like Jacoulet, Hinojosa recovers an almost forgotten artistic tradition, the "*estampa*," a sixteenth century Spanish narrative genre, and uses it to archive the modes of life that are floating away. The place where he was born and raised offers a wealth of writing material and is rich with the human experience and the contradictions and complexities of a borderlands region. *Estampas del Valle y otras obras* manifests the personal intimate relationship between the writer and the place. Hinojosa speaks often of needing a sense of place, of having a strong bond to the Valley and of attempting to capture its history, people and language. "For the writer—this writer—a sense of place was not a matter of importance; it became essential" ("Sense of Place" 21). He comments about the importance of identifying with people's names, of belonging to the Valley and the Border. "For me, then, part of the sense of the Border came from sharing: the sharing of names, of places, of common history, and of belonging to the place; one attended funerals, was taken to cemeteries, and one saw names that corresponded to one's own or to one's friends and neighbors, and relatives" (19). He speaks of " . . . the desire to write about what I know, the place I know, the language . . . the Valley." However, Hinojosa does not refer directly to the real names of the towns and cities of the Rio Grande Valley. "I am not here to report, so I have to use my imagination" (Cedillo 105). Therefore, to give his imagination free rein, he constructs an alternative world. In recalling a story his grandfather shared Hinojosa comments,

> The story is apocryphal; it has to be. But living in the Valley, and hearing that type of story laid the foundation for what I later learned was to give me a sense of place. By that I do not mean that I had a feel for the place; no, not at all. I had a sense of it, and by that I mean that I was not learning about the culture of the Valley, but living it, forming part of it, and thus, contributing to it. ("Sense of Place" 19)

Hinojosa finds complete artistic freedom in his active imagination. He constructs Belken County, an apocryphal place where he recasts and fixes the geography, architecture and way of life of the Rio Grande Valley. In doing so he emphasizes the importance of its history, intra-history, cities, towns and the people. Hinojosa juxtaposes the fixed permanence of the apocryphal world of his written text to the inevitable changes that have happened, are happening and will happen to the place and to the Chicanos living in the Valley. Certainly other writers have created apocryphal countries, worlds to parody reality. They juxtapose different kinds of worlds and question what happens when boundaries between these worlds are violated. In Hinojosa's apocryphal cosmos, life in Belken County parodies life in the Valley.

Hinojosa, like William Faulkner, describes his storytelling in reference to the aesthetics of his written texts and the relationship between empirical Hidalgo County and apocryphal Belken County. In referring to Faulkner "An 'apocrypha' suggests an alternative to orthodoxy, especially in regards to ways of perception and presentation; and as such, Faulkner may have found the term a more accurate description of his literary ambitions" (Hamblin and Peek 17). The same can be said of Hinojosa's heroic desire and attempt, like that of the artist Paul Jacoulet, to save in a more permanent form the intra-history of the Rio Grande Valley and also to present Belken County as an "alternative to orthodoxy." On the one hand Hinojosa does not want to lose the orthodoxy of inherited traditions and social customs handed down from generation to generation but on the other hand, his main characters witness and contribute to the dissolution of these long cherished behaviors and social structures. They gladly and fully participate in a more inclusive Anglo hegemony. "Most of Hinojosa's characters—and certainly the main characters—no longer have to worry about the conditions of migrant life or overt racism. The admirable characters now could be any American anywhere who has 'made it'" (Lee 168). Faulkner's statement in explaining the meaning of Yoknapatawpha—"I created a cosmos of my own" (Kerr 115)—might also hint to a better understanding of the significance of Hinojosa's idea of Belken county.

In "Faulknerian Elements in Rolando Hinojosa's *The Valley*," Mark Busby points to the similarities between Yoknapatawpha County and Hinojosa's Belken County, one of which is the strong sense of place found in both, but he argues that in Hinojosa's novels it is the importance of the people and their intra-history that trumps sense of place for the writer. Busby finds that " . . . both writers concentrate on the theme of human endurance" (Busby 103). They put " . . . emphasis on the positive nature of human endurance brought on by hardship and travail." Hinojosa underscores the theme of endurance at the end of "Round Table," a sketch in *Estampas del Valle y otras obras*: "The three old men thank him, as usual, and don Manuel Guzmán leaves to stroll through the streets of Klail City, one of many towns in Belken County, Río Grande Valley, Texas" (90). Ten years later Hinojosa recasts this sketch as "The Squires at the Round Table" and places it at the end of the of *The Valley* his self-translation of *Estampas del Valle y otras obras*. In the recasting the sense of endurance is made even stronger. "The *viejitos*—the old men, thank him, as always; and don Manuel Guzmán, native born Texas mexicano, looks out into the night and cuts across Third, a side street in Klail City, a town much like any other in Belken County down in the Valley" (112). Busby comments that "while Hinojosa makes it clear that age and death will take them all, it is also clear that their enduring spirits have helped them to prevail; there's nothing such characters can't handle" (108). He ends his essay declaring "Hinojosa is especially good at rendering the Mexican American's ability to endure . . . and Hinojosa's work shows every sign of a long life" (108).

Hinojosa will reside forever in the enduring world of Belken County. Here is where he will make his stand, where he will resist the disappearance of a transitory way of life outside in the real world of the Rio Grande Valley. The *KCDT* becomes a fantastic, mythical journey through an imaginary space where the author guarantees a recasting of characters and their enduring spirits, their family history and their intra-history. At the end of the *KCDT* Hinojosa will conquer death and will live on. Ironically, the *Klail City Death Trip* is a journey of survival. Hinojosa's and that of his characters' enduring spirits constitute a re-memory, an energy of a person, a place or an event fixed in permanence that exists independent of human consciousness, an energy that can impact the author's physical and psychological existence. Hinojosa has on many occasions run into the re-memories of life and people of the Rio Grande Valley. He has chronicled in his novels what he has seen, heard, smelled, touched and tasted in his encounters with these re-memories. His creations constitute a primary original permanent artistic archive that he himself has "translated" and his readers are asked to also participate in their recreation.

In an interview with Manuel M. Martín-Rodríguez, Hinojosa comments on the origin of the title of the *KCDT* and mentions the importance of Michael Lesy's *Wisconsin Death Trip,* a book that deals with the lives of Scandinavian immigrants in Wisconsin.

> Y el título de ese libro era *Wisconsin Death Trip*. Entonces me cayó bien y asentó perfectamente [con mi proyecto] . . . porque yo venía pensando en la muerte de esta gente y viendo la vida nuestra, del chicano, como un largo viaje hacia la muerte. (Martín-Rodríguez 73)

> And the title of that book was *Wisconsin Death Trip*. The title really hit me and it fit perfectly [with my project] . . . because I continued to think about the death of these people and to consider our life, of the Chicano, as a long journey toward death. (My translation)

For Hinojosa the people of the Rio Grande Valley will pass on and their way of life might disappear in the real world, in the floating-world, but an account of their existence will survive, endure in Hinojosa's other world that the reader will find in the *KCDT*. Hinojosa is a writer battling against time and change that he considers the only constant in the Rio Grande Valley.

The *KCDT* ends (thus far) in Belken County. Ultimately Belken County is a place of salvation, a paradise, a sacred place at the end of the journey. Hinojosa has recorded its way of life in his memory and in his books to preserve forever for future generations. The reader of the future will find Hinojosa here doing what he likes best, conversing with neighbors and writing to save the transitory world beyond the borders of Belken County. Today Hinojosa lives in the interstice, the borderlands between two worlds: the real world, the empirical world of Austin and of the Rio Grande Valley and the fixed fictional written world of his characters residing in Belken County. These two worlds are constantly overlapping. Not respecting any kind of border, Hinojosa at will moves back and forth. On occasion, incognito, he crosses over into the world of Belken County as "Romeo Hinojosa." He cherishes his characters, for many he has documented a biography to which he keeps adding more information; everyday he speaks to at least one of them; there are occasions where he seems preoccupied, he has no time to talk, not because he is being rude or disrespectful but because he is with one or perhaps a group of his creations. Hinojosa cares for his characters, enjoys their company and wants to preserve their fixed reality, not the fast-changing world, the real world, the empirical world of the Rio Grande Valley from where they have emerged. He understands that the empirical world is fast disappearing and thus Hinojosa creates a changeless place, the written fixed fictional world of Belken County, for his characters to reside and for him to take eternal refuge. A place whose sacred written chronicles only he can recast.

Works Cited

Busby, Mark. "Faulknerian Elements in Rolando Hinojosa's *The Valley.*" *MELUS* 11.4 (Winter 1984): 103-109. Print.

Cedillo, Wendy F. "Location of Writing: A Reading and Conversation with Rolando Hinojosa." *Hipertexto* 5 (Winter 2007): 100-108. Web. 9 Sept. 2010.

Foucault, Michel. "Society Must be Defended." *Lectures at the Collège de France 1975-1976.* Eds. Mauro Bertani and Alessandro Fontana. Trans. David Macey. New York: Penguin, 2004. Print.

Hamblin, Robert W. and Charles A. Peek, eds. *A William Faulkner Encyclopedia.* Westport: Greenwood Press, 1999. Print.

Hinojosa, Rolando R. *Estampas del Valle y otras obras.* Berkeley: Quinto Sol Publications, 1973. Print.

___. "A Sense of Place." *The Rolando Hinojosa Reader: Essays Historical and Critical.* Ed. José David Saldívar. Houston: Arte Público Press, 1985. 18-24. Print.

Huyssen, Andreas. *After the Great Divide: Modernism, Mass Culture, Postmodernism.* Bloomington: Indiana University Press, 1986. Print.

Jameson, Fredric. "Postmodernism and Consumer Society." *The Anti-Aesthetic: Essays on Postmodern Culture.* Ed. Hal Foster. New York: New Press, 1983. Print.

Jung, Carl G. *The Structure and Dynamics of the Psyche.* New York: Pantheon, 1960. Print.

Jurkevich, Gayana. "Unamuno's Intrahistoria and Jung's Collective Unconscious: Parallels, Convergences, and Common Sources." *Comparative Literature* 43.1 (Winter 1991): 43-59. Print.

Kanada, Margaret M. *Color Woodblock Printmaking: The Traditional Method of Ukiyo-e.* Tokyo: Shufunotomo, 1989. Print.

Kerr, Elizabeth M. *William Faulkner's Yoknapatawpha: "A Kind of Keystone in the Universe."* New York: Fordham University Press, 1983. Print.

Lee, Joyce Glover. *Rolando Hinojosa and the American Dream.* Denton: University of North Texas Press, 1997. Print.

Martín-Rodríguez, Manuel M. *Rolando Hinojosa y su "Cronicón" Chicano: una novela del lector.* Sevilla: Universidad de Sevilla, 1993. Print.

McHale, Brian. *Postmodernist Fiction*. London: Routledge, 1987. Print. *The New American Bible*. "Revelation 2:19." New York: Oxford University Press, 2004. Print.

Unamuno, Miguel de. *En torno al casticismo*. Madrid: Alianza, 2008. Print.

Wells, Florence. *Paul Jacoulet, Wood-Block Artist*. Tokyo: Foreign Affairs Association of Japan, 1957. Print.

Zilles, Klaus. *Rolando Hinojosa: A Reader's Guide*. Albuquerque: University of New Mexico, 2001. Print.

II. Specialized Studies of the *Klail City Death Trip Series*

Time that Remains in Time: The *Estampas*[1] of Rolando Hinojosa-Smith

Eduardo Espina
Texas A&M University

> *"Recuerde el alma dormida, /avive el seso e despierte/contemplando/ cómo se passa la vida, /cómo se viene la muerte/ tan callando; /cuán presto se va el plazer, /cómo, después de acordado, /da dolor; /cómo, a nuestro parescer, /cualquiere tiempo passado/fue mejor."*
>
> "O let the soul her slumbers break, /Let thought be quickened, and awake; /Awake to see/How soon this life is past and gone, /And death comes softly stealing on, /How silently! /Swiftly our pleasures glide away, /Our hearts recall the distant day /With many sighs; /The moments that are speeding fast /We heed not, but the past,—the past, /More highly prize."
>
> —Jorge Manrique
> (Translated by Henry Wadsworth Longfellow)

Dutch writer Cees Nooteboom relates that when he visited the grave of Ludwig Wittgenstein (1889-1951) in the Cambridge cemetery, he saw the headstones of many individuals who today are completely unknown despite having once been distinguished researchers and professors at the prestigious British university. Death had robbed them of the time and importance they enjoyed when they were alive. Even there, in the house of the dead, in that great equalizer of a place, time was different. While Wittgenstein's time was still living, that of those others buried there had been devoured by anonymity. There are occasions when the time of life and the time of death are the same. Some day we will know. Time without time, time without past or future, an illusory sequence. That is the time in which we reside: a time gap, at odds with its duration, inserted between the various lives of the same man, time that spans a separation and a lapse, a censure of its own existence.

German writer Ernst Jünger (1895-1998), a master at the art of writing diaries and surviving bullet wounds and cannon blasts, tells an incredible tale. This man, who had been a great soldier and a warrior of a thousand battles, was wounded countless times. One of these wounds came while he was in a trench during World War I. The bullet perforated his stomach and he thought that his time had come and that he would die. As he later wrote, however, the nearly fatal wound was painless, and even brought extraordinary relief. What paradoxical agony. Jünger states that those minutes (he never really knew how many) between the instant he was wounded and when he lost consciousness, were the happiest of his entire, long life. This was due to the fact that, with the certainty that death was imminent, the notion of time disappeared, just as happens in Horacio Quiroga's "The Dead Man" ("El hombre muerto"). He felt that he had ceased to belong to the world.

Is "pure" time a place outside of time? One of the characters on the popular television show *Lost*, after losing the same notion of space and temporality, wonders aloud during one of the last episodes of the final season: "Guys, where are we?" Without time there can be no place, and there are places like the unknown island on *Lost* that can exist outside of time, at least until commercials and real life interrupt.

From time one can also escape being in time all the time, just as the character of another magnificent television series, Jack Bauer, on *24*. A day of his is not equal to a day as experienced by the rest of us mortals. A Jack Bauer day can begin and then not stop until long after the corresponding chronology has ended. It is time saturated with more time, a morass of temporality in which all the minutes are so close together that they come one after the other, almost one on top of the other, overlaid, as if it were nothing, without even giving time to the previous and coming hours to find their place in the corresponding duration.

This kind of time, which might just be the opportune time for literature, the time of love and of death (and also that of *Lost* and *24*), is the temporality of imagination. The remnants of existence and thought that it carries with it are so strong that not even memory has time to know how little or how much it did a week ago, and even less so an hour ago. Art tends to climb up and perch itself on this time—which is there, suspended but in force because we once presumed it to be similar, almost like a time from another time, before and after—as if trying to say in its own way, *I only exist if I can guarantee an existence outside of time*. What does such a thing mean, to be "out of time?" It means that time exists, ergo it has something "within," meaning that permanent time has an interior. Could it be the time of now, that time which includes the minutes that are inserted into life with great intensity, which can be measured two ways, one psychological and one chronological?

Time, an armor-plated entity that accompanies us from the time we learn to remember and to recognize a something prior to "having been," can on occasion be a reversible signal, as is the soft watch in Salvador Dalí's painting "The Persistence of Memory." And if time can be bent, then its chronology is not as linear or straight as we were made to believe in different ways by life and sports. Muhammad Ali said that the only difference between him and all other boxers was that he had absolute control of time, meaning that he knew mentally how to make it to the second-to-the-last round tracking the temporal weakening of his opponent and then achieve his objective. This was demonstrated in his memorable bout against George Foreman in October of 1974, when he patiently waited for Foreman's time to run out while he, Ali, made use of the time he still had saved up in his mind and was transferring in eyedropper amounts to his body, until landing the well-placed blow that left his fatigued rival on the canvas.

Muhammad Ali, a king on par with Cronus, had that which so many characters throughout the years and on the printed page have shown themselves to have in Latin American literature: the capacity to detach themselves from time. This ability was possessed by the likes of Martín Fierro, who returned to his home so many years after everything had taken place, as if nothing had happened, including time. Because he had been absent (from time), he did not simply state but rather cried out, "Here I come to sing" ("Aquí me pongo a cantar").[2] This ability was shared by Rubén Darío, who stated, "I am the one who just yesterday spoke" ("Yo soy aquel que ayer no más decía"),[3] a past transformed into a today yet to be lived, like the one that granted existential identity to the dead man in Quiroga's above-mentioned story. This man, as he died, knew that he had earlier died in time, in the middle of the jungle on his mental island. Likewise possessing this capacity was Jacob Van Oppen, the protagonist in Juan Carlos Onetti's story "Jacob and the Other" ("Jacob y el otro") who tended to forget that tomorrow is always today and that age does not count. There is also Torito, from Julio Cortázar's pugilistic tale of the same name, who was a Muhammad Ali of fewer pounds, with a River Plate accent. Then there is Florentino Ariza, the sentimental hero in Gabriel García Márquez' *Love in the Time of Cholera* (*Amor en los tiempos de cólera*), who was so in love that he was able to continue to the end of the world, that is, to where time will never be able to go. For this reason, Florentino, as an elderly lover, felt eternal, at least while the desire for survival urged him to continue loving. For how long?

"Forever," is the answer of Diego Samaritano, the captain of the boat taking the elderly lovers Florentino and Fermina toward some unnamed place, because in this way, going no place, time will also not be able to find either the lovers nor, ah!, the love that is shining between them, which is also not going anywhere. This is like the time in the life of the characters on *Lost*, which was also going nowhere. These people, just as Florentino, were also surrounded by water, which is the water of the beginning and the end, the same as always, eternal water by design, because time is a river which, besides flowing, gets things wet. Heraclitus well knew that we do not step twice into the same river. For this reason, Florentino prefers to stay out of the water, dry, on a boat, desiring to deceive his own temporality, even though he is unlikely to achieve this. No one manages to escape from it. Time passes; it passes all the time. We know this all too well, and yet, how exactly does it flow? Is it always the same? Does it always go at the same speed? Or does it sometimes go faster and then suddenly slow down? And what does this depend on? Life is a place where time entertains itself asking questions that no one, among the living, knows how to answer.

As a platform of repetition, a synthesis of sensations, time is the shortcut to abandon events and to transition into living in an arithmetic that is adrift in the fragments of a partial temporality. We are time (which is why we have created verbal forms), and time needs us too in order to exist and to justify its definition in the dictionary:

> Time. Noun. \'t m\ . . . 1 a : the measured or measurable period during which an action, process, or condition exists or continues : DURATION; b : a nonspatial continuum that is measured in terms of events which succeed one another from past through present to future; c : LEISURE <*time* for reading> . . . Middle English, from Old English *t ma* . . . " (*Merriam-Webster Online Dictionary*).

In the duration perceived in its successive sequences, we proffer an attempt at reconciliation with temporality. We make concessions, we depend on intervals of discontinuity, and we accept that life is no more (nor less) than a livable concept to whose rules we must conform. Saint Augustine was also right about this: "that if nothing were passing, there would be no past time: and if nothing were coming, there should be no time to come: and if nothing were, there should now be no present time" ("si nihil praeteriret, non esset praeteritum tempus, et si nihil adveniret, non esset futurum tempus, et si nihil esset, non esset praesens tempus"; *Confessions* Bk. XI, Chap. xiv, 238-39).

"Ah, Time, all is now understood" ("Ah, el Tiempo, ya todo se comprende") wrote Gil de Biedma in one of his poems,[4] even though in truth nothing in this life is completely understood, least of all time. "For what is time?" ("*quid est enim tempus*"), wondered Saint Augustine in a confessional tone, responding: "If no one asks me, I know: but if I were desirous to explain it to one that should ask me, plainly I know not" ("si nemo ex me quaerat, scio; si quaerenti explicare velim, nescio"; *Confessions* XI.xiv, 236-39). And if a saint, capable of accessing mystic atemporality, a sacred aura, did not know, we will know even less. Time is a vague reference to which we do justice by not speaking, and even more so by not asking. We should heed Saint Augustine in at least something, and he gave us a valuable hint in this regard. All the time since human beings have inhabited the planet, entire centuries, has led them to attempt to define time (which, along with love and death, are the only questions without answer).

When speaking of time, questions are as unnecessary as the projected answers that come more as a sense of obligation to rational thinking than as a result of common sense when faced with the difficulty of the question. Here we may profit by returning to the words of Saint Augustine: "If no one asks me [what time is], I know" what it is, but if I wish to explain it to him who asks me, "I know not." Maybe that is why the saint sought access to sacred things, since he lives in eternity, in a time that disappears due to an excess of time. God lives outside of time, in eternity, and for Him there are no problems. But when He began the work of creating the world, He did not have any other option but to resort, just like the rest of the world, to an earthly week. This is why He worked intensely for six days and rested on the seventh (maybe it was His way of saying that time is the same for all). Does time move forward, in a straight line, like William Tell's arrow before piercing the apple, or does it follow a singular circularity in which repetition does not rest? Philosophers have never come to an agreement regarding the definitive answer, or if such an answer even exists. Many have offered their opinion, from Plato to Heidegger to Kant, the latter of whom believed that time is nothing more than a category of thought.

Marilyn Monroe said that she liked poetry because "one saves time." In the reading of the *estampa*, that little-studied literary genre, one saves time. This time not only represents savings but also salvation, movement outside of continuity or, rather, continuity abbreviated by its hurried resolution, which demands a greater degree of concentration, of careful consideration—fixation, I would say—on the core. The *estampa*, an amphibious genre—situated between poetic prose and minifiction, between the note and the aphorism, between the joke and the breviary, between the fable and the parable—establishes an intermediate space between what is and what perhaps is not, where the contradiction of continuity and the restriction of literary time is resolved.

The definition of developing events comes from the very act of canceling the expectations of temporal succession, expectations that promote an interpretation with conclusive finality. Therefore, according to these considerations sponsored by fiction, what is the time in which the *estampa* begins and ends? The horizontality of its movement toward an elastic caesura, different from the vertical temporality of poetry, displays features—as affirmed in Rolando Hinojosa-Smith's work—of a combinatorial analysis of factors both documentary and confessional.

What is the relationship between the texts of *Platero and I* (*Platero y yo*), by Juan Ramón Jiménez, and *Ocnos*, by Luis Cernuda, and Hinojosa-Smith's *Estampas del Valle*? There is one, and it is found in the expressive brevity at play, and the articulation of a series of questions regarding formal characteristics of the genre. In the early 20th century, Julio Herrera y Reissig wrote texts similar to the *estampas*. This poet from Montevideo, ahead of his time in many ways, called these works of his "snapshots" (*instantáneas*) long before the invention of the Polaroid camera. In fact, in these very *instantáneas*, just as in Hinojosa-Smith's *estampas*, there repeatedly appears peculiarly expressive information, such as the tendency of the popular theater of the grotesque, with snippets of oral-tradition street speak, as seen in his complete works:

> Bang!! From the right comes the sound of a punch that makes a hundred heads turn in unison. Don Sebastián moves over nervously, looking to see if the table has been broken. It is Ramón the fat man, a casino Hercules, the most radical economist and sociologist from the shoe factory . . . (*Pum!! Por la derecha suena un puñetazo que hace girar cien cabezas al mismo tiempo. Don Sebastián acude nervioso, husmeando si la mesa ha quedado rota. Es el gordo Ramón, un Hércules de Casino, el economista y sociólogo más radical de la fábrica de alpargatas* . . . [*Poesías completas y prosas* 643]).[5]

In the 1960s, beginning with the Cuban Revolution, the literary specificity that we could consider to be the *estampa* underwent a period of hatching in Latin America. What is more, I would venture to say that it experienced a premature "golden age," its first moment of popularity and acceptance as a genre with its own rules. It was an idiosyncratic form of writing. Julio Cortázar wrote *estampas*, but he called them by a different name. Based on the traditional model (a model that is not easy to characterize), he invented these texts outside the script and without an *a priori* cannon. They displayed moments of dazzling literary imagination, which is the case of those in *Cronopios and Famas* (*Historias de cronopios y famas*, 1962) and *Around the Day in Eighty Worlds* (*La vuelta al día en ochenta mundos*, 1967) from where the following example is taken:

> After his sixth glass of grappa, Drinks deigned to accompany Solano in order to raise his spirits, and they arrived at the wake in a high state of ethylic emotion. Drinks entered the funeral chapel first, and even though he had never in his life seen the dead man, he drew near to the coffin, saw him lying there peacefully, and, turning to Solano, said to him in that tone that is only aroused and perhaps heard by the deceased:
>
> —He looks the same.[6]

> A la sexta grapa Copitas condescendió a acompañar a Solano para levantarle el ánimo, y cayeron al velorio en alto grado de emoción etílica. Le tocó a Copitas entrar el primero en la capilla ardiente, y aunque en su vida había visto al muerto, se acercó al ataúd, lo contempló recogido, y volviéndose a Solano le dijo con ese tono que sólo suscitan y quizá oyen los finados:
>
> —Está idéntico. ("De la seriedad en los velorios") ("On Seriousness at Wakes")

In Cortázar's work, *estampas*—those stories to be read at the speed of imagination—appear in that indefinable but thoroughly premeditated region whose base, both formal and argumental, comes from vignettes, short stories and jokes to which each new teller adds details, both heard and seen. The brevity of *Cronopios and Famas* and *Around the Day in Eighty Worlds* generates moments of writing outside the genre, texts that had not completely begun when they already started to end. According to the *Diccionario de la lengua española* (Espasa-Calpe), an *estampa* (in one of its meanings) is a "Scene, an image that is typical or representative of something" ("Escena, imágen típica o representativa de algo").[7] And the verb *estampar* means to make, reconstruct, or write an *estampa*, to capture an alternative look, hearing and procedure.

Along these same lines, with marked restrictions, are the *estampas* or "minifictions" of *Falsifications* (*Falsificaciones*, 1966 and 1969) by Marco Denevi, who also wrote *Rose at Ten O'Clock* (*Rosaura a las diez*, 1955). In this same register are the texts contained in Eduardo Galeano's books *Vagabond* (*Vagamundo,* 1973) and *Days and Nights of Love and War* (*Días de noches de amor y de guerra*, 1978)—the latter a volume presented as a novel, but which in truth is comprised of minichapters that exist separate from one another—as well as the three volumes of *Memories of Fire* (*Memorias del fuego*, 1982-86). In these titles Galeano's narration centers on small, daily events which the reader is invited to consider from a later perspective. The written word hears and represents "intra-history," that which George Perec called "the infra-ordinary." The unclassifiable *estampas* of Ariel Méndez are imbued also with this element of that which is partially "unseen" but which is there, and may be best read in his 1982 collection *Chocolate with Sardines* (*Chocolate con sardinas*). This book by this strange, brilliant but forgotten man, includes examples such as the following: "I wanted her to cheat on me so I would have a reason to leave her, but the lousy bitch never cheated on me" ("Quería que me engañara para encontrar un motivo para abandonarla, pero la muy hija de puta nunca me engañó" 18).[8]

In the *estampas* genre the narrated time belongs to the life of others. It is for this reason, and because of the demiurgic condition of the one who dramatizes it, that it is so easy to abbreviate this time and manipulate its influential impact on the succession of moments. Writing favors a time that is "unreal." It is a time that is the enemy of duration, a time that the past has neglected.

Juan Ramón Jiménez suggests, without saying so explicitly, that *estampas* are written for children. This is how his *Platero and I* (*Platero y yo*) is read in the America south of Mercedes, Texas: as an ideal book for those who are just beginning to read and seek in literature a reason to keep reading. Therefore, could the *estampa* not be the childhood of a developing, older text that at a certain point in time intentionally stopped growing? The *estampa*, the Peter Pan of literature, the same as childhood itself, demands to be read in its own nontransferable time, one that does not give any warning about its accelerated duration. It is a time that transpires without it being noticed, a temporality that does not seem to indicate where it is going, and it is rechristened, since the present can be the past, and the past can influence the future.

In the brief introduction to *Estampas del Valle*, Hinojosa explains that among these *estampas* there are "some short, some long" ("unas cortas, otras largas"; *Estampas* 15).[9] Their length, just as with obituaries, depends on the character or characters in question. In fact, "Beto Castañeda," an *estampa* belonging to the section "Lives and Miracles" ("Vidas y milagros"), can be read as an obituary. This story refers to a restricted time that can be chosen and improved upon, since for Hinojosa time is the intermediary that turns life into the action of a continuity, a state that is livable, and when not, at least writable. It is not for nothing that the time of obituaries—a lifetime written after the life is over—is that of the beginning and the end; it covers the stretch between parentheses. It is a time at the disposal of the mind, a time that is still, like a taxidermied animal. It is time that the past has completely erased, even though the same thing does not always happen.

On other occasions, the time of an *estampa* arrives "already begun," and the text starts with the name of the *estampa* itself, as if the story had begun to be told before and something was missing, or rather, as if the synchrony between the rhetorical space and the real duration of the reading belonged to an oral moment being manufactured. This happens in "Coyotes" (*Estampas* 131-32, 152-53) where the written word seeks to capture the representation of the voice, that is to say, to fulfill the impossible discursive task of translating one duration to another (a transposition), the one that best corresponds to that which cannot be counted because it is not necessary to count and recount everything.

There appears what we could consider an "onomatopoeic" time that does not imitate that which it describes, since it is not known precisely what it is that is being described. It is a time supported on the specific path where speech falls into ruin before collapsing. It is a time of noise, accustomed to that which cannot be silenced because it has not yet been expressed. This stretch between word and deed facilitates the presence of a guttural murmur composed of seventeen m's in a row (*Estampas* 131, 153), which in this case is something more than the "m" sound that characterizes a surprise reaction (Mmm!), since the mechanism includes the emergence of the temporal paradigm as the duration of speech is lost.

The use of onomatopoeia does not enrich the narrated action, because the sound plays a more deactivating role for any subsequent rhetorical resonance. Reference is vaguely made to temporality in an immeasurable lapse. "This happened a long time ago" ("De esto ya hace tiempo"; *Estampas* 131, 152) states the narrator, who earlier, in his great eagerness for precision, had said: "so far" ("hasta la fecha"; *Estampas* 131, 152). But what is that date, especially if that is the least important thing? Also unimportant is an exact determination of how much time will go by before the event takes place, since it will not be "until the end of the year" ("hasta el fin de año"; *Estampas* 132, 153) without it being known in what month the perspective of the narrator is situated, since neither the present, past, or future have a traceable trail. In the *estampa*, time simply transpires, and with its passage it gives rise to a fortuitous order. Reading cannot exist outside of temporality because its form lives by succession, by adding or taking back time à la Parmenides, which can exist exclusively because it does.

The *estampa*, with that temporal instantaneousness contained in a single moment (analogous only to itself), forces the present to live from its resurrections, to depend not on another existence beyond the one that emerges from this moment. The text becomes the architect of a possibility carried out in semi-fullness, a possibility about which inquiries are made and into which are introduced stories belonging to a desire that is not necessarily meant to be fulfilled. Time is much more than a metaphysical intermediary that is carried from one word to another, and from one phrase to the next.

As a result of depending unremittingly on brevity, the *estampa* gives temporal material a facilitating condition that lacks direction during the course of reading. In other words, it instills the belief that one moment of the narration can substitute for another, and that the last instant can be the beginning of the next. Reading is an intensity with its own panorama, one whose sparkles assume as their own all that could be said of them, without the necessity of discarding something or of denying the tentative conclusions of the previous reading. Therefore, regression, that is to say rereading, will not be asymmetrical because there emerges a different verisimilitude based on what is already realized.

Just as with the time that is spent reading an *estampa*, the *estampa* itself is brief. There is no time (nor does any remain) for its possible meaning to grow old or to be accessed. Therefore, the sparkle, the residual or primordial effect that it highlights, is poetic. The paradox rises to the surface to establish its purposes. The *estampa*, as if it were a poetic object (or objective) whose present spreads out in a space of minimal diction, erases the possibility that the plotline in the making be the only hub of attention.

In this fashion, the story occupies the place of that which is told. It pushes its hypothesis, disintegrating the anecdotal plane. The entity that prevails is that of writing itself, the discursive procedure in action. The effect is poetic, as the feint toward resolution occurs due to incompleteness, due to a lack of data in the information provided by the story. This, therefore, prevents a consideration of the *estampa* as a fragmentary form of writing, since it emerges as an open parenthesis of thought, along the lines of an ellipsis of ideas that embarked upon a quest for other, future ideas, and that along the way met with a story that distracted them.

In the *estampas*, since there is no beginning or end (the segment is from before and is moving toward an after that is barely discernable), time is all in (for) itself. It denies its future, but even more so its past, in order to be present until it no longer can, until it can exist outside of itself. It is a truly enormous desire (only in literature can such things happen): time also wants to exist outside of time.

Long before quartz and digital watches, Aristotle said "the time marks the movement, since it is its number, and the movement the time" (*Physics* IV.12). In an attempt to represent the figures of temporality, the scandalous behavior of *tempus fugit*, Jorge Luis Borges turned to an Indian aporia that helps, in part, to negotiate insurmountable logical difficulty, putting forth at the same time the idea that even the present is nonexistent: "The orange is about to fall from the branch or it is already on the ground, state those strange simplifiers. No one sees it fall" ("La naranja está por caer de la rama o ya está en el suelo, afirman esos simplificadores extraños. Nadie la ve caer"; *Obras completas* 354).[10]

To the contrary, in the *estampas* of Hinojosa-Smith, the present remained there so it could be seen unfolding in the writing, whose main difficulty consists of existing in a time which—because it is always the same, redundant right down to the core, because it persists too much in its being—becomes something rather different. It is somewhat like a motionless tree (not necessarily in an orange grove) that changed time and, as a result, changed place for having made possible different angles of observation. Without knowing how to do it, words venture forth to capture the process of becoming, and they are partially successful in achieving this.

Given the stated epistemological circumstances, the *estampa* demands only one thing of the reader: that he or she exist in complicity with the time of words, in a synchrony devoid of either an after or a before, in a present of right now that does not desire to share its time with any other time, but which requires that it be known in the immediate now of thought, where all the other things in the world can and must be left for later. The act of reading defines its argument and is that which is in play. There are no parts to join together, nor is anything anticipated beyond that which is already there. In this simultaneous present, the right now follows the still current moment.

The spectacle unveiled by minimal narration imposes a strange premonition that the reading will need to confirm. The *estampa* contains the time that cannot change, that has come to language to preserve the present as a guardian between the minutes, even if in some cases the reading requires less of one in order to be completed. The successive and the simultaneous, when they coincide, establish a halo of representation exhorted by that which cannot be outside of the narrated temporality, by that half knowledge of duration that feigns being complete. As with the works of Robert Rauschenberg, another Texan, the *estampas* are what could be called "souvenirs without nostalgia."

The minimization of the story prevents the inclusion of modifications to all that may occur after the events in the reading. It is that sort of hiatus from perspective, a catalyzing detour from all that which is allowed to be expressed in order to make clear that we are reading "time," that we are not reading only literature, and that the representation comes from a carelessness of indifference, which is worried this time over paying attention to all that it does not know about the immediate reality. It is a reality that does not need to be imagined since it is there to overcome fiction.

Through this strategy, the *estampa* appeals to a preserved time that transcribes itself, a time where that which is oral allows itself to be written, showing itself to be intentionally violated; it has opened the way to a type of uncommon literary expression where that which is expressed is the way of being, turned into the spectacle of its game and its rules. Could the ungrammaticality of time be the main subject matter of the *estampas*? Could it be that they turn to the stories of others like bait, and to the page—even if the content of its expression is minimal—like a space of sedimentation for a logos that is, of all things, the least ineffable?

The desire of the *estampa* to restore an eagerness for realistic fiction radicalizes the act of beginning and ending the story, of being an indication and a challenge. This is because outside of time reality gives language a new look, which testifies of its existence, narrating that which it saw and even that which it might see, in the event that the past was not an appearance that presents the pause in knowledge as the only proof of its existence. Perhaps in order to better understand the resonance of its format, the *estampa* should be read aloud, as its time is that of a countdown (ten, nine, eight . . .), time that comes to an end but never concludes since it complies with a plan of reminiscence in perpetual motion. This vaulted time, whose alias might be hyperbaton, is made of inclusion and proliferation in synthesis, not of conclusion.

This time highlights the expressed representation of an immediacy that cannot be sustained at the very moment that the look occurs (since the duration is not a fixation of instants, but, to the contrary, is their pulverization), and it likewise highlights its irrepresentability. In the itinerary between beginning and end (itinerary or attempt, itinerary and attempt, which is nothing but a way of insisting on its staying power), in the little time that it has to invent a figure of speech of its own, the resident of a perspective, time fulfills the trajectory of a temporal levity that has not occurred in vain. In spite of having begun and ended before expected, it fulfills the poetic illusion of thought, just as did Zeno of Elea's turtle and Heraclitus's water. This water is also that of Jorge Manrique's rivers, which are flowing to the sea that is life, water that expresses itself as it flows to find its course at the level of an improbable plan, that plan which fulfills expectations after having first created them.

Time is the awareness of a concept that defines our temporality, and which is not necessarily (even if time is the most necessary thing) the time that transpires objectively in chronology. This is how writing duplicates its audacity and learns to live with counted minutes and the existential triviality that surrounds it. It is not for nothing that it deals with stories that are of interest to time only. This is the way it takes care of its unresolved business. "The newspaper said nothing about you or me" ("En el diario no hablaban de ti, ni de mí")[11] says Joaquín Sabina's song, and the *estampas*, those of Hinojosa-Smith, as well as those of Galeano, Cortázar, and Ariel Méndez, deal with the vital time of characters about whom no one speaks, much less newspapers.

It is a time that withdraws in the face of requests made by words. Such words might well be those of a bolero, and not just any bolero, but "The Clock" ("El reloj"), by Roberto Cantoral: "Clock, stop your forward march" ("Reloj, detén tu camino").[12] But here psychological temporality does not stop (nor does chronological temporality), since time flies, and it is good that this is so, since it refers to the heterogeneity of the perspective of an intense but ephemeral experience, concentrated in its exclusivity, in a vertigo that at some point ceased to know where it should go. How can one stop time except by writing it, giving it a future in another time, one that passes in a different way?

What happens in Time stays in Time. The issue, therefore, is not how to remove it, how to pull time out of the time that it is in, but rather how to represent it and tell of that merger of effusiveness where temporality stops counting when something is being recounted. Yes, but how? As accounts that count time, the *estampas* are the countdown to a finality returning to its flowing course. In one of Hinojosa-Smith's most eloquent *estampas* in this regard, "Death Once Again" ("Otra vez la muerte"; *Estampas* 28, 67), time exemplifies a vague curiosity of the mind that seeks to find a replica of its abstractions. In this *estampa*, time has an uninhibited presence, as all the references that could be made to it are mere approximations: "Around that time." The temporal vagueness, in fact, sums up a great irony, since one of the characters has a Swiss watch sent to him by his father-in-law (*Estampas* 31, 70). The catalogue of temporal references in this particular story includes temporal references such as the following: "Three years . . . had gone by as if they were just a day" ("Había pasado tres años como un día"; *Estampas* 28, 67); "had once" ("en un tiempo"; *Estampas* 28, 67); "a few years before" ("unos años antes"; *Estampas* 28, 67) ; "After a few months" ("Pasando unos pocos meses"; *Estampas* 31, 70).

In this time, transpiring adrift toward its mobile isles of elusive sense, not all passes and not all remains, though there is sufficient remanence to be able to speak of the ephemeral based on the word's resistance to time. What we are witnessing is a time that is the time of Medusa's look, a time of freezing, which prevents the use of temporal adverbs because nothing exists sooner or later but rather right then and there, a repetition in perception like a Hydra with one of its heads cut off. This idiosyncratic temporality drives an approximate perception of all that occurs, and even more than the occurrence itself. In this temporality, just as is the case with nearly all of the *estampas*, the references to temporal moments are present in the present, in an adverbial time situated in the superimposed moments of now. This, precisely as the end of the story relates, is because time, like life itself, comes in to anchor.

In the *estampa* entitled "Tere Noriega," the eponymous character states "I get tired of the same old life" ("una se cansa de la misma vida"; *Estampas* 56, 17). Italian Cesare Pavese wrote that "work is tiring" ("lavore stanca"), and Argentine Oliverio Girondo, in his poem "Tiredness" ("Cansancio"), wrote: "Tired, /above all, /of always being with myself" ("Cansado/sobre todo,/de estar siempre conmigo").[12] The *estampas*, I would venture to say, represent the exhaustion of time, which is tired of working and of always being with itself. In the just-cited *estampa*, Tere herself ends by saying: "I get tired and that's it, you know?" ("Una se cansa y ya, ¿sabe?"; *Estampas* 56, 17). Yes, it is known, but what of it? What can be known in time, and especially in such a short narrative time where life fits into a gerund ("passing time"), in a moment in which "it will be seen in due time"?

In another *estampa*, "Learning the Profession" ("Aprendiendo el oficio"; *Estampas* 25, 64), the narrator recommends: "Don't waste your time" ("No malgaste su tiempo"; *Estampas* 26, 65). Time—just as with the *estampa*, that nearly-literary genre that represents so well the perception that we have of temporality—exists between speech and silence, between atemporality and a time that cannot be preserved as a continuity without interruptions, because its chameleonic specificity is made of constant fleeing. The author himself understands it this way, which is why the *estampa* "Roque Malacara" only has fifty-four words and can be read in only eighteen seconds. Occupying its throne in language, time practices a vile type of blackmail with us and shamelessly exhibits its haste. The gods, Cronus and Saturn, are not angry, they are in a hurry. The time that guides the blazing word is a sprinter, which is why inside the *estampa* anything and everything can happen before we realize it.

In Hinojosa-Smith's *estampas*, the word is installed in a process dealing with the synthesis of temporalities, favoring with its timeless mission the three reunifying "ecstasies" of temporality to which Martin Heidegger referred ("having been," "presencing," and "coming-towards"), which do not necessarily represent the past, present and future. The concepts "coming-towards," "having been," and "presencing" correspond to a fulfilling moment of Being. They constitute temporality, not separately but together (the three in unity), in what could be considered a coinciding concurrence of the past with the present and the future in a synchronic stratum in full.

In its spiral ellipsis of intertwinings and dispersions, time is individualized: it becomes intimate time, non-transferrable time, subjective time. All of these times are characteristic of thought and of the body, and not of astronomical, galactic, or universal temporality. The word promotes an absolute Unitarian intimacy, which is why it also becomes part of a "homochrony," of a time that gets confused with other times, since it is always chameleonically the same, all the time, but different.

Writing, or better yet the act of telling, happens in time, no matter how much it ends up transgressing against it in its final trajectory. The episodic plot—and I would go further and even say spasmodic plot—which does not even give one time to read it by the time it has already finished, fosters formal (special) and conceptual (temporal) conditions by which language accesses the "ecstasies of temporality" through its own dynamics. Even though the *estampas* take place in the definite finiteness of time, the word, due to its own teleological tendencies, desires that which is perpetual and which perhaps—what a paradox!—has not yet come to be completely present. In its sameness, the word becomes the intermediary of the flow of permanence, of that which can only demonstrate perseverance in language. As a consequence, or rather as an inescapable attribute, Hinojosa-Smith's *estampas* articulate strategies to detemporalize time itself, seeking simultaneously to escape time.

Between the beginning and the end of the charted narration, which concludes when it is just getting started, chronological time turns into purely psychological (psychophysical) temporality. This temporality is incomprehensible in its unity of meaning and produces a digression of meaning warned of in the writing. It is non-specific but besiegeable time, because in this particular writing format there emerges a past tense (the ideal sum of all tenses, both past and future) that projects itself onto a (non-ecstatic) present that, due to its implicit, mobilizing, dynamic function can be considered a "continual present," since it includes that which has gone by, that which is presently here, and that which will come.

In that which is narrated, not the narration, the characters manage to detach themselves from chronological ligatures. The writing, therefore, acquires timeless vestments that turn objective (measurable) time into another that is absolutely imaginary, radically literary. Due to their perseverance with the aim of achieving the dismantling of reality, words learn to take advantage of an invented and complex truth by which literature speaks of life as if it knew what it was talking about.

Translator's note

While this essay was translated by Travis Sorenson, it contains certain quotes from other works that had been translated from Spanish to English previously. The following list of translation references (which correspond to the superscript numbers throughout the text) makes clear which translated quotes meet this description and which ones were not located in other sources and were therefore translated as part of this project. The websites listed for the previously translated material were accessed on or around 15 September 2010. See note 8 below for more precise information on the translation of the Hinojosa quotes taken from *Estampas del Valle.*

Notes

1The Spanish word *estampa*, which can denote a picture, a print, or a similar image, is a reference to Rolando Hinojosa-Smith's book *Estampas del Valle y otras obas* (1973), a title translated as *Sketches of the Valley and Other Works* in the first, bilingual edition. Of the four sections of the book, we concentrate on two "*estampas*"-rich sections: "Estampas del Valle" ("Sketches of the Valley") and "Vidas y milagros" ("Lives and Miracles"). At the same time our discussion may be applicable to some of the "*otras obras" ("other works")* constituted by "Por esas cosas que pasan" ("One of Those Things") and "Una vida de Rafa Buenrostro" ("A Life of Rafa Buenrostro").

2Translated by Travis Sorenson; http://users.telenet.be/Tango-E-Vita/tango/Fierro.htm

3Translated by Travis Sorenson; *Cantos de vida y esperanza* 25.

4Translated by Travis Sorenson.

5Translated by Travis Sorenson.

[6]Translated by Travis Sorenson.
[7]Translated by Travis Sorenson.
[8]Translated by Travis Sorenson.
[9]Translated by Travis Sorenson. In this essay, citations from *Estampas* will be made from the first bilingual edition of 1973; it contains Hinojosa's original Spanish text and the Valadez translation into English. The English translation will normally be that of Valadez; the Sorenson translation will be cited only when it better catches the time-related nuance of the Spanish that is being studied here. *The Valley*, what Hinojosa calls his "recreation in narrative prose" of *Estampas* (*The Valley* 3), is a cultural as well as linguistic recreation of *Estampas*. In practice this means often that Hinojosa's English-language text has no direct equivalent to words, phrases and information in his original Spanish text. Likewise, *The Valley* sometimes introduces material for which there is no equivalent in *Estampas*. In this context, then, the English of *The Valley* is not authoritative as respects the Spanish of *Estampas*; and, for that reason we must use the English words—either those of Valadez or Sorenson—which most literally communicate the time-related information of the original Spanish.
[10]Translated by Travis Sorenson.
[11]Translated by Travis Sorenson.
[12]Translated by Travis Sorenson.
[13]Translated by Travis Sorenson.

Works Cited

Agustine. *St. Augustine's Confessions with an English Translation by William Watts*, Vol. II. Cambridge, MA and London: Harvard UP and William Heineman Ltd., 1968. Print.

Aristotle. *Physics*. Trans. R.P. Hardie and R.K. Gaye. *The Internet Classics Archive*. Web Atomic and Massachusetts Institute of Technology, 13 Sept. 2007. Web. 15 Jan. 2012.

Borges, Jorge Luis. *Obras completas 1923-1972*. Buenos Aires: Emece, 1974. Print.

Cantoral, Roberto. "El reloj." Perf. Los tres caballeros. *Los tres caballeros*. Discos Musart, 1956. LP.

Cernuda, Luis. *Ocnos*. Madrid: Huerga y Fierro, 2002. Print.

Cortázar, Julio. "De la seriedad en los velorios." *La vuelta al día en ochenta mundos*. Mexico: Siglo XXI Editores, 1967. *Literatura.org*. Web. 15 Jan. 2012.

___. *Historia de cronopios y famas*. Madrid: Alfaguara, 2006. Print.

Darío, Rubén. *Cantos de vida y esperanza*. Madrid: Espasa-Calpe/Austral, 1971. Print.

Denevi, Marco. *Falsificaciones*. Barcelona: Thule Ediciones, 2008. Print.

Galeano, Eduardo. *Vagamundo y otros relatos*. Mexico: Siglo XXI, 1973. Print.

___. *Días y noches de amor y de guerra*. Buenos Aires: Siglo XXI, 2005. Print.

Girondo, Oliverio. "Cansancio." *Persuasión de los días*. Buenos Aires: Losada, 1942. *A media voz*. Web. 15 Jan. 2012.

Heidegger, Martin. *Ser y tiempo*. Santiago de Chile: Editorial Universitaria, 1997. Print.

Herrera y Reissig, Julio. *Poesía completa y prosas*. Ed. Ángeles Estévez. Paris: ALLCA XX / Mexico: Fondo de Cultura Económica, 1998. Print.

Hinojosa, Rolando. *Estampas del Valle y otras obras/Sketches of the Valley and Other Works*. Trans. Gustavo Valadez. Berkeley: Quinto Sol, 1973. Print.

___. *Estampas del Valle*. Tempe, AZ: Bilingual Press/Editorial Bilingüe, 1994. Print.

___. *The Valley*. Tempe, AZ: Bilingual Press/Editorial Bilingüe 1983. Print.

Jiménez, Juan Ramón. *Platero y yo*. Madrid: Editorial Edaf, 1984. Print.

Manrique, Jorge. *Coplas de Jorge Manrique*. Trans. Henry Wadsworth Longfellow. Whitefish, MT: Kessinger Publishing, 2004. Print.

Méndez, Ariel. *Chocolate con sardinas*. Montevideo: Imago, 1982. Print.

Nooteboom, Cees. *Grave of Poets and Thinkers*. New York: Random House/Mondadori, 2009. Print.

Perec, Georges. *La vida, instrucciones de uso*. Barcelona: Anagrama, 2006. Print.

Sabina, Joaquín. "Eclipse de mar." *Mentiras piadosas*. BMG / Ariola, 1990. CD.

The Wounds of War
Mapping Geographies of Trauma in Rolando Hinojosa's *Korean Love Songs*

María Herrera-Sobek
University of California, Santa Barbara

Korean Love Songs (1978), the third installment of Rolando Hinojosa's *Klail City Death Trip* series, is a collection of poems that, as the author himself has stated, is written in "narrative prose in verse form" (Jason 2).[1] Published after *Estampas del Valle y otras obras* (1973) and *Klail City y sus alrededores* (1976), it is an extraordinary collection of poems depicting the Korean War experience that features as its central narrator Rafa Buenrostro, one of the main protagonists appearing repeatedly throughout the *Death Trip*. *Korean Love Songs* (*KLS*) focuses on a three year period, 1949-1952, while Rafa (aka Rafe) is stationed first in Allied-occupied Japan and then transferred to Korea at the beginning of the Korean conflict. The small fifty-three page chap book of narrative verse highlights in thirty-eight fairly short poems the traumatizing events American soldiers were experiencing during those Korean war years when Rafe was in the military serving his country. Philip K. Jason has stated in an interview he did with Hinojosa for the *Bilingual Review* in 2000 that Hinojosa "may be the only writer in any language who has written both a novel [*Useless Servants* (1993)] and a book-length poetry sequence [*KLS*] about the Korean War" (1). The uniqueness of this accomplishment as well as the significant literary merit of the *KLS* motivated the writing of this study. Some biographical and historical background may be in order.

Hinojosa experienced first-hand the Korean War. He was in the U.S. Army from 1946-1949 and was later reactivated in 1950 to serve in Korea in a reconnaissance unit (Jason 1). However, Hinojosa did not write about the Korean War until he began his creative writing career with his first book *Estampas del Valle*. After that book and *KLS*, Korea and the war experience continue to surface. For instance, Rafe's life as a soldier is one of the important narrative threads of the novel *Rites and Witnesses* (1982); and it centers the action of the novel *The Useless Servants* which is presented as the journal or diary of Rafa who is also the protagonist of *KLS*.

The Korean War began on June 25, 1950, and featured North Korea fighting against South Korea. In this conflict the Republic of Korea (South Korea) was supported by the United Nations and the United States while North Korea (The Democratic Peoples' Republic of Korea) had the Peoples' Republic of China on its side and received additional aid, mainly air support, from the Soviet Union. The roots of this conflict can be traced to the division of the Korean Peninsula and its peoples after World War II. Korea had been a conquered colony of the Japanese Empire since 1910 and when the Japanese fell after World War II, they lost all their former colonized territories, including Korea. The former Japanese colony was thereafter divided into two countries and these were to be ruled under the guidance of the two major super powers: the United States and the Soviet Union. The northern part of Korea at the 38th Parallel was to be under Soviet Union control and the Southern part below the 38th Parallel line was to be under US control.

As might be expected, the unification of the two Koreas was greatly desired by nationalist parties on both sides of the Korean border and constant skirmishes and incursions became frequent at the 38th parallel, the dividing point between the two countries. Eventually, North Korea (the Korean Peoples' Army) invaded South Korea by crossing the 38th Parallel on Sunday, June 25, 1950, and began a war that lasted until an armistice was signed on July 27, 1953. The war, lasting three years, was a devastating event for all the people involved: civilians and soldiers alike. The soldiers from the United States, the soldiers from the Peoples' Republic of China and the North and South Koreans all suffered grievous losses in life and limb as well as resources. The various battles that took place decimated people in extraordinarily high numbers. The casualty numbers given for the Korean War are all approximate since due to the extremely high number of casualties it was difficult to keep accurate statistics. The numbers cited here provide an insight into the human toll taken by this war: U.S.: 36,940 soldiers killed; People's Republic of China (same as People's Volunteer Army, China): 152,000 dead; Democratic People's Republic of Korea also known as Korean People's Army (North Korea): 215,000; Republic of Korea (South Korea): 137,899 dead. It is estimated that the total number of civilians killed or wounded was a staggering 2.5 million.[2]

Given the enormity of the numbers of people killed and wounded (physical trauma), it is not surprising that soldiers, and of course civilians, would suffer also unspeakable psychological traumas. Hinojosa's multiple cast of characters in *KLS* suffer both kinds of trauma, but here I shall use literary trauma theory in order to explicate and delve into the various responses to the psychological trauma inscribed in this creative work. In this way I shall expand both the meaning and scope of the theoretical model related to psychological trauma in the novelistic genre.

Of particular interest in *KLS* is that each poem encompasses a particular traumatic experience of the Korean War and hence provides a model for further conversations and elucidations on literary trauma theory. Hinojosa's war poems both further complicate and clarify important issues associated with literary trauma theory as they relate to race, ethnicity and place. My study maps out what I call the "geographies of trauma" and utilizes literary trauma theory in the analysis and hermeneutics of the *KLS* poems. In mapping the geographies of trauma, I focus on specific poems that highlight traumatic events experienced by the soldiers featured in the collection and I demonstrate both the different degrees of traumas experienced and the responses the soldiers had to the events described. It could be further posited that Hinojosa's poetry and the traumatized soldiers depicted within the poetic verses serve to harshly critique the Korean War effort and, in fact, all wars. Moreover, the analysis of Hinojosa's poems could help to expand literary trauma theory to encompass ideological formations presented in literary works based specifically on the structuring of trauma to encode social critiques and ideological positions. In the case of *KLS* it would be a critique of government policies, of racism and world governments involved in violent actions without thinking or not caring about the human tragedies their political policies engender. But the study of ideological formations which underlie the *KLS* goes beyond the purview of this study. Our analysis here of psychological trauma in *KLS* reveals instead Hinojosa's quiet and elegant manner—sometimes incorporating dry humor—of making present the great suffering of all involved in war.

In mapping the geographies of trauma in *KLS*, I found Michelle Balaev's essay "Trends in Literary Trauma Theory" (2008) particularly useful for its discussion of contemporary trauma theories and their application to the trauma novel. For Balaev's purposes, trauma is perceived mainly as a psychological response that can happen to an individual or a group including populations in entire countries; for example, those that suffer natural disasters such as floods or earthquakes. A key conceptualization of trauma theory that I will be using in my analysis is the proposition, articulated by Balaev and other trauma critics such as Cathy Caruth and Bessel van der Kolk, that "trauma creates a speechless fright that divides or destroys identity" (Balaev 1). This has a corollary related to identity formation and suggests "identity is formed by the intergenerational transmission of trauma" (1). I will be focusing on trauma as creating "speechless fright" as well as some aspects of transhistorical and intergenerational transmission of trauma which I will elaborate in my analysis of some *KLS* poems that relate to these specific areas of trauma theory. Balaev expands on her definition of the trauma narrative, stating that it is

> a work of fiction that conveys profound loss or intense fear on individual or collective levels. A defining feature of the trauma novel is the transformation of the self ignited by an external, often terrifying experience, which illuminates the process of coming to terms with the dynamics of memory that inform the new perceptions of the self and world. (1)

Balaev challenges literary trauma theory in its narrow conceptualization of trauma arguing that: "a discursive dependence upon a single psychological theory of trauma produces a homogenous interpretation of the diverse representations in the trauma novel and the interplay that occurs between language, experience, memory, and place" (1). She contends that we should be aware of the "multiple models of trauma and memory presented in the trauma novel" and particularly to "the role of place, which functions to portray trauma's effects through metaphoric and material means. Descriptions of geographic place of traumatic experience and remembrance situate the individual in relation to a larger cultural context that contains social values that influence the recollection of the event and the reconfiguration of the self" (1).

In *KLS,* the focus is made on individual soldiers and officers experiencing different traumatic events and offering various responses to their traumas. The collection of poems is divided into three sections: Section I encompasses the dates December 1949 and June-December 1950. The first date, December 1949, features only one poem: "The Old Army Game." It is short because it is the period preceding Rafe's transfer to Korea. The second set of dates cited in Section I encompass more action. The dates cover June to December 1950 and refer to the beginning of the Korean offensive. Section II covers the period January-May 1951 and has the greatest number of poems—fourteen poems total. Section III encompasses two periods: September 1951 and January-March 1952 and in a final poem, "Vale," Rafe summarizes his stint in the Korean conflict.

Critics have not paid *KLS* the attention it deserves; few scholars have analyzed the collection and those that have, have done so only in passing. Some of these critics who have included short sections in their books within their discussions of Hinojosa's other works are: Ramón Saldívar in *Chicano Narratives: The Dialectics of Difference* (1990); Manuel M. Martín Rodríguez in *Rolando Hinojosa y su "Cronicón" Chicano: Una novela del lector* (1993); Joyce Glover Lee in *Rolando Hinojosa and the American Dream* (1997); and Klaus Zilles in *Rolando Hinojosa: A Reader's Guide* (2001). However, the discussions related to *KLS* within the above works are very brief and are not a sustained analysis of the complete collection. As a result, there are very few extant studies focusing on this important collection of war poems. Ramón Saldívar has offered an interesting reading of the poems positing that the collection bears the structure of the corrido and thematizes similar concerns to that of the traditional Mexican ballad, mainly in the context of border conflict and the struggle for social justice. In *Chicano Narrative: The Dialectics of Difference* he argues:

> The Hero in this case, however, is not an idyllic figure of communal solidarity like Gregorio Cortez, but rather the orphaned and eccentric Rafa Buenrostro, one of the two Janus-like protagonists of the Klail City Death Trip. The issue is not the conflict inherent in a cultural and political border but a real war precipitated from an abstract conflict between world powers and their surrogates. (136)

Nevertheless, Saldívar perceives the connection to the corrido tradition in the "poem's thematization of cultural integrity, communal identity, and social justice" (136). He further views the *Korean Love Songs* as related to "South Texas and Mexican American life in a moment of crucial self-formation" (136). In an analogous manner to the corrido, Saldívar explains, "*Korean Love Songs* is an example of Chicano narrative struggling to maintain its existence as an expression of an organic social life. In Hinojosa's poem we are offered a moment in this struggle to understand and retain a genuine cultural and historical class consciousness within the ever-encroaching insistence of late capitalist social life" (136-137). He further points out that the collection of poems is not necessarily folk art while taking inspiration from it nor is it modernist poetry even though influenced by it. And Saldívar emphasizes that

> unlike its own folkloric base, Hinojosa's poem must enact its representation of this struggle not from the outside, as one between Anglo-American cultural and political institutions and Mexican American ones, but from within, as the central Chicano characters become representatives of American cultural and political power as embodied in its armed forces. (137)

Although Joyce Glover Lee does not view *KLS* in the same light that Saldívar does, especially its association with the corrido, I do agree with Saldívar that *KLS* indeed shares many similarities such as, for example, a narrative structure as well as the theme of war, bellicose encounters, and the focus of specific experiences of the characters that populate his creative universe (see Lee 157). In fact, one could go so far as to assert that many of the poems could be characterized as mini corridos since they depict the death of individuals or traumatic events transpiring in the war effort and are told using similar narrative structures, i.e. a narrating voice, via poetry.

My conceptualization and expansion of trauma theory in my analysis of *KLS* creates three categories of traumatic experiences as manifested in Hinojosa's characters and the poetic narratives in which they appear. These are: (1) catastrophic trauma responses, (2) medium trauma responses, and (3) light trauma responses. In the catastrophic trauma response category, the emotional response is so severe and the trauma is so unspeakable and unbearable that the protagonist commits suicide. This would be related to the "unrepresentability" and "unspeakability" of trauma since suicide silences the individual forever. Although I should underline that the event of suicide in itself speaks volumes. This most severe traumatic shock is found in the poem featuring the death of the forward observer Lt. Brodkey titled "Above All, the Waste." We read in the poetic lines that: "Lt. Phil Brodkey up and shot himself two days ago / We found his helmet, the binocs" (30). And the poetic voice comments:

> He was very good at his job
> And yet, he cracked,
> As I imagine many of us will,
> In time. (30)

Trauma theory, as quoted earlier, posits the "speechless fright that divides or destroys identity" (Balaev 1), but in the conceptualization of contemporary trauma theory as posited by various literary critics, including Balaev, it does not encompass suicide as the ultimate response to trauma or psychic suffering. Hinojosa's depiction of what I call catastrophic trauma leading to suicide adds to the conversation of literary trauma theory in the novel. He adds to this conversation in other *KLS* poems such as "Chinaman's Hat" and "Rear Guard Action I."

During the Korean War, victory oscillated between the United Nations-U.S.-Republic of Korea (ROK) armed forces and the North Korean—Peoples' Republic of China armies. At different times during the armed conflict, one military power had the upper hand and had almost the whole Korean peninsula under its jurisdiction. On several occasions the UN-U.S.-ROK forces retreated in almost apparent defeat but always managed to regroup and recover until eventually securing the stalemate that resulted in the 1953 armistice agreement that restored the political division between North and South Korea at the 38th parallel. In "Chinaman's Hat" (11) Hinojosa, who had carefully researched the history of the Korean War before composing the texts collected in *KLS* (Jason 2), based his poem on the Chinese's Third Phase Offensive known as the "Chinese New Year's Offensive." The war was going badly for the ROK and its UN/U.S. allies, and on 26 December 1951 a new commander, Lieutenant-General Matthew Ridgway, was assigned to lead the U.S. Eighth Army. Treated in the poem is what transpired five days after Ridgeway's appointment when the 88th Field Battalion "cut and ran; worse: / They abandoned their guns and shells" (*KLS* 11). This dereliction resulted from the tactics employed by the Chinese during their nocturnal attack where they employed

> loud trumpets and gongs, which fulfilled the double purpose of facilitating tactical communication and mentally disorienting the enemy. UN forces initially had no familiarity with this tactic, and as a result some soldiers "bugged out," abandoning their respective weapons and retreating to the south. The Chinese New Year's Offensive overwhelmed the UN Command forces and the People's Volunteer Army and the Korean People's Army in the conquered Seoul on 4 January 1951. ("Korean War")

Hence in both the historical record and in *KLS* we witness a major, collective traumatic response by U.S./UN soldiers in Korea.

Following the poem "Chinaman's Hat" comes "Rear Guard Action I" which offers a representation of catastrophic trauma in the case of the death of a soldier who is primarily a non-combatant. The narrative recounts how "Mr. Company Clerk" was left behind by his battalion as it was being overrun by Chinese troops:

> The company clerk whose company
> Abandoned *him*; he was left to guard
> Cabinets crammed with shot, leave, and pay records along with the usual morning reports.
> He carried an unloaded carbine, and there were no rounds on his person. (13)

When found physically unharmed later by U.S. soldiers, the clerk seemed to be totally disoriented after having just stood by the cabinets while the Chinese soldiers not only let him be, but also waved to him as they pressed forward! At the end of *KLS* the poetic voice, Rafe, gives an update on the clerk. We find out in the poem, "Vale," how "the sad-faced Company Clerk . . . finally found a loaded carbine" (53), intimating how this hopelessly traumatized soldier did to himself what the Chinese soldiers had not.

The case of Louis Dodge is another excellent example of a catastrophic traumatic response to the war experience (32-35). Dodge joined Rafe's Division as a replacement for the fine officer, but eventual suicide Lt. Brodkey. Louis had assumed the code name of "Red George Three" and he turned out to be a big "talker." However, as we read further, the very next poem suggests that his excessive talking and blustering was a traumatic response to his army war experience. In the poem "One Solution" the poetic voice narrates: "Early this morning, Louis Dodge jumped into the latrine, / Sat down, and refused to come out / Threats and direct orders couldn't budge him" (33). Evidently, Louis had a nervous breakdown and no one could talk him into coming out of the latrine until a captain arrived and ordered him to leave the latrine immediately. Louis was removed from combat and classified as a war casualty. He left silently sitting in the jeep that was transporting him to the hospital with tears streaming down his face. The poem's caustic, and at the same time, humorous title, "One Solution," i.e. to sit out the war in a latrine, evidences the continuing portrayal of the many forms of psychological trauma and how Korean War veteran Hinojosa's dry humor, apparent throughout the poetry collection, is just one more response to the trauma he himself must have suffered.

As for Dodge himself, the company clerk and Lt. Brodkey, according to trauma theory some events are so catastrophic to the psyche that the individual is left "speechless." It will be remembered that Balaev states that "trauma creates a speechless fright that divides or destroys identity" (1). Hinojosa skillfully constructs in Dodge, the company clerk and Lt. Brodkey literary representations of severely traumatized individuals who have lost their identity. Balaev views this literary technique as a "shattering trope" (1). She uses this trope to describe "the damage done to the individual's coherent sense of self and the change of consciousness caused by the experience" (1). Cathy Caruth, in her edited book *Trauma: Explorations in Memory* (1995), expounds on trauma and its destructive power. She comments on how trauma today has replaced the words "shell shock," "combat stress," "delayed stress syndrome," and "traumatic neurosis" (vii). Indeed, we often speak about "post-traumatic stress disorder," where the effects of trauma are delayed and one day they surface unexpectedly. This seems to have happened to Louis Dodge and the company clerk. Caruth also posits the "unrepresentability" of trauma throughout her book *Unclaimed Experiences: Trauma, Narrative, and History* (1996). Catastrophic trauma, nevertheless, provides the author strategies through which he/she demonstrates the "unrepresentability" of trauma in its most extreme manifestation since the characters die or are reduced to a subhuman condition that leaves them unable to articulate their trauma. The response to trauma, as embodied in Hinojosa's characters Louis Dodge, the company clerk and Lt. Brodkey, is evident and is eloquent: all incarnate the mind-destroying effects the unspeakable horrors of war have on individuals.

The fourth character in Hinojosa's *KLS* narrative poem I wish to discuss, since he too exhibits a catastrophic response to war, is David (Sonny) Ruiz. Sonny is a Rio Grande Valley boy from the same area in South Texas where Rafe and his other war buddies, Rosalío (Charlie) Villalón and José (Joey) Vielma, are from. His story is narrated in the poem "Nagoya Station."

> Sonny, of the *old*, old 219th and twice wounded made corporal and stopped;
> One day he filled out and signed his own Missing-In-Action cards,
> Just like so much equipment;
> He personally turned them over to battery HQ,
> Then simply walked away to the docks. (43)

The traumatic response to war from Sonny is to assume a complete and new identity, changing race, name and country. He appropriates the identity of a Japanese man; the young man from Klail City, Texas-born David Ruiz becomes Mr. Kazuo Fusaro and takes up residence in Nagoya, Japan. He is soon to be married to his live-in Japanese girlfriend. Sonny's response to trauma, as constructed by Hinojosa, is to lose his complete identity, although consciously doing so. His character becomes a foil for the representation of political issues Hinojosa wishes to highlight via this particular person. In the poem "Brief Encounter" the military police (MP) stops Rafe in Japan as he is about to take his Rest & Recuperation (R&R). The MPs are checking his documents to make sure he is not Absent Without Leave (AWOL). While the MPs are interrogating Rafe, Sonny passes by with a huge flower bouquet and one of the MPs makes a racially derogatory remark: "Pipe the gook and them flowers" (45). In this manner the MPs articulate an offensive racial epithet for Asians for whom, ironically, the U.S. is supposed to be fighting. The joke is of course on the racist MPs since Sonny has actually gone AWOL, but because the MPs cannot differentiate between a Mexican-American and a Japanese person, Ruiz is able to safely thumb his nose at them even waving to them and smiling.

Sonny also serves as a foil for a moral/ethical discussion of what is morally right or wrong in times of war. According to literary trauma theory, "The trauma novel demonstrates how a traumatic event disrupts attachments between self and others by challenging fundamental assumptions about moral laws and social relationships that are themselves connected to specific environments" (Balaev 1). A traumatic event indeed can provide a new consciousness and a different evaluation of the world as well as the cultural milieu into which one has been thrown. War rearranges moral certitudes since confronting death can immerse the individual in philosophical introspection and analysis about the very meaning of life and the standards by which we comport ourselves.

In the poem "Up Before the Board," Rafe's traumatic experience with war injects a dose of cynicism in the young man. Rafe is in his early twenties, as are most recruits, but his encounters with death have left him cynical of the war, the military and even his country. For example, *KLS* begins with a biblical quote: "And Jehu said, What hast thou to do with peace?" (4), thus castigating all those involved in war. In the poem cited above he is brought before the Board of Inquiry to testify regarding Sonny Ruiz's death. Rafe knows Sonny is alive in Japan under an assumed name but his concern is for "old, mad, Tina Ruiz," Sonny's mother—and her economic situation—who is the sole beneficiary of her son's estate should her son be declared dead. The Board of Inquiry will take Rafe's word because he is considered "a good man" (40). "A good man. Yessir. One of the best. / And so, I lie" (40).

Rafe recalls all the violent deaths he has witnessed, including those of his very close friends: Hatalski, Frazier, Brodkey, Joey Vielma and Charlie Villalón. His introspective meanderings into trying to make sense of the meaning of those deaths lead him to change his moral stance and opt for helping "old mad, Tina Ruiz," who is being left in economic straits resulting from her oldest son's death in WWII and because now her youngest son is lost to her for the rest of her life. And so Rafe lies.

Hinojosa's brilliant intuition as an author conceptualizes yet another tenet related to literary trauma theory and this is in relation to how memory functions after experiencing a traumatic event. He does this in the poem "Jacob Mosqueda Wrestles with the Angels." Caruth describes the nature of a traumatic experience thusly: "the experience of a trauma repeats itself, exactly and unremittingly, through the unknowing act of the survivor and against his very will" (*Unclaimed Experience* 2). We have often seen this transpire in those individuals experiencing flashbacks after a traumatic event. These flashbacks can appear over and over again with the individual unable to prevent them from manifesting themselves in dreams, nightmares or even hallucinations.

The poem "Jacob Mosqueda Wrestles with the Angels" presents a traumatic experience which I posit is representative of the "medium degree trauma category (as opposed to the previous catastrophic trauma or the soon-to-be examined "light" traumas). The possibility of Jacob Mosqueda suffering from post-traumatic flashbacks is discussed in detail in the poem which features him as a protagonist. In Mosqueda's horrific experience he is subjected to the destruction and mayhem an exploding rocket bomb has on him and his friends during combat. When the rocket sent by the enemy explodes nearby, the flesh emanating from the fatal wounds of his friends is splattered on his sleeve. The poem details how Mosqueda "Screamed and fainted / And soiled his fatigues" as he swears "he'll never forget it" (36). Nevertheless, the poetic voice contradicts Mosqueda's will to remember through repeated insistence that "Mosqueda will forget." Yet this assertion is not convincing and, in fact, the constant repetition contradicts the poetic voice's statement. Mosqueda has been so traumatized that the reader agrees, he will never forget. Nevertheless, the poem is interesting for its discussion regarding the nature of forgetting. The poetic voice insists that because Mosqueda did not lose sight or limb and in fact was not hurt at all, although he fainted, he will soon forget. The traumatic event was of major proportions, since at least three of his friends were killed including Joey Vielma who was just visiting and "caught it in the chest and face" (37). The poetic voice insists that there is a difference between actually losing a limb or other parts of the body and only experiencing a horrific event. Mosqueda is certain that he will never forget the event, and trauma theory tends to support him.

The third category of trauma depicted in *KLS* is the "light" trauma response. It differs in intensity and in the response the fictional characters have towards it. The poem "The Eighth Army at the Chongchon" encompasses not only an example of a traumatic experience that is "light" or fairly innocuous, but that is related to the literary trauma theory known as transhistorical trauma and intergenerational trauma. According to Balaev,

> The theory of transhistorical trauma indicates that a massive trauma experienced by a group in the historical past can be experienced by an individual living centuries later who shares a similar attribute of the historical group, such as sharing the same race, religion, nationality, or gender due to the timeless, repetitious, and infectious characteristics of traumatic experience and memory. (2)

Transhistorical trauma is passed on from generation to generation through narrative, that is, history, stories, literature, myth, folk narratives and any medium that conveys information from one human being to another. Identity formation is linked to both intergenerational trauma and transhistorical trauma due to the individual's close attachment and identification to his/her group via gender, ethnicity, race, religion and so forth.

In the poem "The Eighth Army at the Chongchon," Rafe is shocked to hear the highest ranking commanding officer in the Korean War effort make a demeaning remark about Mexicans in a public forum. General Walton H. (Johnny) Walker, in trying to boost the morale of his troops and lessen the potential power the Chinese Peoples' Army possessed in the eyes of his troops, articulates the snide remark that: "We should not assume that (the) / Chinese Communists are committed in force. / After all, a lot of Mexicans live in Texas" (11). Rafe chafes under the gratuitous remark made by the General and sarcastically adds: "And that from Eighth Army Commanding / Himself. It was touching" (11). The stinging remark brings to bear the trauma of the Alamo, the loss of Texas and the U.S. Southwest in the U.S. Mexican War of 1848, a transhistorical and intergenerational trauma experienced by Mexican Americans.[3]

The concepts of transhistorical and intergenerational trauma have been critiqued by some scholars including Balaev due to the mistaken view, in my opinion, that it is essentialist since the concept entails a linkage by race, ethnicity, gender, nationality, religion and so forth. Nevertheless, the poem points out splendidly how transhistorical trauma works; it is not passed on by genetic transmission but can be transmitted through continued reminders by hegemonic society regarding the inferior position of a group, in this case, the Mexican American. Here, General Walker is not even viewing Mexican Americans as "Americans" but as Mexicans living in Texas and traitors or cowards at that. The poetic voice bitterly states:

> And yet, the 219th
> Creating history by protecting the world from Communism,
> Brought up the rear, protected the guns, continued the mission,

And many of us there
Were again reminded who we were
Thousands of miles from home. (11)

The poem clearly elucidates on the Chicano involvement in the war, sacrificing their very lives, and yet still demeaned in public and not considered "American."

A few pages later in the poem titled "Rest Due and Taken," we read that General Walker dies meaninglessly:

General Walker is dead; killed in a road accident,
What a way to go
No grudges about the Mexican crack;
We don't have to prove anything to anyone here. (16)

Now, the death of General Walker actually happened as described in the poem; he was killed on December 23, 1950 in a head-on jeep crash ("Korean War"). This death is best understood, perhaps, in connection with Hinojosa's final poem in the *KLS* collection, "Vale." This closing poem summarizes Rafe's stint in the Korean War, and is one last farewell to those who perished in the War.

Literary trauma theory posits that a character experiencing a traumatic event may be subjected to having his/her identity destroyed. For Rafe as central protagonist in the *Korean Love Songs* poetry collection, the traumatic experience served to transform him, yes, but he is ultimately a stronger, more matured person as evidenced in the last poem. The poem's title, "Vale," conveys an affirmation in closing *Korean Love Songs*. "Vale," is a Spanish word with multiple connotations, some of which include: "OK," "It's worth it," and "Yes!" or, simply, "Yes." Because of Korea and all the traumatic events experienced, Rafe seems only to be able to mourn the dead and accept all that has happened. For his/her part the reader absorbs the trauma Rafe records and experiences, and then, perhaps like him, is left with the emptiness of the horrors and destruction, "Above All, the Waste" (30), which war in Japan, Korea and everywhere else leaves in its wake.

Notes

[1] Hinojosa details in the interview with Philip K. Jason for the *Bilingual Review* (Sept.-Dec., 2000), how he came to write a full-length book on the Korean War citing the major influences for his work: "In 1976 I read Paul Fussell's *The Great War and Modern Memory*, and this led me to write a third work expressly on Korea. It didn't go anywhere. I tried Spanish, and that didn't work. I then tried to translate what I had. Again nothing, I decided to reread Robert Graves's *Goodbye to All That*, and from there I went to Siegried Sasson's prose and poetry. I also looked at the poetry of Isaac Rosenberg and David Jones, and finally some created by Wilfred Owens. I realized I'd tried to write in the wrong language and in the wrong genre. Narrative verse was the ticket, and *KLS* came as a result of all that" (2).

[2] These approximate figures can be found on the "Korean War" Wikipedia page, http://en.wikipedia.org/wiki/Korean_War, accessed on 6 August 2012.

[3] It is interesting to note that General Walker also might have been suffering from intergenerational prejudice; that is to say, he had "inherited" via historical, printed, and oral repetitions the prejudice exhibited against Mexican and Mexican American especially in Texas since he was a native Texan, born in Belton in 1889—a mere 41 years after the United States war with Mexico in 1847-48.

Another interesting point can be made regarding intergenerational prejudice and General Walker: he himself was the victim of such prejudice given that he came from a military family whose members fought for the Confederacy, and yet this Texas southerner went to and graduated from West Point (1912). Most humans are likely to be exposed to intergenerational prejudice. How we react to it and come to terms with it, especially how we can escape it, is an interesting question. Intergenerational prejudice/racism is not destiny. For example, one wonders how this intergenerational trauma plays out in the case of General Walker. Did he have to question Mexican Americans; i.e., their loyalty and patriotism because he himself was questioned as a "southern rebel" who wanted to be a "Union officer"? Freud would of course label this a case of "projection." That is to say, the General was projecting his own insecurities on Mexican Americans.

I thank Stephen Miller for pointing the above interesting set of questions regarding General Walker to me and providing me with some of the above data.

References

Balaev, Michelle. "Trends in Literary Trauma Theory." *Mosaic* 41.2 (June 2008): 149-166. Print.

Bousin, J. Brooks. *Quiet as It's Kept: Shame, Trauma, and Race in the Novels of Toni Morrison.* Albany: SUNY Press, 2000. Print.

Caruth, Cathy. *Unclaimed Experience: Trauma, Narrative, and History*. Baltimore: The Johns Hopkins University Press, 1996. Print.

Hinojosa, Rolando. *Estampas del Valle y otras obras*. Berkeley: Quinto Sol, 1973. Print.

___. *Korean Love Songs*. Berkeley, CA: Justa Publications, 1978. Print.

___. *Klail City y sus alrededores*. La Habana: Casa de las Américas, 1976. Print.

___. *Rites and Witnesses*. Houston: Arte Público Press, 1982. Print.

___. *The Useless Servants*. Houston: Arte Público Press, 1993. Print.

Jason, Philip K. "A Conversation with Rolando Hinojosa." *Bilingual Review / Revista Bilingüe* 25.3 (Sept.-Dec. 2000): 298-305. Print.

Johnson, Erica L. "Forgetting Trauma: Dionne Brand's Haunted Histories." *Anthurium: A Caribbean Studies Journal* 2 (Spring 2004): n. pag. Web. 30 Aug. 2010.

"Korean War." *Wikipedia: The Free Encyclopedia*. Wikimedia Foundation, Inc. Web. 6 Aug. 2012.

LaCapra, Dominick. *Writing History, Writing Trauma*. Baltimore, MD: The Johns Hopkins University Press, 2001. Print.

Tal, Kali. *Worlds of Hurt: Reading the Literatures of Trauma*. Cambridge: Cambridge University Press, 1996. Print.

Lee, Joyce Glover. *Rolando Hinojosa and the American Dream*. Denton: University of North Texas Press, 1997. Print.

Martín-Rodríguez, Manuel M. *Rolando Hinojosa y su "Cronicón" chicano: Una novela del lector*. Sevilla: Secretaría de Publicaciones de la Universidad de Sevilla, 1993. Print.

Randolph, Donald A. "Eroticism in War and the Eroticism of War in Hinojosa's *Korean Love Songs*." *Revista Monográfica* 7 (1991): 218-26. Print.

Saldívar, José David. *The Rolando Hinojosa Reader*. Houston: Arte Público Press, 1985. Print.

Saldívar. Ramón. *Chicano Narrative: The Dialectics of Difference*. Madison: University of Wisconsin Press, 1990. Print.

___. "*Korean Love Songs*: A Border Ballad and Its Heroes." *The Rolando Hinojosa Reader*. Ed. José David Saldívar. Houston: Arte Público Press, 1985. 143-57. Print.

Van der Kolk, Bessel A., Alexander McFarlane, and Lars Weisaeth. *Traumatic Stress: The Effects of Overwhelming Experience on Mind, Body, and Society*. New York: Guilford Press, 1987. Print.

Zilles, Klaus. *Rolando Hinojosa: A Reader's Guide*. Albuquerque: University of New Mexico Press, 2001. Print.

Critical Regionalism and the Literature of Texas: The Comparative Case of Rolando Hinojosa and Larry McMurtry

José E. Limón
University of Notre Dame

What follows in these pages is taken from a book in progress called *Neither Friends, Nor Strangers: Mexicans and Anglos in the Literary Making of Texas*, a title fashioned from those of two major narratives about Texas: respectively, *All My Friends are Going to be Strangers* by Larry McMurtry and *Anglos and Mexicans in the Making of Texas, 1836-1986* by David Montejano. The well-known McMurtry will be one of the two principal novelist subjects of this essay, but the distinguished historian Montejano will also make an appearance as is almost requisite in any writing on Texas history. My book seeks to provide an analytical treatment of two major literary traditions, Mexican American and Anglo-American, that have spoken from, about and to Texas but also to the world.

I am partially preceded in this effort only by Tom Pilkington and his 1998 *State of Mind: Texas Literature and Culture*, a book that differs from mine in three important respects. First, it is a running survey of a great variety of such writing with little extended focus on important writers. Second, he deals mostly with Anglo-American writing; Mexican American writers merit three pages at the end of a 169 page book with the startling omission of all of Américo Paredes' creative writings appearing from 1990 to 1994, especially *George Washington Gómez*. Finally, the book offers little by way of a comprehensive and comparative conceptual interpretive framework offering instead broad thematic categories.

Mexican-American and Anglo-American writing in Texas ought not to be treated as separate and unequal domains. From the beginning of what is now called Texas, these two peoples have been quite aware of and involved with each other, often painfully so; that is, they have not particularly been friends, but nor have they been strangers to each other. Even in hostility both have had to share Texas and what Texas has gone through historically as it has had to come to terms with yet a third force, not ethnic but economic, as Texas gradually came to be incorporated into the United States, but more fundamentally, and for better or worse, into the economic and cultural world system of capitalism. The latter is a theme implicit in all histories of Texas but which Montejano has made explicit in his history. In these terms, I would then argue that Anglos and Mexicans *share* Texas even as they are simultaneously divided within it and the best of Texas literature speaks to this multi-dimensional state of affairs. The other writerly subject of the present chapter is the distinguished Rolando Hinojosa, the principal subject of this collection. While much better known as a writer of prose, he does have a long poem to his credit, *Korean Love Songs*, based on his experience as a combatant in the Korean War (1950-1953). At the end of the poem, a Mexican-American speaker, having suffered the battlefield agony of the Korean War, says, in English:

> Home to Texas, our Texas
> Hell and heaven on earth
> And land of our fathers.

The lines could have been uttered by an Anglo-Texan speaker as well, except that for Mexican Americans in Texas, hell has always been a bit hotter.

Therefore, rather than structurally separating these two ethnic communities, in my view, Texas writing is much better understood by *pairing* Anglo and Mexican-American writers who, over time and out of a history of Anglo-Mexican conflict, speak of their own cultures but also to each other's even as they respectively articulate a comparative vision of the onset of capitalist modernity and postmodernity in Texas. The first half of my book develops more or less chronologically by pairing Jovita Gonzalez and Laura Krey and then moves on to Américo Paredes and J. Frank Dobie, followed by Tomás Rivera and Katherine Anne Porter. In the second half, I then move more decisively into our time with Rolando Hinojosa and Larry McMurtry followed by Shelby Hearon and Sandra Cisneros, and concluding at the turn of the twentieth century with John Phillip Santos and Mary Karr and, finally, a reprise of McMurtry this time paired with Oscar Casares. These writers also represent two different regions of Texas, which is to say south Texas, on the Mexican American hand, and the rest of Texas on the other, the latter with some interesting emphasis on East Texas. In this instance and constrained by space considerations, I offer only a portion of the chapter entitled "Imagined Communities . . . and Not: Rolando Hinojosa and Larry McMurtry," and I will concentrate on one each of their early books, Hinojosa's *The Valley* and McMurtry's *The Last Picture Show*, although I will at least reference their other mostly later work.

Critical Regionalism

To place these readings in a broad and conceptual interpretive context, I turn to the notion of critical regionalism. For to say that these writers and certainly Hinojosa and McMurtry represent different regions of Texas is not to say enough; it is to lapse into a simple and traditional literary regionalism: this writer writes about the customs of his region and this other writer about hers. The concept of "critical regionalism" has been developed by Herr and Powell but also Jameson (*The Seeds of Time* 129-205). It seems to me to vastly improve matters interpretively allowing us to grasp two or more regions in one comparative but also conceptual move. Critical regionalism is simultaneously a theory, methodology and praxis for recognizing, closely examining and indeed fostering localized identities especially as these stand in antagonistic, yet also negotiated relationships with late capitalist globalization. More specifically, critical regionalism focuses on the array of resources—or not—available to a region for coming to terms with such globalization including but not solely literary practices. In contrast to a traditional sense of the self-enclosed "regional," within critical regionalism, such local identities and practices, however, are not statically fixed although they often do retain their distinction and discretion over against a globalizing "outside." Such a negotiated yet fundamentally adversarial relationship is conducted with an openness—or not—toward globalizing elements and processes but with a critical selectiveness relative to their contribution toward the local identity and its perdurance in such a globalized existence. By these measures, I evaluate how the writers in my book, but in this instance, McMurtry and Hinojosa, have addressed or evaded the other's culture but also addressed or evaded the problem of capitalist and post-capitalist modernity and its incorporation of Texas into the world-system.

My working thesis is that in this comparative instance, both writers are instruments of their respective cultures for critically diagnosing and responding to the onset of a largely inimical capitalist and Anglo generated modernity. In Hinojosa's case, the battle is joined but skillfully negotiated with and against such modernity; whereas with McMurtry, it is as if defeat is wholly conceded leaving a wasteland whose very pervasiveness speaks to the total, if satirized, victory of such a modernity. Thus it can be said that my approach is that of political economy though encompassing both structural and cultural dimensions, and as such, I am anticipated, but only to some degree, by previous and major critics.

Politics and Interpretation

The present volume is dedicated to the work of Rolando Hinojosa, so I will say little about critical work on McMurtry's fiction except to note that with one exception, none addresses it in terms of political economy and region. Reilly does offer a brief, but suggestive, appraisal of the *Lonesome Dove* series in Marxist terms (112-114). Critical appraisals of Hinojosa's work also offer a variety of perspectives and approaches, several captured in the 1985 volume edited by Saldívar. Some of these will be deployed in what follows, but, for my interpretive purpose, clearly the most extended and influential readings are those offered by José D. Saldívar and Héctor Calderón in their respective, separate extended treatments. I depart principally from these.

Saldívar puts Hinojosa's work in conjunction with that of other and largely southern hemispheric writers such as Gabriel García Márquez as mutual exponents, says Saldívar, of a critical vision based on a *nuestra América* opposed to the United States (*The Dialectics of Our America* 62-82). For him, it is as if the sole signification of Hinojosa's work is, as he says in another place, that it "resists, limits, and alters the cultural domination or hegemony of the ruling culture in the United States" ("Preface" 9). But this, almost exclusively ideological comparison, is one that, in keeping with current fashion, is not closely attentive to the texts or their national contexts. Elsewhere, I have offered a more extended critique, and I am not alone in this discomfort with Saldívar's approach (see Limón, 2008 and Karem, 2001).

Saldívar's comparisons and his ideologically-centered readings of these largely Latin American authors have always seemed to be a bit forced and certainly for Hinojosa whose vision of the United States, like the man's intellect, is far more complicated. It is not a matter of ignoring the obvious, namely that there is indeed a politics in Hinojosa that speaks to social conflict, for that is my concern as well. Rather, I do not find in Saldívar's relatively compact reading of Hinojosa's prodigious project a sufficient appreciation of the subtleties, nuances and sometimes contradictions through which Hinojosa addresses such matters as social conflict but others as well.

For his part, Calderón is much more appreciative of that complication. Practicing a more classical biographical and inter-textual criticism, he literally spends more time with Hinojosa's total project showing us the relationship of this work to his marvelous and detailed documentation of the author's life and regional history (139-166). He also reminds us that our author is a learned, well-read and well-traveled man who draws many and disparate literary and cultural traditions into his work. Yet, because it cannot be overlooked, Calderón is also well-aware of the politics in Hinojosa's work, but this understanding is even-tempered as when he reminds us, for example, of Hinojosa's Anglo character, the Michigan school teacher, Tom Purdy, "who, along with his wife, helped Mexican farm workers in the early sixties" (161). If something is missing here—and it is only a book chapter—it is a continuing close attention to the nuances of the individual texts and any sort of comprehensive interpretive framework.

Comparative Hinojosa

Saldívar's comparative approach and Calderón's intertextual assessment raise another issue as well, namely that of comparison itself. One can certainly understand an effort to place Hinojosa in conjunction with writers of Latin America, for after all, not only does he hold the Ph.D. in Spanish and knows well the Latin American canon, but a great deal of his initial work was first written in Spanish, and as Calderón has shown, it can also be formally compared to certain writers of Spain such as Benito Pérez Galdós. But Calderón also offers another brief comparative move as he reminds us that Hinojosa's project and title is also comparable to an American text, Michael Lesy's 1973 *Wisconsin Death Trip*.

But, more importantly, it is Hinojosa himself who has candidly acknowledged that his multi-volume project centered in the fictive Belken County is comparable to that extended and famous literary project, that of William Faulkner and his Yoknapatawpha

County ("A Voice of One's Own" 16). I am not aware that this particular comparison has been pursued at length or in-depth on a par, let us say, with Ramón Saldivar's reading of Faulkner and Américo Paredes (1995). However, as far as I know, another axis of comparison has been wholly overlooked. As I noted at the beginning, Texas, a very large and complicated space, has been home to two substantial and literate yet very different Western cultural traditions since before there was a United States. These two peoples have experienced each other, but also the world, over a shared terrain. Out of that experience and literacy, literatures have emerged that speak to that shared experience, sometimes in similar ways, sometimes not. I suggest that such a comparative analysis may be in order, one more grounded and that returns "home to Texas, our Texas."

I turn now to the two texts. My interpretive strategy will be to closely and comparatively read through scenes from each book, scenes that resemble each other yet are very different if understood as responses to the question of Anglos, Mexicans and capitalist modernity in Texas. Let us begin with Hinojosa.

Texas Texts

The Valley begins with a remembrance of things past rendered in three of those small, tight, but evocative sketches that Hinojosa does so well. The first is one-page long and titled "Braulio Tapia" (*The Valley* 12) in which an initially unidentified male speaker, at his doorstep, greets a younger man named Roque Malacara. The speaker sees Roque as squat, "what the Germans call *diecke*," he thinks. Roque has come to ask for the hand in marriage of the speaker's daughter, Tere, apologizing that he "has no money for sponsors," but that the speaker did give him permission to call on Tere, and that it has been a year and a half. But the speaker then turns his head and thinks he catches a glimpse of "my late father-in-law, Don Braulio Tapia: long side-burns and matching black mustache à la Kaiser" (probably of an old picture or in his mind's eye). He continues with his remembrance: "Don Braulio raises his hand to shake mine as he did years ago when I first came here to this house to ask for Matilde's hand." He also recalls that Don Braulio was a widower at that time as the speaker himself is now having lost his wife, Matilde or Matti. But in closing, the speaker also wonders: "Who did Don Braulio see when he walked up these steps to ask for his wife's hand?"

History is not a small matter in this scene in a specific and a broad cultural sense. The vignette and those that will follow are set in the Lower Rio Grande Valley, if the accompanying map in the book is to be taken as part of the text. But where are we historically in a specific sense, or as Jameson might say, where history is understood "in the narrow sense of punctual event and a chronicle-like sequence of happenings in time" (*The Political Unconscious* 75)? One clear indicator is the reference the speaker makes to things German—the word *diecke* and the Kaiser's side-burns and moustache—which, unless he is being performatively anachronistic, like Prince William, currently second-in-line to inherit the British throne, dressing as a Nazi officer for a party, places the speaker circa the first World War or soon thereafter, possibly as late as the 1930s. As a reference, the image of the Kaiser would have been readily available in newspapers and magazines at that time even in the Valley, but the word, *diecke*, on the lips of this presumably Mexican-American native speaker in the Valley at this time is intriguing, for it suggests either a learned man or a veteran of World War I in Europe or both, a very real possibility as Emilio Zamora has recently shown us in south Texas, World War I veteran, educator and activist, José de la Luz Sáenz (2002). Hinojosa himself offers such a veteran in Don Genaro Castañeda, the master housepainter of Belken County.

But the sketch also reveals history in a somewhat broader sense "where the individual utterance or text is grasped as a symbolic move in an essentially polemic and strategic ideological confrontation between the classes" (Jameson, *The Political Unconscious* 85). While such a confrontation is not yet immediately evident, the cultural base for it is being laid in the two overlapping dimensions: (1) the cultural semi-imperative that a young man needs socio-cultural references by way of sponsors—responsible members of the community—when asking for a woman's hand in marriage and, (2) the almost infinitely receding reference as to the different men that came to this doorstep to ask for a hand in marriage, backward through time at least to the early Spanish settlement of the Lower Rio Grande Valley and southern Texas as the northern portion of the province of Nuevo Santander in the mid-eighteenth century.

The next two sketches move us forward in time and bring to the fore class and ethnic antagonism. The first of these, also one-page long, called, "Tere Malacara née Vilches Noriega" (*The Valley* 13) allows us to identify the speaker in "Braulio Tapia": he is Tere's father, with the surname Vilches. More importantly it opens up a window on the kind of relationship that was developing in Tere's generation *vis-à-vis* the Anglo-American in the Valley. With the coming of the railroad to the Valley in 1906, there was a mutual agricultural development of that region into an Anglo-dominated agri-business and racialized social formation (Montejano). Again, *el maestro* Hinojosa needs only a few words to speak vividly to this double reality of agri-business capitalist development and Anglos as Tere speaks for many Mexican Americans, mostly farm laborers at that time: "I'm bushed, beat, and dead to the world; know what I mean? I'm a dollar short and three days behind, and I can't even blame it on staying up, which I don't anyway. It's this life, that's all. It's hard." But she reasons, others have it harder: "Maybe worse, the housemaids . . . I mean there is the Mister and the Mister's son . . . ," and here we come to the single word, "Mister." Even before *gringo, bolillo* or *gabacho*, or at least along with them, "Mister" also names the Anglo both racially but also in terms of class in a way that the others do not. Tere concludes: "I'm just plain tired." We can thus quarrel with Rosaura Sánchez's critical reservation, namely that *The Valley* ignores class oppression (79).

Finally, in the third, one-page sketch in this opening series, "Roque Malacara" (*The Valley* 14) the eponymous character speaks as he acknowledges his wife Tere's fatigue which "S'got every right to be so." The dropping of the "h" and "e" in the word "She" perhaps voices micro-linguistically his own fatigue. He then fondly recalls his now late father-in-law, Mr. Vilches. He sees him as "a good man . . . in the best sense of the word *good*, as Machado once pointed out." Machado, the early twentieth-century Spanish poet? On the lips of a common Mexican-American worker? But, why not, for a generation which had available newspapers like *La Prensa* of San Antonio with its *Lunes Literario* and its reprints of the works of Latin American and Spanish writers? He recalls that his father-in-law loved to fish the Rio Grande for the sly gray catfish hiding in the *tules*, fishing with his little grandson, his namesake, Jehu, as the also sly Hinojosa finally provides us with a first name for Mr. Vilches. That Hinojosa makes us work to piece together all of these names and relationships is exactly to the point as he enlists us in imagining and making this community. But as he names Jehu as a child, Hinojosa, of course, introduces us to one of the two young protagonists, the other being Rafe Buenrostro, who will appear in and thematically structure most of the rest of the *Klail City Death Trip* beginning in their childhood circa the early 1930s.

Keeping in mind, then, (a) paired young protagonists and (b) the first half of the twentieth century, we can now, by comparison, turn to the opening pages of Larry McMurtry's *The Last Picture Show* set in a fictive place called Thalia, said to be close to Wichita Falls up in northern Texas about as far away as one could get from the Valley in Texas if you don't count the panhandle, that odd extension of Texas imperialism. The time appears to be in the late 40s and early 50s. Paralleling Hinojosa's *The Valley*, here we also have two young protagonists who, when we meet them, are about the same age as Rafe and Jehu in their own narrative time frame. The first, Sonny, appears immediately in this fashion in the book's opening lines:

> Sometimes Sonny felt like he was the only human creature in the town. It was a bad feeling, and it usually came on him in the mornings early, when the streets were completely empty, the

> way they were one Saturday morning in late November. The night before Sonny had played his last game of high school for Thalia High School, but it wasn't that that made him feel so strange and alone. It was just the look of the town. (1)

As with Rafe following Jehu, shortly thereafter we will meet Duane, Sonny's best friend, and together they will, like Rafe and Jehu, thematically structure the rest of the book, another coming of age story for these two young men; but, as we have already seen with vastly different beginnings and, as we shall soon see, very different middles and ends. In sharp contrast to Hinojosa, history and culture are almost vacated in McMurtry's opening scenes and throughout most of the narrative as if having given way to a pervading sense of emptiness, accentuated by the menial work occupations these two boys will have after high school graduation; their broken homes causing them to live together in a rooming house; less-than-inspiring sexual experiences; a hard-drinking macho culture among the older men and some of the women; and, a stultifying and depressive educational system.

By contrast, recall the manner in which history community and family sustain Jehu after the early death of his parents and the decisively affirmative intervention in his young life of the quite wonderful Don Victor Pelaez and his circus, "an upright, honest man who took his liquor, his friendships and his responsibilities straight, which is to say, without benefit of water" (*The Valley* 27). And, upon Don Victor's death, Jehu has an opportunity to read Don Victor's diary wherein he discovers a rich autobiography of Don Victor's important involvement in the Mexican Revolution. As for Rafe, even as the theme of class conflict continues, he will later tell of such cultural support as well, such as going up to Michigan as a young boy to pick cherries, when his Dad would take him for doughnuts to a roadside place in Monon, Indiana called Myrtles (*The Valley* 47). (One wonders if they drove through Thalia!)

Back in Thalia, the general depression is only partially relieved by four other characters, who appear early and throughout the story, and an incident. Sam the Lion is a gruff but kind-hearted old man who owns the local pool hall, café and movie theatre, simply known as the picture show. Sam provides a tenuous link to the largely missing history and culture as the story briefly tells us that he lost the first of three sons "when he and his son were trying to drive a herd of yearlings across the Little Wichita River. . . and the boy had been knocked loose from his horse, pawed under and drowned" (4). Genevieve, the waitress at Sam' café, is also a kind person who acts as a surrogate mom for the two boys although she is inconsistently deployed in the narrative. On the other hand, Ruth, the depressed and sickly wife of the high school football and basketball coach, figures more prominently especially when she and Sonny begin an affair that will last to the end of the narrative. But it is the fourth character that is perhaps of more central interest.

Billy, a mentally-handicapped boy about ten years old whose mother died at childbirth, now lives with Sam and sweeps Sam's places for his keep. Only trouble is that he does not know when to stop sweeping and, unless stopped, will continue outside sweeping the streets to the edge of town and beyond. Billy also speaks to the ethnic dimension of my argument as McMurtry obliquely acknowledges that there are Mexicans in Texas. Shortly after Billy's birth, his no-good father, a transient railroad worker, largely abandoned him to be raised "by the family of Mexicans who helped the old man keep the railroad track repaired" (5). But the old man left for another job in Oklahoma "leaving Billy with the Mexicans," and then they also left to pick cotton in Plainview and "snuck off one morning and left Billy sitting on the curb in front of the picture show" (5-6). Later in the story, at what appears to be an attempt at humor, McMurtry has Sonny, Duane and other adolescents hire a local prostitute for two dollars and trick the totally innocent Billy into wholly failed intercourse with her. She has consented to having Billy because she "just as soon it was an idiot as not . . . the only thing I draw the line at is Mixicans and niggers" (107). However, McMurtry is not yet done with Mexicans and prostitution as we return to Hinojosa's Valley by another route.

Humor is not at all unknown in Hinojosa as Teresa McKenna has shown. In comparison to McMurtry, *The Valley* offers a rich, multi-faceted, and diaglossic world that would certainly win Bakhtin's approval (McKenna 73-102). Centrally, of course, in the sketch on Bruno Cano, but also in smaller speech acts such as my personal favorite, the little boy, Leo Pumarejo, who, unlike the little *vendidita*, Lucy Ramirez, tells Miss Bunn, their teacher, that for breakfast he ate, "one flour tortilla WITH PLENTY OF PEANUT BUTTER!" (43). Even here, in child language the idiom of class/ethnic conflict continues, if we recall that in the 1930s, peanut butter was one of the federal government commodity foods for the poor. And that his humor is directed at an Anglo teacher is not to be missed as Hinojosa does not fail to remind us that a racial divide continues in the Valley: "At sundown our fellow Texans across the tracks close their shops and head for home . . ." (*The Valley* 109).

Sex and prostitution are also not absent in Hinojosa's account of Rafe and Jehu's development. There is a local prostitute, Fira, who "carries her whoredom as school girls carry their tote bags: naturally and with no affectation," and is "simply put, the most beautiful woman in the Valley" (*The Valley* 103) but, I would further add, a woman who exists on a higher moral plane than most of McMurtry's non-prostitute women in Thalia. As teenagers, in time-honored Valley and south Texas ritual fashion, Rafe and another friend get what appears to be their first sexual experience across the river where they are greeted by the madam of the house "as two young American gentlemen to see us" to which Rafe thinks: "Gentlemen? Americans? Shoot, it was just Monche Rivera and me and we were going on sixteen at the time . . . and I was game but scared" (*The Valley* 48).

This adolescent encounter across the Rio Grande also allows us to return to Thalia, or rather to bring Thalia to the Valley as McMurtry and Mexicans cross paths once again. In a kind of moral mid-course correction to McMurtry's narrative of Anglo-Texas degeneration and decay, one day with no particular motivation save life in Thalia, Sonny and Duane decide to take off for the Lower Rio Grande Valley and Matamoros, Mexico in that so oft-repeated American quest for adventure, i.e. liquor, sex and just plain difference; but in this case, something else is learned. In Matamoros, they "entered the cabaret timidly, expecting to be mobbed at once by whores or else slugged by Mexican gangsters, but neither thing happened. They were simply ignored," probably because "most of the people in the club were American boys, sitting around tables." Sensing lots of competition, the boys drink too much and are soon propositioned by a woman named, of course, Juanita who "squeezed Sonny intimately through his blue jeans." They find her unattractive and dismiss her, but she leaves them with a parting shot: "Texas is full of queers," she says. So Sonny sets his now bleary eyes on "a slim, black-headed girl who spent most of her time on the dance floor, dancing with boys from Texas A&M. There were a good many boys from Texas A&M in the cabaret" (137).

Before much longer but after more beer, Sonny goes off to a small house with the slim, black-headed girl whose name is, of course, Maria, but the result of what is supposed to be a night-long liaison momentarily alters the moral and political trajectory of *The Last Picture Show*. As they prepare for sex, Sonny realizes that Maria is pregnant, experiences shame, and with that and the plentiful beer, "to Maria's amazement he simply stopped and went to sleep." Morning brings a greater awareness. After getting up, Sonny walks out into the street, kneels and vomits, and then sees an old man driving a water wagon "drawn by a decrepit brown mule," an old man whose "grizzled whiskers were as white as Sam the Lion's hair." The prostitutes come out and they "seemed much happier than they had seemed the night before. They chattered like high school girls and came lightly to the wagon to get their water. The old man spoke to them cheerfully" (175). The old man and his mule then move along and

> . . . when he passed where Sonny was kneeling the old man nodded to him kindly and gestured with a tin dipper he had in his

> hand. Sonny gratefully took a dipper of water from him, using it to wash the sour taste out of his mouth. The old man smiled at him sympathetically and said something in a philosophic tone, something which Sonny took to mean that life was a matter of ups and downs. (175)

In keeping with a long tradition in American letters, Sonny seems to see another Mexico on the border of his Texas but also an alternative, affirmative way of life to that which he has known all of his life in Thalia. Yet, as much as this Mexican imagery might be taken as a stereotype, we cannot be entirely sure, for just who is this old man who resembles Sam the Lion? What is his history, his life? Hinojosa would know what to make of his life in his final section of *The Valley* called "Lives and Miracles," that rich compendium of stories and anecdotes in which the fullness of life in *Klail City y sus alrededores* is vividly recovered.

Sonny meets up with Duane and they slowly make their way back to Thalia. I like to imagine that if they used the fastest way to Thalia, then Texas Highway 183, they would have passed through Mercedes and could have stopped at a local cantina, perhaps at Hinojosa's *Aquí me Quedo*, and perhaps had a hair of the dog, maybe one of those warm Pearl beers that Echevarria will later be served by Rafe (*The Valley* 52). As they near Thalia, they are momentarily pleased to be back in familiar surroundings, but they, especially Sonny, soon discover that little has changed and that what has changed is not for the good. During their absence, Sam the Lion has died and with him, the only living link to anything like an affirmative past and present culture.

Life continues much as before with McMurtry's remaining narrative perversely structured mostly by failed, slightly sordid sexual/marital experiences including Sonny's on-going affair with Coach Popper's wife, Ruth. For critic Reilly, "it is a function of the theme of an absence of cultural or familial moorings," that led McMurtry "to present the characters stripped of any other terrain for defining the self and reduced to strutting themselves largely in the roles of sexual players alone" (45). Only four other events relieve the sexual tedium, if relief is even the right word. The picture show closes down after Sam's death; in the midst of his affair with Ruth, Sonny has an unconsummated one day marriage to the prettiest, richest girl in town which somehow winds up with Sonny having sex with Lois Farrow, the girl's mother, like Dustin Hoffman in *The Graduate*; Billy is killed by a cattle truck while sweeping the street; and, Duane joins the army and is off to Korea. McMurtry does not give us a date, but since the last films shown at Sam the Lion's Picture Show before it closes are *Winchester '73* and *The Kid from Texas* with Audie Murphy, both from 1950, we can safely assume that Duane is about to meet the North Korean Army crossing the 38th parallel and/or the Chinese army rolling down from the Yalu River. The rest of the youngsters in Thalia disappear into insignificance at the story's end, the future of Anglo Texas, if you will.

For his part, Hinojosa does not ask us to imagine the North Koreans and their Chinese allies, as in this early book we get a sharp glimpse of Rafe Buenrostro who has again left the Valley, not for Michigan, but to fight as an artilleryman in the same Korean War that will soon greet Duane. But what happens to Rafe after Korea is perhaps more telling, for it will provide the forward chronological impetus to the *Klail City Death Trip* series that will eventually bring us to *Partners in Crime* and *Ask a Policeman*—but also to the next major transformation of the Lower Rio Grande Valley. After coming back from Korea a little worse for wear, Rafe visits with a VA adviser, in the 1950s likely an Anglo, and the ethnic/class struggle continues. The man suggested that Rafe "sign up for a two-year course in boat-building; after that, he said, I could then use the remainder of my G.I. Bill in another form of carpentry: cabinet making" (*The Valley* 53). The adviser then endorsed his counsel by adding that "He'd done right well—his words—without college, and it was his honest opinion I'd waste my time there" (53), to which Rafe comments, "Some adviser, some advice" (53). The sketch then closes with: "Leaving the Valley for awhile; I've registered at the University up in Austin. It'll be a new town for me. Will it be a new life? We'll see" (54).

Texas, Our Texas

Thus we have two regions in the hands of two Texas authors who yield very different visions of their respective places, both relative to each other but also to the common problem that will affect and shape both regions, which is the coming of capitalist modernity to Texas.

That Hinojosa lays implicit claim to the idea and practice of region is evident in his very title, *The Valley*, and elsewhere he has spoken eloquently about his "sense of place" ("A Sense of Place" 18-24). Such a claim is not anywhere as evident in McMurtry's narratives, although he certainly does confine most of his narrative to a region if only in geographical spatial terms. Yet, elsewhere one has the clear sense that McMurtry clearly recognizes his region and its history referencing it as Archer County, Texas. He speaks of his grandparents as "pioneers" who came to Archer County out of Missouri after the Civil War, of their hunger for land, of the McMurty men as cowboys, of losing their land and having only the memory of having been cowboys to sustain them, and finally of an early storytelling culture lasting into his early childhood in the late 30s and early 40s, which in the 1980s he tries vainly to recapture in the gossiping at the local Dairy Queen (1999). Yet, in contrast to Hinojosa, it is as if McMurtry is therefore consciously intent on *not* working such material into his early Texas books and indeed into his later Texas books which continue the narrative of emptiness of *The Last Picture Show,* albeit in new places like Houston. His *Lonesome Dove* will, of course, return us to this culture, but displaced into the 19th century. Mark Busby, the foremost critic of McMurtry's work, explains this foreclosure of history and an older culture as McMurtry's need to carve out his own original creative space in reaction to the work of J. Frank Dobie, drawing on Harold Bloom's anxiety of influence. On the other hand, McMurty having little choice for such bleakness may be all that remains of Anglo-Texas.

Busby is certainly aware of the negative uses of history in this novel as he cites another of McMurtry's critics, Raymond Neinstein, who says that the book is "about the disappearance of land as a force of stability and tradition in people's lives" (105). Or as Lois Farrow, the woman who takes Sonny to bed late in the novel, says to her daughter, Jacy: " . . . life's too damn hard here . . . the land's got too much power over you. Being rich here is a good way to go insane. Everything's flat and empty and there's nothing to do but spend money" (48).

But Lois is not specific enough. It is not so much the land that thus produces various forms of insanity, but rather what's underneath the land. As historian Campbell puts it: "Even while Texas remained essentially agricultural, rural and southern into the early twentieth century, certain developments pointed toward a very different future. The first can be summarized in one word: oil!" (326). By the 1930s and certainly with the coming of World War II, oil became the primary economic commodity in an increasingly capitalistic Texas, even with the Depression which was only a temporary setback, and even as most workers in the state did not even have the compensation of participating in its full benefits as most of the profit went to the big oilmen. Therefore, and usually overlooked by the critics, it is not at all surprising that both Sonny and Duane work as roughnecks and that another of Sam the Lion's sons died in an oil well explosion. But it remains to another character in another of McMurtry's novels, *Horseman Pass By*, to put the matter succinctly. A figure much like Sam the Lion, Homer Bannon says:

> What good's oil to me . . . what can I do with it? With a bunch a fuckin' oil wells. I can't ride out every day an' prowl amongst 'em like I can my cattle. I can't breed 'em or tend 'em or rope 'em or chase 'em or nothin'. I can't feel a smidgen a pride in 'em cause they ain't none of my doin'. Money, yes. Piss on that kind of money. (106)

Although oil represents the disruptive advent of late capitalism in the lives of McMurtry's people, commentators of his work tend to take such disruption in critical stride, with "the anxieties and discontents of individuals defined simply as contemporary American" (Reilly 41). One supposes that the recent Gulf oil disaster is also simply American.

For better or worse, the Lower Rio Grande Valley did not become part of the new oil economy although upper south Texas did, and even if it had, the racial segregation that prevailed in most parts of the Valley into the 1970s would have assured an unequal distribution of wealth paralleling that of the agri-business industry that did and continues to prevail in the Valley (Zamora, 2009). We have already seen evidence of that in Hinojosa's work. Yet, perhaps it is this non-participation that also allowed the perdurance of the native, affirmative culture that Hinojosa also so deftly records for us and which is almost wholly absent in McMurtry. None of this means, however, that the Valley was divorced from the world at large if only through the migrant labor circuit that Hinojosa also glimpses for us. And, as Hinojosa also demonstrates here and in his later work, the Valley also connects with the world by way of the military and education as at least some of its children garner such experience and, in some instances, bring it back to the Valley although we must remember that there is Rafe who, after Korea and higher education (and, unlike George in Paredes' *George Washington Gómez*), will return to the Valley in *Partners in Crime* and *Ask a Policeman* to struggle against new and insidious forces of post-modernity threatening his beloved Valley represented by the drug trade that today threatens to engulf all of Mexico. Yet we see no such enriching and complicated dialectic of departure, return and resistance in McMurtry. He offers *Texasville* populated by migrants from *The Last Picture Show* now older and even more depressed. As Janis Stout has noted, McMurtry uses journeying as "a metaphor for modern life itself, which is seen as being impoverished by the demise of the old traditions and the lack of a new structure of meaning and allegiance" (38).

Thus, within the concept of critical regionalism, we may conclude that the uneven impact of capitalist modernity in these two different regions has allowed Hinojosa to offer a more subtly nuanced and complicated response. Indeed that subtlety also extends to his vision of the Anglo, from the perspective of the Valley, perhaps one and the same—that is, modernity and Anglos; a subtlety and nuance that perhaps, is congruent with his chosen form of the *estampa*, an interesting kind of ideology of form (Jameson, *The Seeds of Time* 98-99).

On the other hand, it is as if the heavy hand of capitalist modernity has fallen hard on McMurtry's regional world, which is to say pretty much the Texas north of the Nueces River. While he may be credited with rendering its baleful consequences in what Fredric Jameson after Bill Burford has identified as "dirty realism," McMurtry refuses, almost pointedly so, to offer any modicum of critical difference or creative negotiation with its presence (*The Seeds of Time* 145-159). The only exception where the "dirty" is magically cleansed is, perhaps and ironically enough, in the one journey that Sonny and Duane take out of Thalia to Rolando Hinojosa's Valley. In his historical Valley and even later, there do remain, again, in Janis Stout's words, "structures of meaning and allegiance," in contrast to McMurtry's world where there is little sense of any roots that clutch or branches that grow in the stony rubbish of modern Anglo Texas.

Works Cited

Busby, Mark. *Larry McMurtry and the West: An Ambivalent Relationship*. Denton: University of North Texas Press, 1995. Print.

Calderón, Héctor. *Narratives from Greater Mexico: Essays on Chicano Literary History, Genre and Borders*. Austin: University of Texas Press, 2004. Print.

Campbell, Randolph B. *Gone to Texas: A History of the Lone Star State*. New York: Oxford University Press, 2003. Print.

Herr, Cheryl Temple. *Critical Regionalism and Cultural Studies: From Ireland to the Midwest*. Gainesville: University Press of Florida, 1996. Print.

Hinojosa, Rolando. *Ask a Policeman*. Houston: Arte Público Press, 1998. Print.

___. *Korean Love Songs*. Berkeley: Editorial Justa, 1978. Print.

___. *The Valley*. Tempe: Bilingual Press, 1983. Print.

___. "The Sense of Place." *The Rolando Hinojosa Reader: Essays Historical and Critical*. Ed. José David Saldívar. Houston: Arte Público Press, 1985. 18-24. Print.

___. "The Voice of One's Own." *The Rolando Hinojosa Reader: Essays Historical and Critical*. Ed. José David Saldívar. Houston: Arte Público Press, 1985. 11-17. Print.

___. *Partners in Crime*. Houston: Arte Público Press, 1985. Print.

Jameson, Fredric. *The Political Unconscious: Narrative as a Socially Symbolic Act*. Ithaca: Cornell University Press, 1981. Print.

___. *The Seeds of Time*. New York: Columbia University Press, 1994. Print.

Karem, Jeff. "On the Advantages and Disadvantages of Postcolonial Theory for Pan-American Study." *The New Centennial Review* 1.3 (2001): 87-116. Print.

Lesy, Michael. *Wisconsin Death Trip*. New York: Doubleday, 1973. Print.

Limón, José E. "Border Literary Histories, Globalization, and Critical Regionalism." *American Literary History* 20 (2008): 160-182. Print.

McKenna, Teresa. *Migrant Song: Politics and Process in Contemporary Chicano Literature*. Austin: University of Texas Press, 1997. Print.

McMurtry, Larry. *All My Friends are Going to be Strangers*. Albuquerque: University of New Mexico Press, 1972. Print.

___. *Horseman Pass By*. New York: Harper, 1961. Print.

___. *The Last Picture Show*. New York: Simon and Schuster, 1966. Print.

___. *Lonesome Dove*. New York: Simon and Schuster, 1985. Print.

___. *Texasville*. New York: Simon and Schuster, 1987. Print.

___. *Walter Benjamin at the Dairy Queen*. New York: Simon and Schuster, 1999. Print.

Montejano, David. *Anglos and Mexicans in the Making of Texas, 1836-1986*. Austin: University of Texas Press, 1987. Print.

Neinstein, Raymond L. *The Ghost Country*. Berkeley: Creative Arts, 1976. Print.

Paredes, Américo. *George Washington Gómez: A Mexico-Texan Novel*. Houston: Arte Público Press, 1990. Print.

Pilkington, Tom. *State of Mind: Texas Literature and Culture*. College Station: Texas A&M University Press, 1998. Print.

Powell, Douglas Reichert. *Critical Regionalism: Connecting Politics and Culture in the American Landscape*. Chapel Hill: University of North Carolina Press, 2007. Print.

Reilly, John M. *Larry McMurtry: A Critical Companion*. Westport, Greenwood Press, 2000. Print.

Saldívar, José David. Preface. *The Rolando Hinojosa Reader: Essays Historical and Critical*. Ed. José David Saldívar. Houston: Arte Público Press, 1985. ix-x. Print.

___. *The Dialectics of Our America: Genealogy, Cultural Critique, and Literary History*. Durham: Duke University Press, 1991. Print.

Saldívar, Ramón. "Looking for a Master Plan: Faulkner, Paredes, and the Colonial and Postcolonial Subject." *The Cambridge Companion to William Faulkner*. Ed. Philip M. Weinstein. Cambridge: Cambridge University Press, 1995. 96-122. Print.

Sánchez, Rosaura. "From Heterogeneity to Contradiction: Hinojosa's Novel." *The Rolando Hinojosa Reader: Essays Historical and Critical*. Ed. José David Saldívar. Houston: Arte Público Press, 1985. 76-100. Print.

Stout, Janis P. "Journeying as a Metaphor for Cultural Loss in the Novels of Larry McMurtry." *Western American Literature* 11 (1976): 37-50. Print.

Zamora, Emilio. "Fighting on Two Fronts: José de la Luz Sáenz and the Language of the Mexican American Civil Rights Movement." *Recovering the U.S. Hispanic Literary Heritage*

Vol. 4. Eds. José F. Aranda and Silvio Torres Saillant. Houston: Arte Público Press, 2002. 214-239. Print.

___. *Claiming Rights and Righting Wrongs in Texas: Mexican Workers and Job Politics during World War II*. College Station: Texas A&M University Press, 2009. Print.

Feminine Autonomy in *Becky and Her Friends* by Rolando Hinojosa

María Esther Quintana Millamoto
Texas A&M University

In *Becky and Her Friends* (1990), a Rolando Hinojosa novel that is part of the *Klail City Death Trip Series* (*KCDTS*), the anonymous narrator who presents his account through interviews with Becky Escobar's family, friends and acquaintances starts by asking himself how she should be judged: "What are we to do with Becky? What should we think of such a woman? A Texas Mexican who, apparently, from one day to the next, decides (that power-laden verb) that her husband is no longer going to live with her and with those two children of theirs."[1] The narrator's questions announce what will be the central theme of the novel: autonomy as an act or action that begins with an independent self-reflection based on established values acknowledged as his/her own by an individual (Friedman, "Autonomy, Social Disruption, and Women" 121). The emphasis on the word "decides," through the narrator's parenthetical comment, bestows agency upon Becky; in other words, she is portrayed as a woman in charge of her life. This agency is reiterated later in the novel through comments from the characters who compare Becky's past subordination as Ira Escobar's wife and her later self-assurance as a divorcee. The narrator's questions announce the change in the power relation in Becky and Ira's marriage; a change that began hatching through the protagonist's rebellion (such as not allowing her husband to share her bed).

On one hand, Hinojosa shows how heterosexual romantic love can present a trap for a woman because patriarchal socialization encourages her to cede her wishes and dreams to her partner's. On the other hand, it creates a character who, at thirty years of age, decides for the first time to give priority to her own wishes rather than trying to conform to her society's moral codes. In *Becky and Her Friends,* the protagonist's decision to banish her husband from her house conveys her desire to free herself from a relationship that has led her to pretend to be another person. In this sense, Becky's divorce is an autonomous act and a desire to create a more genuine identity that is not grounded in her role as a dependent wife and obedient daughter. Alternatively, Becky's psychological dependence on her mother (Elvira Navarrete) in the stage that precedes her divorce fictionalizes the continuity of identification between daughters and mothers, which is a major obstacle for adult women who seek autonomy (Flax, "The Conflict between Nurturance and Autonomy" 174-75).

In this essay I propose that through Becky, Hinojosa portrays a Mexican-American woman who defends her personal desires and her wish for autonomy by negotiating at the same time the values that bind her to her family and society. Likewise, the author conveys how crucial it is for women to separate psychologically from their mother in order to be autonomous. Tangentially, I compare Hinojosa's perspective in *Becky and Her Friends* with regard to the negotiation of feminine autonomy in the Texas Valley with two less-optimistic testimonies by women born in that region: Gloria Anzaldúa and Sonia Saldívar-Hull.

In *Becky and Her Friends*, Hinojosa turns to an anonymous narrator whose account includes interviews with Klail City residents who comment on the protagonist Becky Escobar, first introduced in the *KCDTS* as a secondary character in the earlier novel *Mi querido Rafa* (1981), and then referred to again in *Rites and Witnesses* (1982), *Dear Rafe* (1985) and *Claros varones de Belken/Fair Gentlemen of Belken County* (1986). This research will focus primarily on *Becky and Her Friends* and to a lesser extent on *Mi querido Rafa*.

Hinojosa's technique in defining the protagonist through statements made by other characters (as well as through Becky's own interview) creates the false illusion that the anonymous narrator holds a neutral position with regard to Becky Escobar. However, from the beginning of the novel, the narrator evidences his subjectivity when he describes Becky as "[the] wife for a certain time (in these uncertain times) of banker-politician cum horns, Ira Escobar, a native of Jonesville-on-the Rio" (13). The irony used by the anonymous narrator to refer to Ira Escobar expresses the dislike of many residents of Klail City toward him because he is related to the Leguizamón-Leyva clan, one of the wealthiest families of the area who, through shady deals and alliances with Anglos, has obtained land from other Mexicans. The antipathy is above all aimed at Javier Leguizamón, Ira Escobar's maternal uncle and the family's patriarch, in such a manner that some of the characters of the *KCDTS* enjoy the protagonist's unfaithfulness to her husband, for they see it as a lesson for the arrogant Leguizamóns.

Additionally, considering that *Becky and Her Friends* belongs to a series that had been preceded by several volumes, one must take into account that the previous narrators and characters have already established certain trustworthy parameters while others have not. As a consequence, the accounts that reliable characters and/or narrators present, among them P. Galindo, Jehu Malacara and Viola Barragán, are more influential than others such as Polín Tapia, whose statements are evidently misleading when contrasted with other interviewees. The profiles of Becky, Jehu Malacara and Ira Escobar which reliable informants present allow the reader to sympathize with the growth of Becky as she transcends her dependence on Ira, a character who is described as a dull and pusillanimous social climber.

Feminism and Autonomy

Marilyn Friedman considers autonomy as self-determination by an individual self, a person, who plays a decisive role in determining her choices and actions (*Autonomy, Gender, Politics* 5). In turn, John Christman offers a similar definition when he posits that self-government—the capacity to act independently and being what one chooses to be—is the unanimous idea behind the different conceptualizations of autonomy (18). Friedman further posits autonomy as moral judging, as living and acting according to one's decisions but also within the limitations of what one regards as morally permissible (*Autonomy, Gender, Politics* 37).

Christman refers to the reluctance of some feminist philosophers to associate moral autonomy with women, as a result of the powerful and persistent Kantian theoretical influence on this concept according to which judgments and moral actions must be based on reason and should be exempt from feelings and emotions.[2] According to Kantian theory women cannot be responsible moral subjects since they are dominated by their feelings and desires. Since emotions are part of a person's "pathological nature," in other words, since they are contingent and completely outside of the reflective control, women are cast out from the realm of moral autonomy (Christman 20).

The criticism that feminism provides of the Kantian ideal concerning moral autonomy also rejects its exclusion from empathy, care, nurturing and emotions, which are tendencies traditionally associated with women (Christman 20). Christman posits that Kantian-influenced conceptualizations of moral autonomy, as well as the process through which objective moral and rational judgments are expressed—according to *universal laws*—are not truthful to women. This is because women's reasoning in moral situations is not disconnected from their personal relationships nor do their judgments transcend particular situations (23).[3] Friedman also refers to the objections of some feminists to using the notion of autonomy owing to its traditional connection with self-sufficiency and self-realization at the expense of human relationships (*Autonomy, Gender, Politics* 98).

Christman and Friedman suggest that the notion of autonomy should be kept for women by freeing it from the masculine paradigm and redefining it. Christman proposes that the idea that autonomy excludes women because of her alleged inability to suspend her feelings when performing judgments in moral situations can be undermined by claiming that reason should not be regarded as the sole source of moral justification and responsibility. Therefore even if women are more often moved by feelings than by reason, this does not affect their status as moral agents. Moreover, "one can accept the claim that reason ought to be the final arbiter of moral judgment but that it is an archaic myth (born of and fostered by patriarchy) that women are by nature more emotional that men" (20).

Christman concludes by pointing out that one can be autonomous and emotional. He also argues that it is acceptable to include emotions and empathy as factors in moral judging as long as they are approved by the individual after a reflective act (27). The great importance that Christman confers on self-reflection is also acknowledged by Friedman, who states that in recent decades the concept of self-determination has been articulated through the notion of self-reflection (*Autonomy, Gender, Politics* 4). According to this point of view, in order for a person to execute her/his autonomy, the individual must first critically reflect on his/her desires and needs (*Autonomy, Gender, Politics* 4-5). After this evaluative assessment, one can advocate for one's needs and values partially or engage them wholeheartedly. One can also do the complete opposite and partially or completely repudiate them. Friedman argues that by endorsing and identifying with our wants and desires, we incorporate them as more genuinely ours, as an integral part of our identities as distinctive and particular selves (*Autonomy, Gender, Politics* 5). Furthermore she argues that moral judging or "autonomy conferring reflection" encompasses "emotional as well as strictly rational or narrowly cognitive dimensions of personal processes" ("Autonomy, Social Disruption, and Women" 37). Friedman proposes to add also to the notion of autonomy the tendencies that have traditionally been associated with women such as their disposition to nurture relationships. In this sense she recommends an inter-relational focus of autonomy according to which human beings are essentially social beings who develop the competency for autonomy through social interactions with other people. Autonomy is thus fostered within a human context, and likewise self-reflection cannot exist apart from social practices ("Autonomy, Social Disruption, and Women" 38).[4] Friedman concludes that the potential that autonomy has in breaking social relationships does not imply a need to repudiate this ideal since that can also be a catalyst for personal and social change beneficial for women and other subordinate groups ("Autonomy, Social Disruption, and Women" 44).

Becky's Journey toward Autonomy

Hinojosa's novel stages the autonomy dialectic proposed by Friedman as inter-relational—as a result of the fact that a person achieves autonomy within a social group—and on the other hand, as potentially capable of disrupting social relations and values. Friedman indicates that the rupture of a social relationship caused by an act of autonomy does not necessarily mean a total decline in the relations of said society or a drastic break with it ("Autonomy, Social Disruption, and Women" 44). Friedman also argues that a person who questions a commitment, for example a religious obligation, on which a certain relationship in his/her life is based, typically looks for the company of other skeptics whose thoughts encourage her/him to reinforce their own doubts ("Autonomy, Social Disruption, and Women" 44). In Becky's case, she looks for a confidante in Reina Campoy, the oldest woman in Belken County, and one who has much experience, having been widowed and divorced during her long life. When interviewed by the anonymous narrator, Campoy states that she assured Becky that going through a divorce was not something out of this world. However, in contrast to this apparent liberalism, Campoy is inflexible with matters that pertain to unfaithfulness: "What I told Becky was this: One can't do that, one doesn't go to bed with just anyone. Leave your husband or stay. Don't lie to him. Don't lie to yourself, either. And no confessions, to him or to the Church" (110).

Although Becky does not confess to Ira Escobar or a priest, her interview reads like a confession as it relates to Foucault's idea that in the act of confession truth and sexuality are juxtaposed through the revelation of an individual secret (62). Foucault emphasizes that a confession presupposes an asymmetrical relationship of power between the confessor and the one who confesses:

> The confession is a ritual of discourse in which the speaking subject is also the subject of the statement; it is also a ritual that unfolds within a power relationship, for one does not confess without the presence (or virtual presence) of a partner who is not simply the interlocutor but the authority who requires the confession, prescribes and appreciates it, and intervenes in order to judge, punish, forgive, console, and reconcile. . . . (62)

Becky's decision to speak to the anonymous narrator indicates that although she states that her divorce is a matter that only concerns her, her children and her love, Jehu Malacara, she is willing to offer an explanation of her breakup and her current relationship with Malacara. She emphasizes the truthfulness of her account by relating it as if she were revealing a secret, hinting that she previously hid her affair with Jehu only as an attempt to protect him from being fired for moral misconduct. The implicit juxtaposition in Becky's narrative between the truth and her sexual life coincides with Foucault's idea that confession is a mechanism that produces the truth with regard to sex, which is a privileged theme of confession in the form of Christian penance (61). In her interview with the anonymous narrator, Becky states that her affair with Malacara took place while Jehu was dating Olivia San Esteban, a well-liked and respected young woman from Klail City. Becky judges her own actions negatively when she compares herself to Jehu's former lover, Sammi Jo Perkins: "I went to him, even when I knew he loved Ollie San Esteban. And why wouldn't he love her, and yes, I also knew about him and Sammi Jo. . . And well, was I any better?" (157). Becky apparently submits herself to an act of confession and therefore occupies a subordinate position before an authority that demands that she render an account of her behavior, precisely what Reina Campoy advised her not to do. This seems to be reiterated in the judgment that she invites from her interviewer when she asks, "was I any better?" The anonymous narrator, having been born in Belken County, in a metonymic manner represents the Mexican-American community. Becky, conscious of the fact that by being unfaithful to Ira Escobar she committed a moral offense in her society, justifies her actions by saying that she was no longer in love with him and explains that she proceeded with her divorce in a manner that did not affect her children's well-being. Becky's last gesture reveals a desire not to separate from her community, even when she has subverted its moral codes, by declaring that before she divorced she spoke with two of the most respected women in Klail City, Reina Campoy and Viola Barragán, and, then, by implying that she secured their approval of her decision. While being conscious that this strategy will not convince all the residents of her community, such as her mother Elvira Navarrete or her maternal aunt Nora Salamanca, who see divorce as a rupture with a life promise, the protagonist has to negotiate somehow the moral and religious norms by declaring that her marriage was not a wise decision and that her divorce corrected her error. In fact, Becky tries to establish a balance in the asymmetry of power between her as a subject who confesses and the community that symbolically hears the confession through the interviewer. When she asks her interlocutor, "Can't I be allowed to make a decision?" (155) Becky questions her community's authority at the same time that she affirms her right to decide her future. Likewise, she symbolically absolves herself when she comments that her children have adapted to the idea that their mother has remarried and "there's nothing wrong in it" (156).

The priority that Becky gives to her interests and desires over her family's and community's expectations deviates from the feminine parameters for Mexican-American women in the late 1960s approximately, when her divorce takes place. Even when at that time the so-called Second wave of the Feminist movement was gestating in the United States and the U.S. Congress was passing laws in favor of women's equality in the labor and educational spheres (Tobias 73), the politics of gender remain untouched for many years in the Texas Valley. The literary critic Sonía Saldívar-Hull, a native of that region, explains precisely that the climate changes in sexual and gender politics that came into effect in the United States during the sixties and seventies did not immediately change moral codes for women of Mexican descent. Saldívar-Hull evokes a misogynistic incident that she encountered during high school as evidence that the Feminist movement had not reached the Valley in the late sixties. By the end of the school year, her English teacher commented on her diary, a semester assignment; he wrote that she did not have her brother's writing talent but instead she had pretty legs (11). Saldívar-Hull observes that her teacher's sexist comment "speaks volumes about the late 1960s, a time before the Women's Movement reached our South Texas enclave" (10). Now it could be that Becky's challenge to the patriarchal moral power of her community was an extraordinary act that came from Hinojosa's will to create a character who was in tune with the fight of the 1960s for civil rights in the United States. For, in agreement with Joyce Glover Lee (166-67), Becky's challenge may have been more contemporary to the 1990 time when the novel was published than to the 1960s period of the plot.

That said, in spite of the emancipatory impulse of Becky's actions, the fact that the changes in her life have been motivated by her feelings for another man lead us back to the question of whether or not she has truly secured her autonomy or, on the contrary, whether she simply moves from dependence on one man to dependence on another. As a result, it is important to analyze the love relationships of the protagonist to answer the anonymous narrator's question, "What are we to do with Becky?"

Romantic Heterosexual Love and Autonomy

In her analysis on the fusion in romantic heterosexual love, Friedman argues that not all unions are equal: some favor feedback and self-knowledge between partners, helping each other and sharing interests; yet in other couples the values and interests of one—usually the male—subordinate the other's—usually the female (*Autonomy, Gender, Politics* 121). Because women have been exposed to a specific kind of socialization, Friedman states that these unions can often threaten women's autonomy: "For it appears that romantically merged identity can diminish the autonomy of one lover even while enhancing the autonomy of her beloved. Gender identity being what it is socialized to be in our culture, the heterosexual romantic merger of identity compromises women's autonomy more than it does that of their male partners" ("Autonomy, Social Disruption, and Women" 121).[5] Jane Flax also notes that the divergent psychological development of infants based on gender causes girls to have problems when looking for psychological independence from their mothers. During adulthood they confront the dilemma of either keeping the bond with their mother or searching for their independence ("The Conflict between Nurturance and Autonomy" 174-75). Flax states that women tend to look for the maternal love they yearn for in their partners ("The Conflict between Nurturance and Autonomy" 182).

The socialization of Becky Caldwell—maiden name—prepares her psychologically to occupy a subordinate position in her relationship with Ira Escobar. Even though Elvira Navarrete motivates her daughter to go to the university, the pressure that she exerts over her to marry illustrates that her priority is not for her daughter to complete her degree and to put it to use, but to secure an advantageous marriage. As is mentioned above, Ira Escobar is related through his mother to the wealthy Leguizamón clan.

Becky's traditional upbringing, added to her unequal status in her relationship with Ira, fosters an asymmetric power relation in her marriage. This asymmetry is illustrated by the dominant role in Becky's marriage played by Ira's political aspirations. The protagonist's subordinate position in relation to her husband is suggested by Julia Ortegón, Becky's long-time friend, who recalls that in spite of having a degree in music, Becky chose to dedicate her life to her home and family. Lionel Villa, Becky's maternal uncle, also confirms that she enslaved herself so that Ira—whom he describes as an intelligence-challenged man—could obtain and secure the county commissioner position, while she forgot about herself: "And what was she doing for herself, for Becky Escobar? Nothing. Not a thing" (21). Villa points out that although Becky should have realized that she was superior to Escobar, she had not yet matured enough to question her marriage. Villa supports his niece's decision to divorce and provides for her economically so that she does not have to worry about her financial situation. The uncle wholeheartedly praises Becky's independence which he considers an accomplishment that liberated her not only from Ira Escobar but also from her mother: "Becky was going to cut loose from Ira, and she was cutting that umbilical cord from Elvira, too, see?" (22).

It is significant that Villa associates the legal independence that Becky obtains when she divorces from Ira with the psychological freedom that she receives when she disobeys maternal ideology for the first time. The psychological breakup mentioned by Villa coincides with Jane Flax's idea regarding how the continuous bond between mother and daughter hinders women's autonomy. In Becky's case, the psychological dependence on her mother is manifested through the powerful influence of Elvira Navarrete when she makes decisions for her. Julia Ortegón speaks to Elvira's control over her daughter, which extended until after her marriage, "As for Becky, she didn't always take the best course for her. I mean, she would defer to her mother too often. You can't do that with a bully like doña Elvira"; "Becky is too loyal to her mother's wishes. And too, she loves her mother [. . .] Why shouldn't she?

It's her mother after all" (67). Becky's psychological dependence on the maternal figure is also present in the influence her mother-in-law—a woman who belongs to the one of the wealthiest families in Belken County—exerts over her. The protagonist apologetically tells the anonymous narrator that when she was married to Escobar, she wanted to be more like her mother-in-law than her mother: "We were a long way from the first day we'd moved to Klail. . . I cut a ridiculous figure. And for a while there, I even pretended to myself that I wasn't Elvira Navarrete's daughter, as if Ira's mother had raised me" (157).

The psychological and emotional dependence on her mother and mother-in-law shape Becky's identity according to expectations that are foreign to her, and when she understands this, Becky makes the necessary changes to mature and become a more genuine person. Her motivation to change is the love she feels for Jehu, but she is initially incapable of transforming her life because she is paralyzed by fear. However, one day she decides to confront it:

> Finally, one day, I asked myself what it was I feared. The answers came tumbling out, hundreds of them. But then, at that time, I hadn't learned about the ultimate questions . . . oh, yes. When I asked myself the ultimate question, and I answered yes to myself, and I knew I was dead serious, fear, or whatever it was, flew out that front door, through the porch, and away from this house. . . . (156-57)

As Becky uses domestic images to explain the desire to liberate herself from her previous life, Hinojosa has already anticipated in the form of a question her move to abandon the domestic role as Escobar's wife and the social status that she enjoyed through him.[6] Becky's query, "Can't I be allowed to make a decision? Must I always accommodate myself, every time?" (155), challenges the heteronormativity that controls female behavior in patriarchal societies. In them Friedman argues, "Women have been expected to make the preservation of certain interpersonal relationships such as those of family their highest concern regardless of the cost to themselves" ("Autonomy, Social Disruption, and Women" 46).

Becky states that during her marriage, she lived "[in] Denial" (157) and that she had forged an identity that was not hers; "I had made myself into another person" (157). In fact several characters think that Ira Escobar was the primary agent in Becky's self-effacement and the reason why the protagonist was snobbish and not authentic. This lack of authenticity that grew out of her desire to follow Ira Escobar and her social status' expectations resonate with Friedman's idea regarding how a woman in an asymmetrical relationship tends to see herself through her lover's perspective, that is, "Her partner's conception of her nature, her virtues and her shortcomings may become the lens through which they together regard her. She may come to see herself more through her partner's eyes than through her own" (*Autonomy, Gender, Politics* 125).

It is indeed true that Ira's projects controlled the relationship between him and Becky and in that sense it lacked reciprocity, but it is also true that Becky did not respond to his faithfulness since she had a sexual relationship with Jehu when she was still married. Likewise, her abrupt decision to divorce Escobar and her demand for him to leave her home immediately is almost incomprehensible. While Becky mentions that she discussed her plans with Viola Barragán and Reina Campoy, she never tries to discuss them with Escobar. This attitude reveals a lack of communication that is foreshadowed in the novel's opening scene where Becky bids farewell to her husband forever, "I've decided that you are not going to live with us anymore" (9).

In contrast to Ira and Becky's relationship, characterized by the power asymmetry between both of them—until her decision to divorce him—, Becky and Jehu's relationship stands out for its mutual reciprocity. It falls in what Friedman describes as a just loving fusion where lovers support each other to grow mutually in their abilities and self-esteem (*Autonomy, Gender, Politics* 123-4). Becky describes her married life with Jehu as ideal, "And this is my new life, and it's the best one I could have chosen. There's no set routine to our lives"; "For Jehu it's always the family. Me. The children" (158-59). The fact that Becky feels more complete and free of social pressure when she is with Jehu—because of their involvement she resigns from the women's social clubs in Belken County—is because her relationship with him has reinforced, not obstructed, her autonomy. Jehu, quite apart from Ira, does not expect her to work in order for him to be successful in his own occupation and he has a more democratic relationship with her in regard to domestic finances since both of them are employed. Becky discovers a source of personal satisfaction through her work when she manages Viola Barragán's business with success that leads even the wealthiest men in Klail City to recognize her ability and commercial acumen.

Indeed, Becky's divorce had a happy ending but we should ask what, aside from Jehu's love, made her risk losing an identity that revolved around her role as Escobar's wife that at the same time granted her a privileged social status. What were the conditions or reasons that allowed the Valley Texas Mexican to risk going against the social network of the small and traditional community of Klail City?

Although the university education could be a factor that separates Becky from traditional societal rules, nothing in the novel seems to indicate that it led the protagonist to make up her mind to leave Ira. However, the fact that Becky moves to Denton to attend the university symbolizes her superior social status, since Becky's attendance at the University of North Texas meant that her family had the means to pay not only her tuition but also her lodging and other personal expenses. Saldívar-Hull highlights that the opportunities that young Mexican-American girls from her generation—some twenty years or so after Becky's—had for leaving the Valley were almost nonexistent and that only Anglo women sought an education beyond its geographic boundaries. This was not only a result of a lack of resources but because mothers of Texas Mexicans continued to follow rules assigned according to gender, where males enjoyed privileges and women had domestic responsibilities. Saldívar-Hull explains:

> For my mother, however, becoming a full-fledged American never altered her biases against her daughter's attempt to escape traditional gender constraints. The boys in the family could aspire to everything the school system provided, but Mother could not accept a daughter's learning to ride a bike or even to roller-skate. . . The brothers could play, read, and study as much as they wanted—indeed, the status of the family somehow hinged on their success—but as a mujercita, I was needed to perform crucial household and child-care tasks. . . At that time, Mother could not conceive of a different possibility for a daughter. (9)

Saldívar-Hull then adds that in her generation, the highest aspiration for a young woman of Mexican heritage was to work in a bank or to attend the local community college known by Texan-Mexicans as "Tamale Tech" (11)[7].

For her part Chicana writer Gloria Anzaldúa (1942-2004), also a native of the Valley, when speaking of her generation, points out that working-class people from the Valley prioritize feeding, dressing and caring for their children because they did not have the means to provide for a formal education (39). Anzaldúa provides an image that is even more distressing than Saldívar-Hull's regarding sexual politics in her community. She points out that the rebellion that she demonstrated as a young girl when facing family pressures to be docile and obedient garnered her a daily beating:

> Even as a child I would not obey. I was "lazy." Instead of ironing my younger brother's shirts or cleaning the cupboards, I would pass many hours studying, reading, painting, writing. Every bit of self-faith I'd painstakingly gathered took a beating daily. Nothing in my culture approved of me. Había agarrado malos pasos. Something was "wrong" with me. Estaba más allá de la tradición. (39)

Both Anzaldúa and Saldívar-Hull succeed in fulfilling their educational goals after a long fight to impose their wishes regarding others' expectations and needs. In Saldívar-Hull's case, the reading of Chicano literature and postcolonial theory provided by her brothers José and Ramón, established academics, helped her to develop her conscience as a Chicana: "For Chicanas who once could not imagine our way out of the laws of tradition, learning to read from a Chicana perspective altered the path of our lives" (25). The author at that time defined herself as a Chicana feminist because she identified with the Chicano Movement struggle. Nonetheless, her reading of Chicana feminist poetry allowed her to see women's subordinate role within the Movement (25-26). Saldívar-Hull decided to join the academy and other Chicana feminists who explore other ways to express the issues that affect them, "It was time to go beyond the roles of dutiful daughter, sister, and wife" (29). In turn, Anzaldúa also referenced the need she had to challenge the traditional Chicana models which led her to leave the Valley and eventually become a world-renowned feminist, noting "To this day I'm not sure where I found the strength to leave the source, the mother, disengage from my family, mi tierra, mi gente, and all that picture stood for. I had to leave home so I could find myself, find my own intrinsic nature buried under the personality that had been imposed on me" (38).

Becky, like Anzaldúa, searches for a more authentic self which in her case had been hidden under the mask of the politician's wife. Becky's journey to self-knowledge takes her to her Mexican roots, especially in regard to relearning the Spanish that had been buried due to the influence of the Anglo-American culture. As Sammi Jo Perkins—the daughter of the banker Noddy Perkins—explains, Spanish is an important part of Texan-Mexican identity. Nevertheless, children commonly forget it because they are forced to learn English and parents reinforce this in their homes. Sammi Jo praises Becky for taking up Spanish because she interprets her recovery of her mother language as an indication that she wants to reinforce her Mexican heritage. Jehu, on the other hand, in *Mi querido Rafa*—a novel referring to a time previous to Becky's transformation—had considered her as a sellout because she spoke English without a Spanish accent. Jehu, very critical of this attitude, sees it as a common attitude in "*la raza*," and rejects that this is a simple sign of adaptability. Rather he interprets this lack of Spanish accent as an attempt to imitate Anglo Americans (*Dear Rafe/Mi querido* Rafa 160).

The protagonist's transformation is motivated in great part by Viola Barragán's influence, something that is pointed out by E. B. "Ibby" Cooke, one of the major powerbrokers in all of Belken County. As Ibby points out, Becky is becoming Viola while at the same time paradoxically transforming into "her own person" (*Becky and Her Friends* 81). With regard to Viola Barragán's role as Becky's surrogate mother, Adrienne Rich proposes that it is common for women to be inspired by others whose lives are diametrically distant from the maternal role. According to Rich, the alternate model is often made up of "a woman artist or teacher, who becomes the countervailing figure. Often this 'counter-mother' is an athletics teacher who exemplifies strength and pride in her body, a freer way of being in the world; or an unmarried woman professor, alive with ideas, who represents the choice of a vigorous work life of 'living alone and liking it'" (247). Viola represents an autonomous model for Becky since she is financially independent and as a widow enjoys personal freedom. Barragán stands out in the *KCDTS* because she makes decisions that go against public opinion in Klail City—for example, having several lovers—and because she is extremely successful in the male-dominated business world. She advises Becky to disregard nosy people's gossip, something that is difficult to do as Viola has discovered firsthand. The powerful personality of Viola manifests when she instructs Elvira Navarrete—her longtime friend—to respect her daughter's decision to divorce and not make a scene out of it. By supporting Becky's divorce over Elvira's opposition, Viola confirms her role as surrogate mother to the protagonist. She teaches her to be an individual; that is, to forge an identity that is not subordinated by others' opinions, but rather is guided by her own aspirations, without giving up personal relationships.

Viola is a role model for Becky because even though she is not restricted by traditional norms, she stands out by her solidarity with Valley Texas Mexicans. Viola negotiates her ties with the community by demonstrating her loyalty to *la raza* by providing them with employment resources (for example, she finds Jehu a job in the Klail City Bank). She does not allow herself to be manipulated by the *bolillos*—Anglo Americans from the Valley—with whom she mingles for business and, in fact, personal matters.

Becky, who has always accepted without question much of the circumstances that make up her world, for the first time in her life decides that it is about time people accept and respect her right to make moral decisions, among them divorcing Ira Escobar. She declares that her divorce is a matter that concerns only four people: her, her two children and Jehu. Becky concludes her interview by saying, "Let's say I saved myself, and let it go at that" (159), a phrase filled with self-determination and agency emphasized by the narrator's statement about having given her the last word. This implies his recognition of Becky as a moral agent, and suggests that her own narrative is the one that should count the most for her and for the reader.

If autonomy always has the potential risk of shaking up personal relationships and of questioning a community's rules of conduct, Becky's case is a paradigm for a woman who undermines her subordination to her husband's interests. Thus her autonomy defies the rules and values that govern the lives of Mexican-American women in fictitious Belken County. However, does not her final adaptation into the marital relationship normalize her new identity as a married woman, lessening her previous subversion? Could there have been a less predictable conclusion for Becky? For example, to be a single mother, enjoying her financial and personal freedom? We have some examples of Chicana protagonists who choose to live as single women, such as Carmen in *Peel my Heart like an Onion* by Ana Castillo, Tere in *Loving Pedro Infante* by Denise Chávez, or Mary in *Mother Tongue* by Demetria Martínez. Could Becky have chosen at least not to marry Jehu but rather live with him in common law thus demonstrating that she had learned Viola's lesson in autonomy? Evidently autonomy is always relative, and if the person pursuing it reaches a major degree of freedom with regard to the codes of conduct or dictates of his/her society she/he has already achieved a positive change (Friedman, "Autonomy, Social Disruption, and Women" 41). Without drastically questioning the normativity of society's sexual politics, for Becky and Rolando Hinojosa the challenge of personal expectations and social paradigms of what is expected of a woman is already a gain for women and furthermore a revolutionary act.

Notes

[1] Hinojosa, Rolando. *Becky and Her Friends*. Houston: Arte Público Press, 1990. (The quote comes from "The Opening Shot" [9].) All quotes are taken from this edition.

[2] Christman quotes Iris Young who rejects the idea of the need for impartiality in moral judgments: "The ideal of impartiality is an idealist fiction. It is impossible to adopt an unsituated moral point of view, and if a point of view is situated, then it cannot be universal, it cannot stand apart from and understand all points of view. It is impossible to reason about substantive moral issues without social and historical context; and one has no motive for making moral judgments and resolving moral dilemmas unless the outcome matters, unless one has a particular and passionate interest in the outcome." (Iris Young quoted in Christman 28)

[3] Friedman believes that the exclusion of emotion within the concept of rationalizing is less prominent today. She proposes that some feminist and philosophical theories blur the difference between emotions and reason even more, which promises that this dichotomy can one day be transcended (*Autonomy, Gender, Politics* 38).

[4] Jane Flax agrees with Friedman when she rejects the opposition between autonomy and interpersonal relations as proposed by some feminists: "These theorists do not see that, for adults, being in relations can be claustrophobic without autonomy and that autonomy without being in relations can easily degenerate into mastery" (*Thinking Fragments* 181).

[5] When she refers to the issue of the psycho-social development of children based on their gender, Flax also refers to the differences regarding boys and girls' socialization indicating that women are taught to dedicate their lives to harvest relationships with men, especially their husbands ("The Conflict between Nurturance and Autonomy" 182).

[6] The Leguizamóns have a bad reputation as a result of their shady business deals and their relationships with the wealthy Anglo Americans in Belken County that often lead them to turn their back on and even do harm to Texas Mexicans. This relationship between Ira and the Leguizamóns, along with his personal attribute of being weak, allows his supervisor, the banker Noddy Perkins, to transform Ira into the novel's anti hero.

[7] Saldívar-Hull indicates with irony that for a Texas Mexican-American woman a variety of options were useless because she would always end up a housewife: "Tamale Tech it would be. I knew that after the tech, I would be married and my life would be complete, anyway" (11).

Works Cited

Anzaldúa, Gloria. *Borderlands / La Frontera: The New Mestiza*. San Francisco: Spinsters / Aunt Lute Books, 1987. Print.

Calderón, Héctor and José David Saldívar. *Criticism in the Borderlands: Studies in Chicano Literature, Culture, and Ideology*. Durham: Duke University Press, 1991. Print.

Christman, John. "Feminism and Autonomy." *Nagging Questions: Feminist Ethics in Everyday Life*. Ed. Dana E. Bushnell. London: Rowman and Littlefield Publishers, 1995. 17-40. Print.

Flax, Jane. "The Conflict between Nurturance and Autonomy in Mother-Daughter Relationships and within Feminism." *Feminist Studies* 4.2 (Jun. 1978): 171-89. Print.

___. "Mother-Daughter Relationships: Psycho-dynamics, Politics, and Philosophy." *The Future of Difference*. Eds. Hester Eisenstein and Alice Jardine. New Brunswick: Rutgers University Press, 1985. 20-40. Print.

___. *Thinking Fragments: Psychoanalysis, Feminism, and Postmodernism in the Contemporary West*. Berkeley: University of California Press, 1990. Print.

Foucault, Michel. *The History of Sexuality. An Introduction*. Vol. 1. Trans. Robert Hurley. New York: Vintage Books, 1978. Print.

Friedman, Marilyn. *Autonomy, Gender, Politics*. London: Oxford University Press, 2003. Print.

___. "Autonomy, Social Disruption, and Women." *Relational Autonomy: Feminist Perspectives on Autonomy, Agency, and the Social Self.* Eds. Catriona Mackenzie and Natalie Stoljar. London: Oxford University Press, 2000. 35-51. Print.

Hinojosa, Rolando. *Becky and Her Friends.* Houston: Arte Público Press, 1990. Print.

___. *Claros varones de Belken/Fair Gentlemen of Belken County.* Tempe: Bilingual Press/Editorial Bilingüe, 1986. Print.

___. *Dear Rafe.* Houston: Arte Público Press, 1981. Print.

___. *Dear Rafe/Mi querido Rafa.* Houston: Arte Público Press, 2005. Print.

___. *Mi querido Rafa.* Houston: Arte Público Press, 1985. Print.

___. *Rites and Witnesses.* Houston: Arte Público Press, 1982. Print.

Lee, Joyce Glover. *Rolando Hinojosa and the American Dream.* Denton: University of North Texas Press, 1997. Print.

Saldívar-Hull, Sonia. *Feminism on the Border: Chicana Gender Politics and Literature.* Berkeley: University of California Press, 2000. Print.

Tobias, Sheila. *Faces of Feminism: An Activist's Reflections on the Women's Movement.* Boulder: Westview Press, 1997. Print.

Rolando Hinojosa's Klail City Sociological and Demographic Reflections of a Hometown

Rogelio Sáenz
University of Texas at San Antonio

While persons of Mexican origin continue to be seen as immigrants and newcomers to the United States, there are many Mexican Americans that can trace their roots to this country for seven or more generations. The ancestors of many Mexican Americans lived in areas that once belonged to Mexico and eventually became citizens of Texas and later the United States following wars and skirmishes that altered the geo-politics of the Mexico-U.S. border region. The author Rolando Hinojosa is an individual whose antecedents first arrived in South Texas—*el Valle*—in the mid-1700s (on his father's side) and the late-1800s (on his mother's side). Hinojosa's youth and formative years were spent in his hometown of Mercedes and the surrounding area that comprises the region. Hinojosa's *Klail City Death Trip* (*KCDT*) series, consisting of fifteen literary volumes to date, takes place in the fictional Belken County, which has been seen as an amalgam of the counties that form *el Valle* or the Valley of the southern tip of Texas—Cameron, Hidalgo, Starr and Willacy. Belken County contains several fictional towns and cities, specifically Bascom, Edgerton, Flads, Flora, Jonesville-on-the-Rio, Klail City, Relámpago, Ruffing and San Pedro.

The Valley has experienced tremendous political, economic, social and cultural changes since Hinojosa's paternal ancestors arrived in the region around 1750. The history of the region and the transformations that have taken place in the area are aptly illustrated in the *KCDT* series. The city of Mercedes is also my own hometown, the place where I spent my youth and formative years. I was born approximately three decades after Hinojosa. In this essay, I will use my lens as a sociologist and demographer to reflect on Rolando Hinojosa, the person and writer, on our hometown of Mercedes, and I will also provide an overview of the demographic, social and economic changes that have occurred in Mercedes over time.

Mercedes: The Hometown

Our hometown of Mercedes is located within the above-mentioned four-county region of Cameron, Hidalgo, Starr and Willacy known as the Valley on the southern tip of the state of Texas. As illustrated in Figure 1, numerous towns and cities are located along the major routes of state highways 83 and 281 and other smaller roads that form the area. Only a few miles separate neighboring towns and cities. While the Valley had nearly 1.3 million inhabitants according to the 2010 census, it continues to have a small-town rural flavor due largely to the isolation of the region from the rest of the state of Texas.

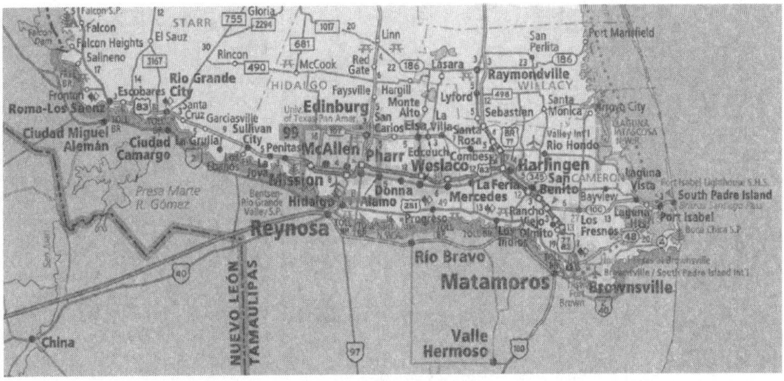

Figure 1. The Rio Grande Valley of Texas.

The history of the Valley extends back to the 1730s and 1740s when Spanish stock raisers settled in the area which at that time was part of Nuevo Santander in New Spain, before Mexico had gained its independence from Spain (Alonzo 1-3). These early settlers found the area's harsh environment useful as pastureland for the raising of stock (Alonzo 1). Rolando Hinojosa's ancestors on his father's side were part of the early settlement in the region. As Spanish settlers tamed the frontier, they "developed a sense of place that made the region Hispanic" (Alonzo 3). The region today clearly shows its deep roots established prior to the arrival of whites or Anglo settlers from the United States. As Alonzo asserts, "Few places in the United States have retained to the present time the influence of Spain and its successor government, Mexico, as strongly as the Lower Valley of Texas" (3). Hinojosa details in his own words the long history of the region and its strong sense of place:

> For me and mine, history, began in 1749 when the first colonists began moving onto the southern and northern banks of the Rio Grande. That river was not yet a jurisdictional barrier and was not to be until almost one hundred years later; but, by then, the Border had its own history, its own culture, and its own sense of place: it was Nuevo Santander, named for old Santander in the Spanish Peninsula. ("The Sense of Place" 19; see also Busby 105)

The site of our hometown of Mercedes was initially settled by ranchers in the late 1770s (*The Handbook of Texas Online* 1). It became part of the Llano Grande Spanish land grant that was issued to Juan José Ynojosa de Ballí in 1790.

White settlers from the United States and Europe began making their way to the region in the 1820s. This movement intensified with Texas independence from Mexico in 1836 and the U.S. annexation of Texas in 1845. It is about this time that the ancestors of Rolando Hinojosa on his mother's side began moving into the region. The Valley was opened up to land development as white land speculators were recruited into the region in the late 1800s and early 1900s (Weber 166). Alonzo points out that with the arrival of whites in the region at this time, a myth emerged emphasizing the contributions of whites to the development and history of the Valley and minimizing those of the original Spanish and Mexican settlers (5-7; see also Weber 166).

In the early 1900s, the site of Mercedes was part of 45,000 acres of land owned by Lon C. Hill, Jr., a land developer, who cleared the land with the purpose of developing it (*The Handbook of Texas Online* 1). Shortly after in 1904 he established the Capisallo Town and Improvement Company to develop the town of Capisallo, which was about a mile east from the site of what is now Mercedes. Drawing on his first name, Hill named the area Lonsboro and sold it to the American Rio Grande Land and Irrigation Company, which renamed the town Diaz (*The Handbook of Texas Online* 1). The town underwent three name changes until it was given the name of Mercedes with the community founded on September 15, 1907. The town was centrally located, being the first town to be part of the Sam Fordyce Branch of the St. Louis, Brownsville, and Mexico Railway and was given the nickname of the "Sweetheart of the Branch" (*The Handbook of Texas Online* 1). It is now commonly referred to as the "queen of the Valley" or "la reina del Valle."

The Changing Demography of Mercedes

The city of Mercedes has experienced population growth over its history. Yet, the fastest growth occurred during the first few decades in the 20th century (Figure 2). Indeed, the population of Mercedes nearly tripled between 1910 and 1920 and almost doubled between 1920 and 1930. This period was associated with movements of whites into the Valley region as well as Mexicans fleeing the Mexican Revolution. The revolution is a major theme in many volumes of the *KCDT* and has as precedent Hinojosa's own father moving to Mexico to fight in the war while his mother remained in Mercedes. A generation after the Revolution Mexicans accounted for approximately half of the population of Mercedes in 1930.

Figure 2. Population of Mercedes, 1910 to 2010.

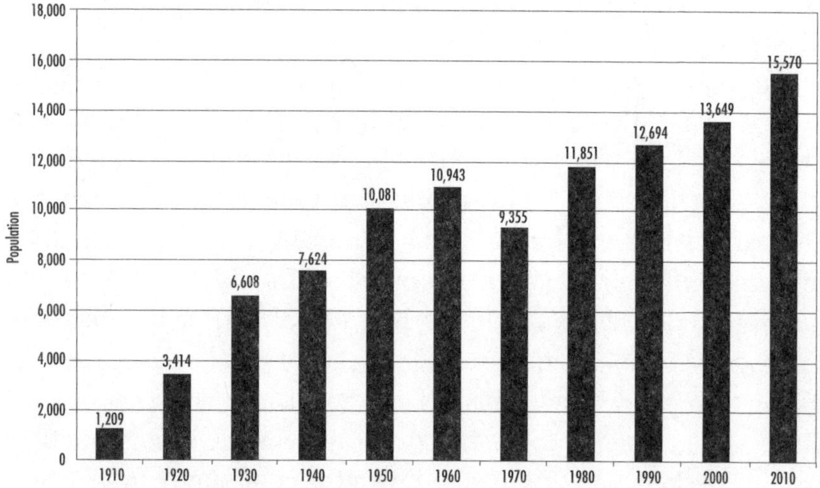

Source: 1910-2000 (Texas State Historical Association 2012); the figure for 2010 is obtained from the 2010 census (U.S. Census 2012b).

Mercedes continued growing after 1930 but at a slower pace. The city population increased to 10,081 by 1950 but has remained relatively stable between then and 2000, when the population stood at 13,649. However, between 2000 and 2010 Mercedes posted rapid growth when its population increased by 14%, the highest percentage change since the mid-20th century. Mercedes experienced its significant revitalization and boost to its economy when Rio Grande Valley Premium Outlet—with its 140 stores—opened its doors for business in November 2006.

Notwithstanding, while Mercedes enjoyed notoriety as a major player in the development of the Valley early in its history, its centrality has declined over time. For example, the population growth of Mercedes pretty much mirrored the level of growth of its county (Hidalgo County) in the 1910-1920 and 1920-1930 periods (data not shown here). Since then, however, Hidalgo County's growth has outpaced that of Mercedes. This growth disparity is particularly evident from the 1970 to 2000 period when the population of Hidalgo County (214% increase) grew nearly five times faster than that of Mercedes (46%). Thus, the Mercedes' share of the overall Hidalgo County population has steadily declined from approximately 9% in 1910 and 1920 to 2% in 2010 (Figure 3).

Figure 3. Percentage of Hidalgo County Population Living in Mercedes, 1910 to 2010

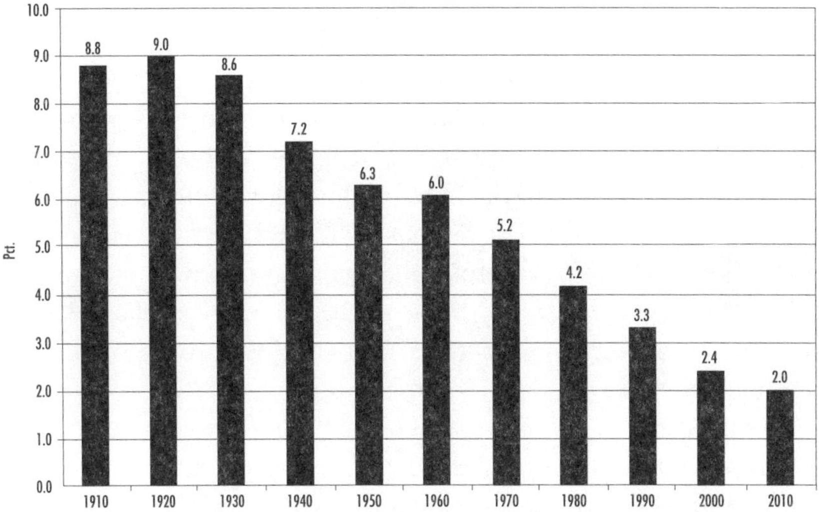

Source: 1910-2000 (Texas State Historical Association 2012); the figure for 2010 is obtained from the 2010 census (U.S. Census 2012b).

Historical Changes in Racial and Ethnic Dynamics of Mercedes

Over its century of existence, the city of Mercedes has experienced major changes in the racial and ethnic dynamics associated with its two largest groups—Mexicans and whites. In particular, the changing dynamics in racial and ethnic relations between these two groups can be divided into two half centuries. The first half century is associated with the entrance of whites into the region, the loss of land among Mexicans, and their eventual subjugation. Two major events occurring in the 1940s and in the 1960s marked the transition of racial and ethnic dynamics in the Valley as was the case in much of the Southwest where Mexican Americans were concentrated. These events were: World War II and the Korean War, which saw Mexican Americans fighting heroically and raising their demands and expectations regarding their social, economic and political standing; and, the Chicano Movement, which saw younger Mexican Americans engaging in confrontational politics to better the conditions of the Mexican American community.

The Chicano Movement was part of the larger Civil Rights Movement that saw blacks, Chicanos, Puerto Ricans and Native Americans making demands for greater equality and inclusion.

Mercedes: 1910-1960

While Mexicans have deep historical roots in the region and have represented the majority of the population throughout the region, for half a century or so Mexicans were absent from many aspects of social and political life in Mercedes (Hinojosa, "Always Writing" 66). As Bruce-Novoa observes drawing from Hinojosa's *KCDT* series, "Anglos control[ed] the centers of power, such as the banks, the government, and the legal system, they are key players in events that directly affect the intimate lives of the Mexicano community" (289).

From early in its history Mercedes, like the numerous other towns and cities that form the Valley, was a segregated community with the Business 83 Highway and the railroad tracks dividing the south and north sides. Virtually all whites lived on the south side and the north side was almost completely Mexican. The nice homes and neighborhoods were located in the south side. An article titled "Honor Roll Announced" appearing in the *News-Tribune* (precursor of the *Mercedes Enterprise*) on April 25, 1941 illustrates the segregation in schools at the grammar school level (1). The South Grammar School honor roll students included forty-six whites and five Mexicans (based on surnames). In contrast, the North Grammar School honor roll students included seventy-five Mexicans and one white. While the schools were segregated at the elementary level, all students attended the same junior and senior high schools. Hinojosa captures this situation and the differences between Mexicans living across the tracks from each other in *Klail City*:

> It was quite a surprise. Here we were, going from the 100% Texas Mexican North Ward Elementary to Klail's Memorial Jr. High and then, just like that, we ran across *other* mexicanos; we later found out that these had gone to South Ward, and they were different from us, somehow. Jehú Malacara, a cousin of mine,

> called them "The Dispossessed." Now, these mexicanos were one hell of a lot more fluent in English than we were, but they came up short on other things; on the uptake, for one, out on the playground, for another. (70)

Furthermore, a perusal of the pages of the *News-Tribune* and *Mercedes Enterprise* extending back to the early 1940s shows whites primarily featured and Mexicans virtually absent. The newspapers report the accomplishments of whites along with the announcements of their rites of passages. Mexicans were under the radar screen of the local newspapers at the time. Hinojosa describes the local newspaper as belonging to whites:

> What we had, both societies [Mexican and Anglo] . . . were separate structures. Not necessarily parallel however. For instance, Mercedes published the *Enterprise* once a week and it was read, predominantly, by the Anglo [or white American] residents. It was a typical small-town newspaper with notes about book clubs, garden societies, visits from out-of-town relatives and such typical fare. Unless the War Department sent a telegram to the family (and to the Mercedes *Enterprise* for propaganda purposes in order to unify the citizenry as Americans), few to no Texas Mexican names appeared in the paper. Those that did, did so usually at semester's end when some of us made the scholastic Honor Roll or when some of us graduated from high school. During the school year, Spanish surnames would also appear when some of us participated in athletic events, school plays or any other extra-curricular activity. In the main, however, the *Enterprise* was their newspaper, not ours. (*A Voice of My Own* 26; brackets used by this author)

White students represented the majority of Mercedes High School (MHS) graduates up to the early 1960s.[1] Over the period from 1941 to 2008, the share of whites among MHS graduates was greatest in the period from 1941 to 1943 when whites constituted approximately three-fourths of all graduates. At the time that Hinojosa graduated from MHS in 1946, whites accounted for nearly three-fifths of all MHS graduates. A newspaper article appearing in the *Mercedes Enterprise* on June 7, 1946, following the graduation of the class of 1946, illustrates the segregated worlds in which whites and Mexicans lived. The article titled "Mexico Party for High School Graduates" reported that:

> Honoring her daughter, Marjorie, Mrs. C. D. MacVean was hostess Sunday afternoon for an unusual event on the calendar of entertainments feting Mercedes girl graduates, when an "Old Mexico jaunt" was enjoyed. The girls met at the MacVean residence early in the afternoon. After a "shopping tour" of the Market Place and Plaza in Matamoros the group returned to Landrum's in Brownsville where a delicious Mexican dinner was served, places being marked by miniature "sombreros" as favors. The guest list included: Misses Laura Nell Lauderdale, Nayon Scogin, Bettye Tullis, Barbara Joyce, Mary Caldeira, Dorinda Schrank, Jo Ann Schwarz, Winona Powel and Mary Jo Wilder. Mrs. C. L. Wilson assisted Mrs. MacVean with the party. (1)

An examination of the roster of girls who graduated in Hinojosa's class of 1946 indicates that ten of the seventeen white graduates attended this celebration while none of the eight Mexican girl graduates were present.

Moreover, over the period from 1941 to 1964, Mexicans were rarely among the valedictorians and salutatorians among MHS graduates. Indeed, of forty-five valedictorians and salutatorians who were listed in newspaper issues and whose race and ethnicity could be identified, only four (9%) were Mexican.

Mexicans also lacked leadership and power in the political arena. Whites held the mayor position of Mercedes for thirty-eight years from 1930 to 1968 before a Mexican was elected to this office.[2] The litany of white mayors during this thirty-eight year reign included E.H. Kasey, W.D. Chadick, D.L. Heidrick, Harold Rowland, G.E. "Buddy" Watson, E.K. O'Shea, Charles A. Ripley, Andrew J. Hagan and John W. Bowe. Similarly, of the thirty-three individuals elected to the Mercedes City Commission between 1930 and 1959, approximately four-fifths (twenty-six of the thirty-three) were white. Indeed, over the sixteen-year period from 1930 to 1946, all city commissioners were white.

It is clear that over the first half century extending back to the founding of Mercedes, Mexicans had relatively little political power and were underrepresented in its leadership positions. This is a theme that emerges consistently in the literary work of Hinojosa. Yet, in many ways, World War II represented a watershed for Mexicans throughout the Southwest. Mexicans exhibited a great degree of patriotism and fought valiantly in World War II and the Korean War. Upon graduation from high school at age seventeen, Hinojosa himself joined the U.S. Army in 1946 and was recalled when the Korean War broke out. Another renowned son of Mercedes, Dr. Hector P. Garcia, fought in World War II after completing his medical degree in 1940 and subsequently his medical internship in 1942, earning honors on the battlefield. In 1948 Dr. Garcia founded the American G.I. Forum, an organization concerned with issues affecting Mexican American veterans and which aimed to better the social, economic and political conditions of Mexican Americans.

Through their participation in World War II and the Korean War, Mexican-American soldiers got an opportunity to see the world beyond the confines of the barrios from where they originated. In addition, having proven their loyalty to the United States, Mexican-American soldiers expected to be treated with respect and dignity when they returned home. Sadly, this was not the case. Rather, the example of Felix Longoria epitomizes the reality that Mexican-American soldiers experienced when they returned from the battlefield. Longoria was killed in the Philippines in 1945. When his body was returned to his hometown of Three Rivers, Texas, the funeral director refused the use of the funeral home for Longoria's wake because he feared that whites would not like it (Carroll 56). This incident galvanized the American G.I. Forum which protested the slap in the face to Longoria and the Mexican-American community. Eventually, the Forum sought the assistance of then-U.S. Senator Lyndon B. Johnson, who intervened and arranged burial of Longoria's body at Arlington National Cemetery.

The frustration of Mexican-American soldiers over persistent inequality on the home front is another theme that is present in the work of Hinojosa. For example, in *Klail City* we amply see the injustice associated with the murder of an unarmed Mexican American World War II veteran, Ambrosio Mora, at the hands of white law enforcement. Early in the book, we learn from the narrator about the murder of Mora:

> . . . Well what the hell happened in the Ambrosio Mora shooting? Young Mora was unarmed. That's right! Van Meers shot young Mora—right there—across those tracks, by the J.C. Penny Store, on a Palm Sunday afternoon as the song says. And you know what? A thousand and one goddam people saw it. And? So? Listen to this: three years! It took the state of Texas three years to get the case going, and when it did, what happened? Well, now: here comes old Choche Markham—that great and good friend of ours—yeah, he came over and he swore in as a witness for Deputy Van Meers! For the man who did the shooting and the killing, for Christ's sakes!. . . . (17)

The narrator provides us more information about the service and sacrifice Mora and other Mexican-American veterans gave to their country:

> Young Mora had been an infantryman in the Second Division (Indianhead) during the French invasion; and, he stood a mere thirty feet away from Chano Ortega, another Klail City youngster, who died during the drive for the Cerisy Forest on D-Day plus two. Young Mora and Ortega were among the numerous Texas mexicanos who'd volunteered for army service a year before this country declared war on the so-called Axis Power. (36)

The anger, frustration, and the seed that portends social transformation stemming from the murder of Mora are evident in the voice of the narrator:

> Ambrosio Mora's murder brought about a change; gradually, but a change. Something. The old men didn't know how to go about making a change, but they *knew* something had to give. They looked to the veterans: yes! This shit's got-to-stop, some of them said.
>
> Sure. But what? A lot of talk and a lot of noise, but first, what with one thing and then another followed by those-oh-so-familiar trial delays, interest began to peter out. The result? Well the trial came out three years later, and Deputy Sheriff Van Meers walked right out of that court house over there. Free as a bird shitting on the house roofs. . . .
>
> This was 1949, a year before Korea, and the mexicano people *again* raised some hell, but no, nothing came of it until don Aureliano Mora [Ambrosio Mora's father] himself took matters (in the shape of a crowbar) into his own hands.
>
> He got himself a crowbar and marched to the old Klail City Park, stood in front of a metal plaque (a County Historical Marker, they called it), and standing there [. . .] he broke that plaque in half; he then proceeded to smash and shatter the damn thing into very small pieces. After this, he ground the pieces into the Bermuda grass; not saying a word. . . . (37)

This incident symbolizes the frustration that Mexican-American soldiers experienced after loyally serving their country and returning home to find "business as usual."

Nonetheless, Mexican Americans were instrumental in the development of organizations, such as the American G.I. Forum, which went on to make demands for the improvement of the social, economic and political conditions of Mexican Americans.

Mercedes: 1960 to the Present

While Mexican-American veterans planted the seeds to bring about improvements in the standing of the Mexican-American community, by the mid-1960s winds of social change blew into places like the Valley and beyond. The period marked a changing of the status quo as well as an alteration of strategy for bettering the conditions of Mexican Americans. Instead of calling for change through traditional routes, the new leadership pressed for change through confrontational means. The Chicano Movement emerged in the mid 1960s throughout the Southwest, especially in California, Colorado and Texas.

In Texas, the establishment of the Mexican American Youth Organization (MAYO) and La Raza Unida Party (LRUP) pressed for radical approaches to bring about change in the Chicano community. Leaders such as José Ángel Gutiérrez, Mario Compean, Willie Velásquez, among others, led this transformation in Texas. In the Valley during this period, important events took place that pressed for change, including farm worker strikes, school walkouts, marches, demonstrations and voter registration drives. Such changes occurred in Mercedes as well, particularly in the form of the opening of the Colegio de Jacinto Treviño in 1969 as part of MAYO activities in the region. The presence of the Colegio along with related activities rankled the white establishment. And, reflecting the larger struggles going on within the Chicano Movement and La Raza Unida Party, internal political disagreements led to the closing of the Colegio in 1975 (Navarro, 2000).

Many in the older Mexican generations were horrified by the militant stand of younger Chicanos during this period. Nonetheless, there was some support among the older generation. David Montejano in his book *Quixote's Soldiers: A Local History of the Chicano Movement, 1966-1981*, draws on an anonymous op-ed appearing in one of the San Antonio newspapers, written by an "oldtimer" who tried to explain the changing of the guard within the Mexican-American community to members of his generation: "We started something right after the war—it was a good thing. It helped make changes; but for the last 15 years after things got a little better for us—after we got good jobs, a law degree, a doctor's license, a nice home, a new car—we let up" (Anonymous 7; see also Montejano, *Quixote's Soldiers* 114). The anonymous writer pointed out that while his generation made some improvements, much was still left undone. He observes that the younger Chicano generation is telling the older generation "You've talked about change. You've had your chance and you've failed. More over [sic] because we're going to get it—now" (Anonymous 7; see also Montejano, *Quixote's Soldiers* 114). The anonymous writer acknowledges the reaction of the older generation: "We are horror-struck. Because our young men—and especially our young women—aren't supposed to talk that way—and act that way. But are we right?" (Anonymous 7; see also Montejano, *Quixote's Soldiers* 114). The writer indicates that the youth are "ruffling feathers—including some of ours" and that they are publicly speaking "the things we used to say in private" and that the younger Chicano generation is challenging authority and that "some of that authority is ours" (Anonymous 7; see also Montejano, *Quixote's Soldiers* 114). The anonymous writer praises some of the successes that Chicanos in San Antonio have accomplished:

> They have opened segregated swimming pools, helped change the school system in San Antonio, organized barrio people to get what's coming to them, registered voters in record numbers all over South Texas, and most important, I suppose, they have given our youngsters a new dignity. (Anonymous 7; see also Montejano, *Quixote's Soldiers* 114)

The anonymous oldster concluded by saying that he did not think any member of the older generation could " . . . stand aside and point our fingers at the young men and women of MAYO. They are doing what they are doing because we failed them. We must take responsibility for that" (Anonymous 7; see also Montejano, *Quixote's Soldiers* 114-115).

The advent of the Chicano Movement and the raising of expectations and consciousness among Chicanos were important in setting a new course for improving the social, economic and political conditions of Chicanos. However, the changing demography of the region also played an important role in improving their lot. In particular, beginning in the 1960s the Chicano population started to grow disproportionately due to a young age structure, relatively high levels of fertility, and increasing immigration.

While there is generally a lack of information on the number of persons who are Mexican or Latino until recent decades, we do know that when "Mexican" was treated as a race in the 1930 U.S. census—the only time ever and a year after Hinojosa's birth—Mexicans accounted for about 54% of the population of Hidalgo County. Unfortunately, such data are not available for smaller places such as Mercedes. Thus, to the extent that Mercedes was similar to Hidalgo County in 1930, we can estimate that Mexicans made up one of every two of its residents that year. By 1990 to the present, Latinos—the large majority of whom are of Mexican-origin—accounted for nine of every ten inhabitants of Mercedes. Thus, through the decades, especially in the second half of the city's history, Mercedes became increasingly Mexicano or Latino. This trend is borne out when we consider the increasing presence of Mexicans in schools and politics.

Though previously Mexican students had been regularly outnumbered among Mercedes High School (MHS) graduates, by the late 1950s there was a significant change. Indeed, the share of Mexicans among MHS graduates rose progressively from about two-thirds in the 1957-1966 period, to four-fifths in the 1967-1970

Figure 4. Percentage of Mercedes High School Graduates Who are Latino for Selected Years.

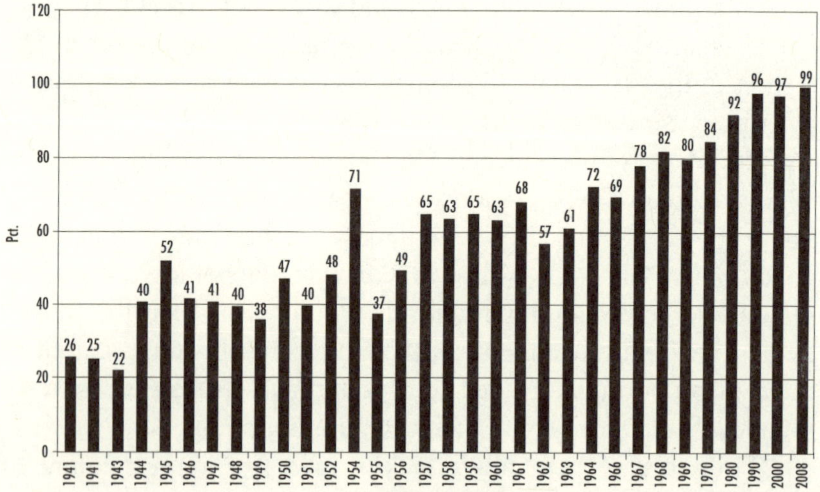

Source: *The Mercededs Enterprise.*

period, and upwards to 90% by 1980 (Figure 4). Latinos accounted for 99% of the 2008 MHS graduating class.

Things changed dramatically in the political arena as well. Over the forty-two year period from 1969, when the first Mexican mayor was elected in Mercedes, to 2010, Mexicans have held the mayoral post for thirty-eight of the forty-two years. The list of Mexican mayors of Mercedes during this period includes Adan Longoria, Liborio Hinojosa, Javier De Los Santos, Gilbert Dominguez, Norma Garcia, Miguel Castillo and Joel Quintanilla. Furthermore, of the forty-one persons elected as Mercedes commissioners from 1970 to 2010, thirty-eight (93%) have been Latinos.

Thus, it is clear that Mercedes underwent a tremendous change demographically with the community becoming increasingly Mexican or Latino. In the first half of the history of the community, despite representing about half of the population, Mexicans were virtually absent from the mainstream leadership of the community. Indeed, the local newspapers at that time rarely featured or reported the accomplishments of Mexicans. In the second half of the history of Mercedes, Mexicans were ubiquitous in the community. Many of the community leaders—educators, politicians, professionals and law enforcement personnel—are Mexican. Today Mexicans regularly populate the pages of the local newspaper. Given these changes, how similar are Latinos and whites today with respect to demographic, social and economic characteristics? Have the major racial and ethnic disparities of the past persisted today?

Demographic and Socioeconomic Differences between Latinos and Whites

To answer these questions, we need to turn to an examination of the demographic, social and economic characteristics of the Latino and white populations of Mercedes. Due to the relatively small size of the population of Mercedes, we must rely on data based on five-year estimates for the 2006-2010 period obtained from the American Community Survey.[3]

Age Structure

One of the major differences between Latinos and whites in Mercedes concerns variations in the age structure. Latinos are significantly younger than whites. In particular, whites are nearly four decades—38.7 years—older than Latinos. The median age of Latinos was 26.5 compared to 65.2 among whites in 2010.

Figure 5 shows the age distributions of Latinos and whites in Mercedes. About half (48.2%) of Latinos are less than 25 years of age; slightly more than half of whites (50.6%) are 65 years of age or older. By way of comparison, only 5.7% of whites are less than 25 years old. Put simply, many Latinos are young, but few whites are young; many whites are old, but few Latinos are old. This variation in age structure portends differential population growth favoring Latinos in the future. Without a major influx of young whites into Mercedes, the white population will virtually vanish from the community.

Figure 5. Age Distribution of Latino and White Population in Mercedes, 2006-2010.

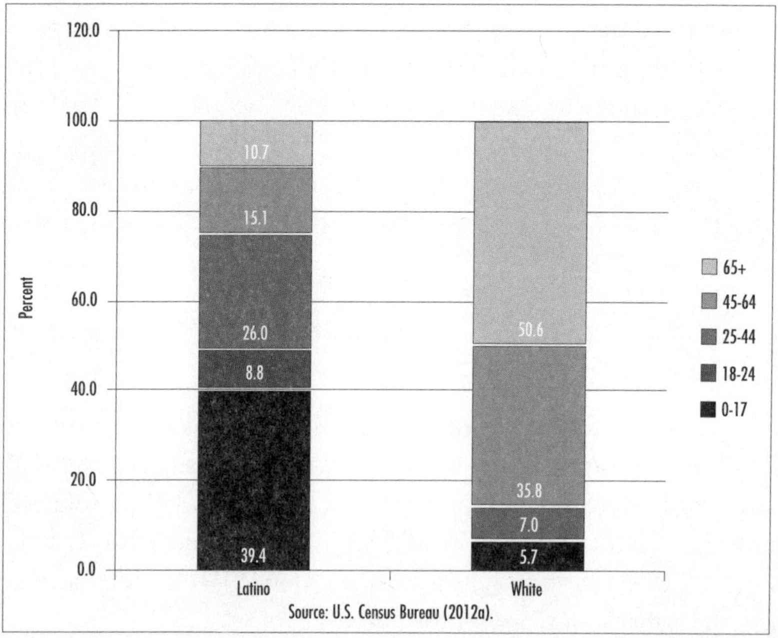

Source: U.S. Census Bureau (2012a).

Fertility

In fact, according to census data for the 2006-2010 period, all births in Mercedes occurred to Latina women. Indeed, approximately 14% of Latina women 15 to 50 years of age gave birth within the past twelve months; in contrast, white women did not give birth during this period (Table 1).

Table 1. Comparison of Latinos and Whites in Mercedes on Selected Demographic, Social, and Economic Characteristics, 2006-2010.

Selected Characteristics	Latino	White
Median Age	26.5	65.2
Fertility		
Pct. of Women 15 to 50 Years of Age Who Had a Birth in Past 12 Months	13.5	0.0
Pct. Born in Texas	69.7	17.2
Language Patterns:		
Pct. Monolingual English	10.1	84.4
Pct. Bilingual	55.3	10.2
Pct. Monolingual Other Language	34.6	5.4
Level of Education among Persons 25 and Older		
Pct. High School Graduates	52.9	84.4
Pct. College Graduates (Bachelor's degree or higher)	8.9	18.6
Pct. of Civilian Labor Force Unemployed	13.6	0.0
Median Family Income	$25,765	$45,769
Pct. of Families with Incomes Below the Poverty Level	40.3	16.7

Source: U.S. Census Bureau (2012a).

Texas Ties

Latinos and whites also differ significantly on the basis of place of birth. Approximately 70% of Latinos were born in Texas compared to only 17% of whites (Table 1). Note that only about one-fifth (21.2%) of Latinos are foreign-born, which is relatively low, given that 31% of Latinos in Hidalgo County and in Texas as a whole are foreign-born. Put simply, Latinos have much more profound roots in the region compared to whites, suggesting that many whites are "snowbirds," who have relocated to the area from, traditionally, the Midwest (see Richardson, 1999). For example, in Hidalgo County, as a whole, two-thirds (66.7%) of whites 65 and older were born in the Midwest with only one-ninth (10.9%) born in Texas.[4]

Language

In the American Community Survey, persons five years of age and older were asked whether they spoke English or another language at home. For individuals who reported that they spoke a language other than English at home, they were further asked to indicate their fluency in English as very good, good, not well, and not at all. This information is used here to create three categories: 1) monolingual English, which refers to people who speak English at home; 2) bilingual, which includes people who speak a language other than English at home and who speak English very well; and 3) monolingual non-English, which represent people who speak a language other than English at home and who speak English less than very well. Given the prevalence of Spanish among speakers in the area who speak a language other than English, the latter group is referred to as monolingual Spanish speakers.

Overall, the majority (55.3%) of Latinos in Mercedes are bilingual speakers, who speak Spanish at home and who are fluent in English (speaking it very well). An additional 35% of Latinos are considered monolingual Spanish speakers, i.e., they speak Spanish at home and speak English less than very well. Whites, on the other hand, tend to be almost exclusively (84.4%) monolingual English speakers, i.e., speaking English at home. Only one-tenth of whites are bilingual speakers. The low prevalence of Spanish among whites reflects the fact that they originate from elsewhere, predominantly the Midwest.

Language is a major theme in Rolando Hinojosa's literary work (Payne-Jackson and Espadas 66). Indeed, Mexican characters are largely bilingual and heavily use code-switching, in which they simultaneous use Spanish and English (Hinojosa, "The Sense of Place" 23). Still, in Hinojosa's work, there are some Mexican characters such as Becky and Ira Escobar, who speak primarily English. In the case of Becky, despite her white father (the retired Army captain Catarino Caldwell) speaking almost exclusively Spanish, her mother (Elvira) strongly encouraged Becky to speak only English. Becky tries to reclaim her Spanish language when she is an adult. In *Becky and Her Friends*, Elvira, Becky's mother, laments that her daughter is learning Spanish: "And now trying to speak in Spanish, yes. She also speaks English just like the Anglos; identically. And she still speaks it, of course, but she says that Spanish is important to her. Is that true? Where did she get that idea?" (139). Some upwardly mobile Mexican families in the Valley through time have encouraged their children to speak only English. Recall that for many years students in the Valley and in many parts of the Southwest were punished—usually through spankings—for speaking Spanish in school. Nevertheless in *Becky and Her Friends*, Sammie Jo Perkins, a white woman from the Klail-Blanchard-Cooke aristocracy who is fluent in Spanish (see below), offers a critique of parents who demand that their children speak English: "What Elvira did . . . was what numerous Mexican families did, rich and poor alike; they pushed English on the kids . . . That's worse than stupid, that's wrong!" (119).

In Hinojosa's literary work a noticeable share of whites speak at least some Spanish. The listener in *Becky and Her Friends* notes that certain white characters in the community "are at home, at ease, both in English *and* in Spanish. They are all Texas Anglos, and they are all bicultural, to use an old term now used popularly" (80). Nonetheless, the listener observes that: "[t]here are Valley Anglos who claim they are bilingual, but aren't. It takes work to speak as a native Spanish-speaker. Then, there are also those Anglos who say they wish they were bicultural and thus bilingual, but they're neither. This also takes time" (80). Three Anglo characters in *Becky and Her Friends* stand out as fluent Spanish speakers: the aforementioned Becky's father and Sammie Jo Perkins, as well as her father, the banker Noddy Perkins. The listener in the book points out that "Catarino Caldwell made himself into a mexicano years ago, before the time Becky was born. Tell you what, I bet there's not a hundred people left in the Valley, farm or city folks, who've heard him say a word in English. God's truth" (20). For his part, perhaps originally because of class reasons associated with his childhood as the orphaned son of an Anglo "fruit tramp" and drunkard (*Dear Rafe/Mi querido Rafa* 12, 149), banker Perkins naturally speaks Spanish as a normal part of his life. His daughter Sammie Jo's case is very different and specifically explained: "Spanish was my first language both in the house and of course out in the Ranch. . . . I learned it at home, first from the maids, their kids, the cowboys, Anglos some but mostly Mexican"; then, showing her family advantages, she learned more "later on in Mexico, Spain, and one summer at Smith's summer program in the Baleares. . . . I must be one of the few Texas Anglos who still speaks Spanish" (118-119). The language data from the 2006-2010 American Community Survey tend to be consistent with Sammie Jo's observation as only a relatively small share of whites were bilingual speakers at that time (10.2%).

Socioeconomic Status

Much of Hinojosa's literary work features the major racial and ethnic inequality that divides Mexicans and whites along socioeconomic lines. The arrival of whites into the region as well as the major loss of land that Mexicans experienced through legal and extra-legal means contributed to the making of the Mexican proletariat in places such as the Valley (Acuña, 1972; Montejano, 1987). Mexicans have historically been disproportionately represented among people who are high school dropouts, the unemployed, persons with low income, and among the poor. While there have undoubtedly been improvements in the socioeconomic standing of Latinos in the area, it is clear that the stratification system separating Latinos and whites persists.

In the area of education, among persons 25 and older in Mercedes, whites (84%) are significantly more likely than Latinos (53%) to have completed a high school degree (Table 1). Latinos with a bachelor's or higher degree continue to be a scarcity in Mercedes, with only one in eleven Latinos 25 and older having such a degree compared to almost one in five whites.

Furthermore, in the period between 2006 and 2010 joblessness in Mercedes was only a Latino problem. Indeed, the unemployment rate among Latinos at that time was 13.6%, signifying that about one in seven Latinos was without a job. In contrast, no white person was unemployed during the same period.

Moreover, when it comes to the median family income, for every one dollar that white families earned in 2006-2010, Latino families earned only fifty-six cents. At the time, the median income of Latino families was $25,765 compared to $45,769 among white families.

Finally, Latino families were nearly 2.5 times more likely than whites to have incomes below the poverty level in 2006-2010. While one in six white families was poor at this time, two in five Latino families were impoverished. Latino families with children who are headed by women without a husband present are especially vulnerable to poverty with slightly more than three-fifths (61.2%) of such families being impoverished in 2006-2010.

Intermarriage

Despite the contentious interethnic relationships between Mexicans and whites in the Valley, there has historically been an appreciable level of intermarriage across these groups. Hinojosa observes the noticeable presence of families which carry Spanish and non-Spanish surnames, as in the case of his family of origin (Hinojosa-Smith). Hinojosa declares:

> I will not pretend I knew each family of Mexican and Anglo parentage, but the following are ones I do remember living in Mercedes: Baum, Billings, Bowman, Brooks, Carr, Carroll, Closner, Foley, Gavlin, Handy, Heath, Howell, January, John-

> son, McGee, McVey, Moody, Parker, Postell, Pue, Rowland, Starcke, Thomas and Werbiski. There may have been others. (*A Voice of My Own* 19-20)

Recall, from above, that Catarino Caldwell, in *Becky and Her Friends,* epitomizes the white man who marries a Mexican woman and "Mexicanizes" himself linguistically and culturally. Nonetheless, given the demographic dictum that small groups tend to be more likely to intermarry than larger groups (Blau, 1977), it is the case that historically a greater portion of whites have married Mexicans than vice-versa in the Valley.

Data from the five-year pooled data from the 2006-2010 American Community Survey public-use files (Ruggles et al., 2012) were used to examine the ethnicity of husbands and wives living in Hidalgo County (where Mercedes is located) to assess the degree to which Mexican and whites marry each other in the early 21st century. Overall, as is expected in the case of members of large ethnic groups in a given setting, Mexicans are largely homogamous (marrying within the Mexican group) with 98% of Mexican husbands and 97% of Mexican wives having a Mexican spouse. Yet, there are no marriages involving white women in Hidalgo County married to a Mexican man. In contrast, white men are much more likely to be married to a Mexican woman with 18% of white husbands having a Mexican wife.

Hinojosa recounts the social relations between Mexican and white youth. He recalls that:

> In my time, during the forties, some Anglo girls dated Mexican boys, although I never knew of Anglo boys who dated Mexican girls. Still, at a recent school reunion, I saw some old Anglo schoolmates who married Mexican women. So, in keeping with border living, the practice of this type of marriage between the two groups continues now as it had in the past. (*A Voice of My Own* 25)

The relatively low prevalence of intermarriage between Mexicans and whites even today—despite what demographic theory would predict—suggests that there are boundary demarcations separating these two groups in the areas of close interpersonal relations.

Conclusions

Over nearly four decades Rolando Hinojosa has developed major literary works which together are referred to as the *Klail City Death Trip*. He draws heavily on material originating from his hometown of Mercedes, Texas, and its surroundings—"what I know," as he states ("The Sense of Place" 24). This region has undergone major transformations over nearly three centuries. The father's side of Hinojosa's family arrived in the region in the 1740s and his mother's side of the family made their way to the area in the late 1800s. In many ways, then, Hinojosa represents a blending of the Spanish, Mexican and Anglo roots that have formed *el Valle* over nearly three centuries. Rolando Hinojosa's origins and his deep sense of place and history in the region spanning across both sides of the Rio Grande/Bravo provides him a unique glimpse into the social life of Mexicans and whites on the Texas-Mexico borderland. In his *KCDT* series, Hinojosa draws on his hometown of Mercedes and its environs encompassed in the four counties (Cameron, Hidalgo, Starr and Willacy) that form *el Valle*.

Drawing on my own reflections of Mercedes, I cast sociological and demographic lenses on the changes that have taken place in this community and how these alterations are mirrored in the world that Hinojosa has crafted in the *KCDT*. The analysis shows a community that has experienced a tremendous amount of change in racial and ethnic relations over its hundred year history. The first half was characterized by the entrapment of Mexicans, indigenous to the Valley, in a position of subjugation at the hands of the dominant white newcomers. As the era was drawing to a close, World War II became a watershed event in which Mexican-American veterans fought heroically in that war and in the Korean War that followed. When they returned home, their demands for equality were largely unrealized. The second half of Mercedes' history saw the advent of the Chicano Movement along with demographic forces which brought about some upward social mobility and entrance into the region's institutions on the part of Mexicans. In this environment, Mexicans became the numerical majority in many avenues of social and political life. Nonetheless, despite their greater entrance into societal institutions, Mexicans still continue to lag socioeconomically compared to whites in the region as well as to their co-ethnics (Mexicans or Latinos) in other parts of the state.

Today, the Rio Grande Valley continues to be among the poorest regions of the country. Sociologists have observed that this area along with other regions like Appalachia, the Black Belt, the Mississippi Delta, Native American reservations, and the Texas-Mexico borderland have long been identified as persistently poor areas. The U.S. Department of Agriculture's (2012) Economic Research Service defines persistently poor counties as those places that have had poverty rates of 20% or higher since 1960. In general, persistently poor counties tend to have certain similarities: a large presence of persons of color, slow population growth or population decline, and absence of job growth. Yet, in some ways, the Valley is different from persistently poor areas, in that the region has experienced a significant amount of population and job growth over the last few decades. For example, the population of Hidalgo County, which contains Mercedes, nearly tripled from 283,323 in 1980 to 774,769 in 2010 (Texas State Library and Archives Commission, 2012).

The location of the region between a rich country and a poor country also creates a variety of unique challenges and opportunities. For example, the Valley region is isolated at a great distance from the federal and even state centers of political power—Mercedes is located some 1,750 miles from Washington, DC and approximately 330 miles from Austin, Texas, the state capital. The Valley region is easily forgotten or left out of policy discussions and debates at the national and state levels. Nonetheless, because of its geographic remoteness and its location straddling the United States and Mexico, as with many border areas throughout the world, historically there have been opportunities to engage in a variety of criminal enterprises involving underground activities like auto theft, drug smuggling, human smuggling and money laundering across international boundaries (see Richardson, 1999). This is a theme that Hinojosa has written about in such works as *Partners in Crime* (1985) and *Ask a Policeman* (1998). In an interview with Danilo Figueredo, Hinojosa makes reference to the crime and violence in the area illustrated in these novels:

> I set Klail City in the Lower Rio Grande Valley. The Valley is tied to the border of the states of Tamaulipas, Coahuila, and Chihuahua economically, psychologically, historically, and culturally. I noticed at the beginning of the 1980s that the economics of the Valley were changing, that there was a large influx of money and an increase in the number of banks. Given the traditional Valley way of life, something else was going on to bring that influx of money.
>
> It was and remains a false economy due to the smuggling of dope and the [drug] money. There is the rivalry of the dope smugglers and the violence it brings. Auto theft, too, is a big business. That's how I present the area. I can do no less since to cheat the reader is to cheat myself as a writer. (27, brackets included in original)

This context of get-rich-quick opportunities alongside entrenched poverty tempt some residents of the Valley, including public officials, to engage in criminal enterprises. In *Ask a Policeman*, Hinojosa also shows the increased militarization of the border which began in the 1990s and which the federal government has intensified after 9-11 (see Zilles, 2001).

Despite the historically high level of impoverishment in the Valley, the region has a hold on many native Latinos born in the area. Indeed, many Latinos find it difficult to break away from familial ties and the unique culture that characterizes *el Valle*. Other Latinos born in the Valley may leave for certain time periods in their lives to work, continue their schooling, enter the military, and so forth, but many eventually move back to the region (Garcia, 2011). For example, the central character, Fructuoso Alaniz García, in Hinojosa's short story titled "Es el Agua" ("It is the Water"), served in France in 1918. He then worked as a migrant farmworker laboring in many locations in Texas, the Midwest and South, but he always returns to live in the Valley. Fructuoso claims that it is the river's water that has a hold on Mexicans in the region. He notes: "We have a saying here in the Rio Grande Valley: *es el agua*; it's the water, the Rio Grande water. It claims you, you understand? It's yours and you belong to it, too. No matter where we work, we always come back. To the border, to the Valley" (*A Voice of My Own* 125). Still other Latinos originating from the Valley, such as Hinojosa and myself, remain tied to the area despite not living in the region for an extended period of time. Such bonds are maintained to the Valley through regular visits. Regardless, even though many of us do not envision living in the region from where we originate, when asked where I am from, I always reply "*del Valle*" ("from the Valley"), despite not having lived there during the last thirty-one years.

It is clear that while Rolando Hinojosa physically left the Valley, in a psychosocial and intellectual sense he never left Mercedes and its surrounding area. Indeed, the memories of his youth about the region and its people, language, and culture consistently emerge in his writings associated with the *Klail City Death Trip* series and beyond. He has a strong sense of place as he says and writes about the place and the people that he knows best (Busby 104-105; Hinojosa, "The Sense of Place" 19-20).

What does the future hold for Mercedes and the larger Valley region? Given current demographic trends, the future of Mercedes will almost certainly be dictated exclusively by the Mexican population. Certainly, with a median age of 65 and only a handful of individuals less than 25 years of age, the white population is expected to decline significantly as it ages even further. Hinojosa reflects on how, in contrast to earlier times, local Mexicans are now predominantly featured in Mercedes' newspaper *The Enterprise*; he remarks:

> And now? The tilt is inescapable; due to the 90% Texas Mexican population; the ads for restaurants, garages, car dealerships and other business establishments are for and by Texas Mexicans. It's a Texas Mexican town; the older Texas Anglo generation still publishes its announcements regarding the book clubs, the garden societies and so on, and this will go on until they die out. As for their sons and daughters and grandsons and granddaughters, the majority no longer live there. (*A Voice of My Own* 26)

In many ways, the demographic patterns observed in Mercedes—in which the community has become predominantly Latino propelled by the youthfulness of Latinos and the outmigration and aging of whites—are similar to trends observed in rural communities in California, where the outmigration of whites resulted in such communities becoming heavily Latino and poor (Allensworth and Rochín, "Ethnic Transformation in Rural California" and "The Latinization of Rural Places in California"). As noted above, Mercedes and other communities constituting the Valley region continue to be isolated from other parts of the state and consistently are among the poorest communities in the country. Yet, despite massive population growth and the large number of jobs and ever-present construction that has taken place in the Valley, jobs employing local Latinos have tended to be low-wage jobs that do not lift people out of poverty.

Finally, the discourse presented here, drawing on social science and humanitics perspectives, is an instructive approach for scholars from these broad disciplines who seek to understand and situate sociologically and demographically the work of literary writers. This work allows us to comprehend more fully the sociological and demographic context that has informed Hinojosa's novels associated with the *Klail City Death Trip* series along with his other writings. Sociologists can also gain a better understanding of the novels of literary authors by examining the places where writers spent their early, formative years.

Notes

[1] Issues from the *Mercedes Enterprise* were examined for individual years (1941 to 1970) and for selected years (1980, 1990, 2000, and 2008). As such, the analysis included 32 years of data. The racial and ethnic designation of graduates was determined roughly with the surnames of the graduates.

[2] A list of mayors and commissioners over the period from 1930 to 2010 was obtained from the Mercedes city government's office to conduct this part of the analysis.

[3] Data for this part of the analysis are obtained from the U.S. Census Bureau's Fact Finder webpage located at http://factfinder2.census.gov/faces/nav/jsf/pages/index.xhtml.

[4] These figures were obtained through the use of the 2006-2010 American Community Survey public-use file obtained from Ruggles et al. (2012).

References

Acuña, Rodolfo F. *Occupied America: The Chicano Struggle Toward Liberation*. New York: Harper & Row, 1972. Print.

Allensworth, E.M. and R.I. Rochín. "Ethnic Transformation in Rural California: Looking Beyond the Immigrant Farmworker. *Rural Sociology* 63.1 (1998): 26-50. Print.

___. "The Latinization of Rural Places in California: Growing Immiseration or Latino Power?" *Journal of the Community Development Society* 29.1 (1998): 119-145. Print.

Alonzo, Armando. *Tejano Legacy: Rancheros and Settlers in South Texas, 1734-1900*. Albuquerque: University of New Mexico Press, 1998. Print.

Anonymous. "¿Por qué MAYO?" *La Nueva Raza* 2.4 (1969): 7. Print.

Blau, Peter. *Inequality and Heterogeneity: A Primitive Theory of Social Structure*. New York: The Free Press, 1977. Print.

Bruce-Novoa, Juan. "Who's Killing Whom in Belkin County: Rolando Hinojosa's Narrative Production." *Monographic Review* 3.1-2 (1987): 288-297. Print.

Busby, Mark. "Faulknerian Elements in Rolando Hinojosa's *The Valley*." *MELUS* 11.4 (1984):103-109. Print.

Carroll, Patrick J. *Felix Longoria's Wake: Bereavement, Racism, and the Rise of Mexican American Activism*. Austin: University of Texas Press, 2003. Print.

Figueredo, Danilo H. "Ask a Mystery Writer: A Conversation with Rolando Hinojosa." *Multicultural Review* 8.3 (1999): 26-27. Print.

Garcia, Jesus Alberto. *Return Migrations, Assimilation, and Cultural Adaptations among Mexican American Professionals from the Lower Rio Grande Valley of South Texas*. Ph.D. Dissertation, Texas A&M University, 2011. Print.

The Handbook of Texas Online. "Mercedes, Texas." Denton: Texas State Historical Association, 2010. Web. 28 September 2010.

Hinojosa, Rolando. "Always Writing: A Chicano Life." *World Literature* 75 (2001): 65-71. Print.

___. *Ask a Policeman*. Houston: Arte Público Press, 1998. Print.

___. *Becky and Her Friends*. Houston: Arte Público Press, 1990. Print.

___. *Dear Rafe/Mi querido Rafa*. Houston: Arte Público Press, 2005. Print.

___. *Klail City*. Houston: Arte Público Press, 1987. Print.

___. "No Furniture So Charming." *ANQ* 10.2 (1997): 42-45. Print.

___. *Partners in Crime*. Houston: Arte Público Press, 1985. Print

___. "The Sense of Place." Saldívar 18-24.

___. "A Voice of One's Own." Saldívar 11-17.

___. *A Voice of My Own: Essays and Stories*. Houston: Arte Público Press, 2011. Print.

___. *We Happy Few*. Houston: Arte Público Press, 2006. Print.

Hinojosa-S.[mith], Rolando R. *Estampas del Valle y otras obras*. Berkeley, Quinto Sol, 1973. Print.

Martinez, Manuel Luis. "An Interview with Rolando Hinojosa-Smith. *Indiana Review* 28.1 (2006): 7-10. Print.

Mercedes Enterprise. "Mexico Party for High School Graduates." *Mercedes Enterprise* 7 June 1946: 1. Print.

Montejano, David. *Anglos and Mexicans in the Making of Texas, 1836-1986*. Austin: University of Texas Press, 1987. Print.

___. *Quixote's Soldiers: A Local History of the Chicano Movement, 1966-1981*. Austin: University of Texas Press, 2010. Print.

Navarro, Armando. 2000. *La Raza Unida Party: A Chicano Challenge to the U.S. Two-Party Dictatorship*. Philadelphia: Temple University Press. Print.

News-Tribune. "Honor Roll Announced." *News-Tribune* 25 Apr. 1941: 1. Print.

Payne-Jackson, Arvilla, and Juan Espadas. "Rolando Hinojosa-Smith's Sense of Place: Sociolinguistic Aspects." *MACLAS Latin American Essays* 12 (1998): 63-82. Print.

Richardson, Chad. *Batos, Bolillos, Pochos, and Pelados: Class and Culture on the South Texas Border*. Austin: University of Texas Press, 1999. Print.

Ruggles, Steven, J. Trent, Alexander, Katie Genadek, Ronald Goeken, Matthew B. Schroeder, and María Herrera-Sobek. *Integrated Public Use Microdata Series: Version 5.0*. Minneapolis: Historical Census Projects / University of Minnesota, 2012. Machine-readable database.

Saldívar, José David, ed. *The Rolando Hinojosa Reader: Essays Historical and Critical*. Houston: Arte Público Press, 1985. Print.

Texas State Historical Association. *Texas Almanac: City Population History from 1850-2000*. Denton: Texas State Historical Association, 2012. Web. 2 April 2012.

Texas State Library and Archive Commission. *Population, Texas Counties*. Austin: Texas State Library and Archive Commission, 2012. Web. 4 June 2012.

U.S. Census Bureau. *2010 American Community Survey 5-Year Estimates*. Washington, DC: U.S. Census Bureau, 2012. Web. 2 April 2012.

___. *2010 Summary File 1 100% Data*. Washington, DC: U.S. Census Bureau, 2012. Web. 2 April 2012.

U.S. Department of Agriculture. *Rural Poverty, Income, and Welfare: Poverty Geography*. Washington, DC: U.S. Department of Agriculture, Economic Research Service, 2012. Web. 4 June 4, 2012.

Weber, David J. *Myth and the History of the Hispanic Southwest*. Albuquerque: University of New Mexico Press, 1988. Print.

Zilles, Klaus. *Rolando Hinojosa: A Reader's Guide*. Albuquerque: University of New Mexico Press, 2001. Print.

Rolando Hinojosa's Texas-Mexican Border Writing the Landscape of Migrants, Mafias and Militarization

Klaus Zilles
Ramon Llull University, Barcelona

> "They're just part of the package of the systematic violence that some of the undesirable element from across the river has been visiting upon us."
>
> Florencio "Chip" Valencia, Belken County District Attorney

Hinojosa's border narratives live off the tension that results from the portrayal of the border as a landscape that denotes separation, but which at the same time constitutes a special geo-political space where interest groups meet and interact in spite of, because of, even regardless of, "the border." In particular, Hinojosa's two mystery novels deal expressly with recent ideological constructions of a border-crisis narrative. The thrust of Hinojosa's account gains remarkable momentum in the sequel to *Partners in Crime* (1985), entitled *Ask a Policeman* (1992), in which he turns the spotlight on the law enforcement efforts directed at illegal immigration, drug-trafficking and organized crime. Hinojosa's main character, chief inspector Rafe Buenrostro, understands that his particular kind of police work not only entails the unraveling of a complex murder plot but also the deconstruction of the simplistic, sensationalist narratives of a border crisis. Aided by his team, he creates a public forum for debate on border issues by actually trying to uncover the motives for border crime, by de-escalating and appeasing the antagonisms, and by scrutinizing the evidence for the elusive truth. What he finds is that the "undesirable element" that is responsible for the violence "from across" are not the wetbacks and the undocumented workers (158).[1] In *Ask a Policeman*, organized border crime is in the hands of a few, traditionally moneyed, Mexican families who own houses in Texas where their money is always welcome. They have impressive bank accounts in Texas, own real estate in plush Klail City neighborhoods, buy their expensive cars from Texas car dealers, send their children to American schools, seek treatment in U.S. hospitals, and satisfy the needs of coke users on the Texas side.

Ask a Policeman is the work of a novelist at the height of his art in that it deals with *the* one most important issue on the border, which is to say it has all the genre specifications of the murder mystery (and may even improve upon a few), and also that it represents a logical continuation of the themes, the generic experimentation, and the thematic foci of his ongoing literary project, the *Klail City Death Trip Series* (*KCDTS*). Although *Ask a Policeman* fairly closely follows the format of the detective novel (the "police procedural" to be precise), the author weaves into his principal narrative a series of subplots and motifs that are designed to make subtle, but forceful, commentary on political and social conditions in the embattled bicultural border region. The incorporation of these elements showcases Hinojosa's writerly control because they neither interfere with the core crime-mystery plot, nor do they take on the form of lectures on racial and social affairs in the Valley.

Hinojosa's acute appraisal of historical and political developments, and the incisive literary treatment he furnishes in his narrative, has been the subject of previous studies. For instance, there is little doubt that David Montejano's 1987 *Anglos and Mexicans in the Making of Texas, 1836-1986,* spearheads revisionist Texas historiography. The particular mode in which "Montejano's self-conscious revisionist history" and Hinojosa's "creative interpretation of a native son" can mutually inform one another has been established by Erlinda Gonzalez-Berry (5). Subsequently, Hinojosa's exploration of the history of landownership in South Texas, and the role it played in the subjugation and segregation of Texas Mexicans over the course of a century and a half, was showcased in a close reading of the *KCDTS* against the backdrop of Montejano's sociohistorical account (see Zilles 145-169).

Foreign Military Doctrine Comes Home

In the case of *Ask a Policeman*, it is another trailblazing study, Timothy Dunn's 1996 *The Militarization of the U.S.-Mexico Border*, which lends itself to the purpose of the present study, in part because the time span of Dunn's inquiry perfectly coincides with the temporal setting of *Ask a Policeman* and, more importantly, because its abundant information on law enforcement efforts and the gradual militarization of the border, as we shall see, tallies significantly with Hinojosa's fictional treatment of the same incidents and phenomena.

Thus, the central subject I would like to examine here is that of border crossers, both undocumented workers and, more closely, organized border crime which has been—and is currently—at the center of alarmist portrayals of both potential and actual crises. My aim is to show how these portrayals tie in with the notion of militarization, and how these—one may almost say archetypical—border topics are treated in Hinojosa's books, and in particular in *Ask a Policeman.*

We shall see, by taking a closer look at the numerous border crossings and cross-border lives portrayed in the book, how Hinojosa crafts a complex account of international border crime that transcends the stories of a one-sided national border security threat as it is routinely touted by politicians and the media. These cross-border lives involve both the novel's main players and secondary and minor characters, and they extend to spheres such as business, education, friendship, adultery, crime, corruption, police work, news journalism, real estate, and even gunshots and floating corpses.

Hinojosa also casts doubt on the stigma of Mexico as a country trapped in a Third-World bubble precariously clinging to the border of the world's last and only superpower. This is executed through subtle but insightful commentary which sets the record straight on Mexico's advances in computerizing the population and modern methods of law enforcement. These observations are interwoven with allusions to computer-based inhabitant registration schemes and public policy issues that differ significantly in Mexico and the U.S. owing to the provenance and history of the two countries' legal systems.

The interlocking sequence of unsuspected, countercurrent eye-openers does not end here. One iconoclastic notion leads to another, and standard objections to computerized registration of citizens and resident aliens, usually on the grounds of invasion of privacy and resulting perils of a police-state, are contextualized—and thus deflated—by portraying the border as a playground for diverse law enforcement agencies jockeying for jurisdiction and, ultimately, for power, often regardless or in detriment of national interest. The law enforcement efficacy resulting from these dynamics is perhaps best described in the words of Theo Crixell, who has just retired from the Federal Attorney General's office after him and his family receiving too many death threats from drug lords: "The truth is that there is so goddamn much dope and shit coming over, that half the time they just stumble over it accidentally, and then they have the unmitigated gall and nerve to call it a haul" (*Ask a Policeman* 61).

Watching the Border

On an earlier occasion I expressed my initial dismay and rejection at the quantity and the graphic nature of the violence depicted in the novel, although I had duly noted the clear stand the book takes on armament and militarization (Zilles 68). However, in hindsight, and in the face of recent events, the violence in *Ask a Policeman* may strike one as downright understated when compared to the massacres occurring on the border currently and in the past few years. Indeed, in the context of border crime, it may seem almost gratuitous to draw attention to both recent atrocities and law enforcement achievements on the border, particularly on the Mexican side. Still, the subsequent list of the most conspicuous incidents that have made the headlines during the composition of this text in 2010 goes some way toward showing how accurate, almost visionary, Hinojosa's narrative is:

- August 26: The mass killing of seventy-two Central and South American undocumented immigrants, both men and women, by Mexican drug gang, 'Los Zetas,' at a ranch in Tamaulipas.
- August 27: the prosecutor of the crime vanishes.
- August 31: Mexican police arrest drug lord Edgar Valdez Villarreal, 'La Barbie.'
- August 31: one tenth of Mexico federal police officers are fired for failing "trust control exams."
- September 8: the prosecutor assigned to the Tamaulipas crimes is found dead.
- September 13: Mexican marines arrest Sergio Villarreal Barragán, 'El Grande,' in Puebla.
- September 20: after the slaying of two of its reporters, *El Diario*, a Ciudad Juárez daily, called for a truce with drug traffickers, asking them what they want the newspaper to report.

These are only a few of the most recent, and most striking, incidents that are symptomatic of the battle involving drug- and immigration-related atrocities and law enforcement efforts which hold the border in sway. The inordinate degree of violence and suffering along the border becomes manifest in a staggering death toll —over 28,000 drug-related deaths since December 2006, when President Felipe Calderón's military offensive against organized drug crime was launched. The number doubled from 2008 to 2009, peaking at 6,300 killed in drug- or human-trafficking- related crimes.

Meanwhile, in the U.S., advocates of anti-immigrant legislation are increasingly giving vent to what David Lloyd has labeled the "monologic desire of cultural nationalism" (quoted in Saldívar 5), culminating in the passage of Senate Bill Arizona. The bill has sparked not only protests against racial profiling, but also demonstrations against the increasing militarization of the border, the very issue chosen by Hinojosa as a central theme in the novel he published twelve years ago. The following excerpt from a July 28, 2010 article by Ed Pilkington in the *The Guardian* reviews some of the main civil rights issues raised by the bill as it was initially passed:

> Under the terms of the original Senate Bill (SB) 1070, Arizona police were obliged to investigate the immigration status of anyone they encounter—whether for a traffic violation, a neighbour dispute or any other minor matter—whom they suspected of not having proper documents.
>
> The law threatened to wrestle immigration policy out of the hands of the federal government and fragment it across the US, with many other states already expressing interest in copying Arizona's example.
>
> [. . .] While some of the most draconian aspects of the law have been blocked, Hispanic groups are unhappy about sections including a provision to make it a crime for undocumented day labourers to get into an employer's vehicle and a vaguely-worded clause against the "transportation" and "harbouring" of illegal immigrants.

Naturally, some argue, none of these measures would be necessary if the U.S. was able to secure its national borders more effectively. The extent to which advocates of "complete border surveillance" believe that it may actually solve any of the problems caused by the immediate adjoining/colliding of what many still call the First and the Third Worlds can perhaps be gauged from a *60 Minutes* feature entitled "Watching the Border," aired January 10, 2010.

In the feature, *60 Minutes* investigates the case of SBInet (Secure Border Initiative Network), a "virtual fence" (so named by President George W. Bush) along the U.S.-Mexico border, commissioned by Homeland Security and contracted to the Boeing Corporation. It consists of electronic observation towers equipped with long-range radar, high-resolution cameras and underground sensors. The report is not really concerned with the underlying causes of border crossing. Instead, it examines the scandalous squandering of taxpayers' money on a billion-dollar surveillance system which was promised to be completed by 2009 and guaranteed apprehension of 95% of all incursions along the *entire* border. After three years' work on the fence, Homeland Security now prefers to call it "a prototype" that is being phased out and is to be replaced with a newer version. Between the lines of the report's "Your tax dollars at work" angle, however, a few glimpses at the true issues may be gleaned.

For instance, Mark Borkowsky, the executive director of SBI-net, responds haltingly, but still affirmatively, when *60 Minutes'* Steve Kroft rephrases the over-zealous objective of the virtual fence: "In simple terms, what you want to do, you want to be able to look at the entire border with Mexico" ("Watching the Border"). Once more, the avowed goal of the project reveals itself as the fanciful idea of wanting to seal the entire border against practically all incursions, a design which smacks both of science fiction and of large corporations securing lucrative government contracts.[2] Similarly, in the same "Watching the Border" segment, *60 Minutes* alludes to the underlying causes of migration and border crossing only in passing: Professor Wayne Cornelius, director of the Center for Comparative Immigration Studies at the University of California at San Diego, ventures that the fence only provides the illusion of border security. The only thing, says Cornelius, that has ever stopped people from crossing the border south to north was the Great Depression. He predicts that illegal border crossers will find ways around this new obstacle just as they managed to elude the previous ones. "They would be crazy not to," Cornelius adds laconically. Indeed, this is the only instance in the entire feature that reminds us of the actual circumstances causing people to risk their lives and freedom in their attempt to enter the U.S. illegally, i.e. sheer economic need or, in the case of drug smugglers, the demand for drugs in exchange for hard dollars north of the border. As things stand now, 90% of those trying to cross eventually succeed, according to a study commissioned by the Border Patrol.

A Slippery Slope

Hence it would be an understatement to say that the Border Patrol and other law enforcement agencies are currently overtaxed by their mission to secure the borders. As a result, the need to call on the military to secure the national border is voiced time and again. However, the *Posse Comitatus* Act, a federal statute, does not allow for military involvement in domestic law enforcement matters (see Dunn 106-08), and in fact, secretary of Homeland Security, Janet Napolitano, told *60 Minutes* in March, 2009 that she considers the involvement of the military at the present time not a matter of urgency but rather "an absolute last resort" ("The War Next Door").

The Secretary's disclaimer notwithstanding, the central premise of this reading of Rolando Hinojosa's *Ask a Policeman* is the *de facto*—albeit creeping—militarization process at the U.S.-Mexican border which undermines the constitutional separation of law enforcement and the military. It is precisely this process that is at the center of Timothy Dunn's 1996 book *The Militarization of the U.S.-Mexico Border, 1978-1992: Low Intensity Conflict Doctrine Comes Home.* The historian compellingly explores the implications of an official U.S. military doctrine which divides armed conflict into high, medium and low. Interestingly, and rather cynically, high, low or medium does not necessarily refer to the actual intensity of the conflict. Rather, conflict is considered low, for example, "because of its implications for U.S. forces—namely, the avoidance of the sustained deployment in battle of U.S. troops and the U.S. casualties that would ensue" (Dunn 20).

While Low Intensity Conflict (LIC) may entail the avoidance of consequential effects to U.S. troops, "the impact of such conflicts can be quite devastating and violent for the local people" (Dunn 20). Dunn identifies the relevance of LIC in the context of the militarization of the U.S.-Mexican border specifically in "the analysis of immigration and drug enforcement efforts," either one having historically been regarded as necessary measures against "Mexican-origin people" (Dunn 19). The term "Mexican-origin people" is crucial here in that it is perhaps the only suitable term under which to group the people that are in effect the near-exclusive target of militarized law enforcement measures on the border. The label comprises "principally undocumented immigrants, smugglers of drugs and immigrants, and *persons suspected of belonging* to either of these categories (with most of the suspects, in the eyes of INS and its Border Patrol unit, being Mexican Americans and Mexican Immigrants)" (Dunn 155, *my emphasis*). This tidy definition of a target is symptomatic of what Dunn refers to as the "construction of an 'enemy,'" which is essential to the process of militarization in that this type of process requires the evocation of a national security threat.

"Ask a p'liceman"

In the novel, the conjuring up a national security threat turns out to be primarily the agenda of politicians such as the district attorney, the sheriff and the congressman who depend on the good graces of the electorate. While persons of this ilk are gung ho about armament, front-line law enforcement professionals are not. Tellingly, Rafe Buenrostro repeatedly cancels on, hangs up on, or dodges his D.A. in order to do "real police work" (*Ask a Policeman* 63, 139, 178-79). For instance, right at the opening of the novel, just after Lisandro Gómez is sprung from the Kail City Court House jail, the team of detectives is hard at work to gather as many fresh leads as possible. Desk sergeant Al Contreras pokes his head into the squad room to give a heads-up to Rafe, and this in the context of establishing from the outset of the novel that misguided militarization efforts are a central theme:

> "Sorry to bother you, Chief. Thought I'd warn you, though. D.A. Chip Valencia's in the hall."
> "We're not here, Contreras."
> [. . .]
> Dorson. [. . .] "What's with the D.A.? Does this have to do with this morning's meeting?"
> "Most likely, and Gómez's escape, I imagine." Buenrostro stared at the parking lot. "He wants the county to buy a tank."
> Dorson: "A tank? What else? A Howitzer? I don't even trust our guys with the .38s we issue them. Good Lord."
> [. . .]
> Dorson poured two cups of coffee. "How do we stop Chip Valencia, Rafe? Can we stop him?" (13)

Further into the novel, when the detectives are setting a trap to lure Felipe Segundo Gómez to the Texas side, which will enable the crime lab to conduct a surreptitious search of his GMC truck, the issue is picked up once again. Here, Hinojosa adds complexity to the subject matter by tying it to the novel's title. The detectives trust that their ruse will work because Felipe Segundo Gómez has a "romantic streak" which forever tempts him to try and lead the police by their noses, presuming that "all policemen are fools" (43). This is when Peter Hauer laughs and throws in the phrase "Ask a p'liceman." Aside from echoing the novel's title, the remark hints at the detectives' stand on mixing law enforcement and military.[3] It's no coincidence that in the midst of doing "real police work" Buenrostro picks up an accordion folder he has brought with him from a meeting with the D.A. Valencia. A "booklet, showing an armed man in a camouflage suit, fell on the floor. He picked it up," and comments: "Just got all this junk from Chip Valencia" (43-44). In response to Rafe's report that Valencia "says there's enough" in the booklet "to come up with an army the size of Costa Rica's," detective Ike Cantú points out that "Costa Rica doesn't have an army" (44). Buenrostro, as he moves to throw the catalog of military equipment in the wastebasket, replies dismissively, "Chip doesn't know that" (44).

Costa Rica is not the only Central American country mentioned in the novel and it will prove revelatory to revisit the significance of Central America in relation with Low Intensity Conflict (LIC) at a later juncture. The immediate implications of the passage, though, point to the incompatibility of the work done by local law enforcement on the ground with the decisions made over their heads by policymakers, lobbyists, and technocrats. In the *60 Minutes* report on SBInet the investigators express amazement and disbelief when they discover that nobody bothered to ask the Border Patrol agents on the ground about the usefulness of the new equipment. In Belken County, too, somehow somebody forgot to "ask a policeman."

In Hinojosa's text, the political affiliations of the advocates of armament and militarization along the border are made plain by D.A. Valencia's display of portraits of presidents Reagan and George H.W. Bush in his office. Also, the hit and miss approach to the militarization process seems consistent with the changeable, populist demands of political campaigning and winning votes, as Dunn indicates:

> The militarization [. . .] reached a high point under the Bush administration, mainly via the expansion of the [Reagan's] War on Drugs. However, the implementation of important characteristics of LIC doctrine in the U.S.-Mexico border region does not appear to have been a conscious, calculated project on the part of either policy-makers or border-area law enforcement officials. Rather, it seems to have occurred in a largely piecemeal fashion, cumulatively resulting in the de facto militarization of the U.S.-Mexico border. This outcome is not entirely illogical, however, given that many policymakers periodically, if not consistently, portrayed undocumented immigration and illicit drug trafficking principally as security issues—indeed, drug trafficking was formally elevated to the status of "national security threat." Consequently, enforcement efforts in the U.S.-Mexico border region

> were expanded and additional resources set in place to further pursue a punitive, coercive, and largely unilateral approach in addressing undocumented immigration and illicit drug trafficking—complex issues that were intimately related to much larger international, social, political, and economic phenomena. (149)

Dunn further describes how a great deal of this process of gradual militarization was initially centered in the Immigration and Naturalization Service (INS) but, after 1986 it increasingly converged with the activities of the DEA, and thus, caught in the slipstream of the "War on Drugs," it took on a decidedly more militaristic quality. This was in part due to the military's considerably diminished areas of activity after the cold war which compelled the armed forces to look for new fields of operation.

Dunn examines three dimensions of border militarization: equipment, operational characteristics and "the overall social control essence of this framework" (151). He provides tables listing the "LIC related hardware" such as military helicopters, night vision equipment, infrared radar and electronic intrusion-detector sensors, aerostat radar balloons, M-16 rifles, a closed-circuit television surveillance system, and the list goes on (151). All these were "on loan" from the military, which meant that they could be operated and maintained by the military itself, which leads us to the second dimension of border-militarization, i.e. the increasing encroachment of military operational procedures on border law enforcement. This process, according to Dunn, reached a first climax with the establishment of Joint Task Force 6 (JTF-6) in 1989, which was set up in Texas "by the Pentagon to coordinate the military's expanding support for the antidrug efforts of border-region police agencies" (153). From 1990 to 1992 alone, JTF-6 carried out 775 missions, about half of them related to drug enforcement. Dunn stresses the fact, though, that many missions went beyond the War on Drugs and involved immigration matters. "Thus," he states, "military troops were at least indirectly involved in immigration and other broader law enforcement concerns in the border region. This development (which was a spillover effect of sorts) illustrates the "slippery slope" or "creeping" dynamic of LIC doctrine-style militarization (153).

The militarization process was not one-directional, though. Aside from the military getting obliquely or directly involved in police work, Dunn cites multiple instances of civilian law enforcement assuming paramilitary characteristics, which culminated in a 1989-90 large scale INS operation to control Central American asylum seekers in the Lower Rio Grande Valley (154). Further instances of the gradual hollowing-out affecting the division of military and law enforcement even saw the increased collaboration between U.S. and Mexican military. Operation Alliance (1986-92) involved law enforcement agencies on federal, state, and local levels plus military support targeting both drug and immigration concerns. "One of the most ominous instances of force integration," Dunn adds, "was the Alien Border Control Committee, a multiagency federal task force created in 1986 and headed by the INS that created an elaborate contingency plan to round up and deport thousands of 'alien terrorists and undesirables' and to supposedly seal the border" (154).

The Border Patrol State

What is remarkable about these operations is their blatant social control agenda, targeting mainly Mexican-origin people, along with Central Americans thrown in among the usual suspects. Aside from the inevitable civil rights infringements suffered by undocumented immigrants, imagine the devastating effect on civil liberties and the self-esteem of U.S. citizens and legal aliens, who are invariably and intrinsically suspect of belonging to the targeted groups.

In fact, Dunn elucidates on this third dimension of LIC, namely the aspect of social control, by providing insight into the mechanics of this process which seems to depend on creating labels such as "criminal aliens." Initially, the meaning of this label extended mainly to immigrants previously convicted of serious crimes, yet subsequently it was also used for those who had committed minor offenses, thus enhancing the capacity for social control (Dunn 155).

The upshot of this gradual three-pronged advance of militarization is that along the border, there gradually developed a joint force of militarized police and, conversely, military performing law enforcement tasks. Together, they were able to act with greatly enhanced authority and power in the supervision and "management" of all those individuals who might reasonably be suspected of being illegal Mexican immigrants. In the context of Rolando Hinojosa's literary project, the historical dimension of control and supervision of the immigrant labor force has been amply documented. Now, with his 1998 detective novel, Hinojosa's South Texas chronicle has arrived on the threshold of the 21st century with a harrowing account of escalating border violence, crime and facile attributions of guilt.

Ask a Policeman offers a shrewd adjustment to the habitual portrayal of one-sided, domestic, border control problems, which more often than not are really predicaments rooted in intricate dynamics involving at least two or more countries. In the novel, the conventional, pedestrian take on border crime invariably comes out of the mouth the aforementioned Belken County D.A. Chip Valencia, who is lobbying for a budget increase in order to buy automatic rifles and a minitank. Valencia does not content himself with continually harping on the "the systematic violence that some of the undesirable element from across the river has been visiting upon us" (158). With a torrent of press releases, he himself actively contributes to the sensationalist portrayal of border crime and the military rhetoric associated with it.

Rafe Buenrostro, for his part, goes so far as to campaign against the attempts of militarizing the border. As chief inspector of the Belken County Police, he is in a position to oppose Valencia's campaign. For instance, he instructs his colleague Peter Hauer to contact the new editor of the local newspaper, invite her to coffee, and create a new message: "We need publicity on the unneeded budget increase and the high risks in the use of the AK-

47s, the Uzis, the lot. How much this would cost the taxpayers. Mention the mini-tank, the County budget, the need for improvement of county roads, pour it on" (44).

A typical misrepresentation of border life and border conflict is denounced in subtle and oblique fashion in a longer passage featuring again Peter Hauer as he visits the INS in the "fortress-like" federal structure behind the Amity Bridge (*Ask a Policeman* 32). The passage culminates in an episode in which Art Styles of the INS jokes about a congressman from North Dakota who has come to visit with local INS officers and businessmen from both sides of the border. Styles quotes the congressman as saying: "Welcome to the hub of activity where we who serve are proud to hold off the hordes of hardened criminals and thus protect the citizens from Mexican banditry" (33). The congressman tells the attendants "that he was well-acquainted with border problems since his own state bordered with Canada" (33). The passage is couched in a portrayal of Art Styles and Peter Hauer as native border dwellers who, speaking Spanish, engage in facetious banter about the incident with the Mexican-American secretaries.

Apart from showing up the politician's misguided officiousness in comparing the Mexican and Canadian border, and even "welcoming" the border dwellers to their own turf, the significance of the passage reaches out in several directions. For instance, as Hauer approaches the headquarters of the INS, the former Fort Jones, a U.S. cavalry outpost on the border, he thinks back on his upbringing as the son of a sergeant-major stationed at the Fort. The significant changes the building and the neighborhood have undergone reveal the pitfalls of viewing border strife as a simple matter of securing a "national border" against have-nots and criminals trying to "get in." Hauer observes that the former 19th-century military border stronghold and the adjacent neighborhood are now,

> a crowded block of cheap stores and fast-food places catering mostly to the Mexican nationals who crossed the bridge daily. Many came to shop and spend American dollars, and more to earn their dollars as maids, store clerks, gardeners, painters, car-

> penters, janitors, and still others to serve as pick-up day laborers paid for work done on the spot. (32)

Similarly, Rafe later observes how on a Monday morning Klail City businesses prepare for the onslaught of "customers streaming across the two bridges by the hundreds . . . ready to spend their money, and the day, on the Texas side" (64). Mind you, not hordes of hardened criminals, but streams of customers and laborers bringing their business and labor to the Texas side. Under careful scrutiny, the text reveals a critique of the unholy dynamics that govern the relationship between militarization on one hand, and on the other the economic asymmetry and the exploitability of Mexican labor and consumption.

The concern with labor control and criminalization of low-wage immigrant labor harks back to previous installments of the *KCDTS* which explore the system of labor control in Texas in the 1930s and 40s that would assure the availability of cheap migrant labor at harvest time. When read side-by-side, novelist Rolando Hinojosa and historian David Montejano provide a harsh account of the practices implemented by the Anglo farmers to achieve these objectives through a wide range of institutionalized, borderline-legal, and outright criminal measures. Montejano shows how the procedures to immobilize Mexican labor changed depending on which level in the administrative hierarchy they were implemented. Criminalization of the workers (mainly through vagrancy laws) proved an effective means of increasing the workers' exploitability. Particularly in *Estampas del Valle*, *El condado de Belken*, and *Claros varones de Belken*, Hinojosa makes frequent references to the plight of the migrant workers, both Texas Mexicans and Mexican nationals, and their annual migration north, using a kind of underground railroad, driving only at night in order to avoid being "immobilized."

A similar composite account of control over civilian populations emerges upon jointly reading Dunn's inquiry into LIC doctrine and Hinojosa's border mystery. The time period Dunn examines, 1978-92, spans three U.S. presidential administrations and is consistent with the clues provided by Rafe's alluded-to-above description of Chip Valencia's office: "Behind Valencia's desk, the usual: a photo of a smiling Chip Valencia shaking hands with Ronald Reagan, another of Valencia with George Bush. The present incumbent was missing" (89). Compare this with the description of Lu Cetina's work place in Barrones, Tamaulipas:

> A portrait of the current president graced two of the walls in the bench-lined reception area; they saw this portrait again along the main hall leading toward Lu Cetina's special office. At forty-three, the youngest president in Mexico's interesting history, his face showed a well-formed mustache over a half-smile. There was a hint of irony in those clear eyes; green eyes which marked him as a North Mexican, a *norteño*. (66-7)

Though never named, the president is obviously Carlos Salinas de Gortari, whose administration lasted from 1988 to 1994. His identity is particularly noteworthy in that Salinas, among many other measures, signed the North American Free Trade Agreement (NAFTA), which had grave consequences for the situation of the labor force on both sides of the Río Grande, as we shall see presently.

The view that the border constitutes a security threat, long before 9/11, is especially noteworthy bearing in mind that in 1992 the U.S., Mexico and Canada signed NAFTA after six years of negotiations. Of the three heads of state who had initiated the process, George H. W. Bush, Brian Mulroney, and Carlos Salinas, only the Mexican President was still in office when NAFTA was finalized and ratified. However, even though Bill Clinton eventually signed the agreement (not without introducing a series of amendments), NAFTA was first and foremost framed in neoliberal terms, and helped "to consolidate and institutionalize the neoliberal economic-reform agenda in Mexico—particularly the sweeping economic changes implemented by the Salinas administration—thereby reinforcing Mexico's status as a lucrative investment site for internationally mobile capital" (Dunn 164).

It begs the question why, in the face of a free trade agreement, which outwardly aims at the international flow of goods, capital, and services, there is any need at all to secure the borders against immigrants looking for work in the U.S.? The notion of "free trade," however, (if "trade" is also meant to include labor) is all but turned on its head in the case of the U.S. and Mexico. In fact, the mechanics of labor "management" are such that it is much more lucrative for the U.S. economy to pit low cost labor on either side of the border against each other. Thus, the Mexican labor force that has situated itself along the border—as in the case of the *maquiladoras*, which almost exclusively exist for, function for, and depend on U.S. markets—enters into a *de facto* competition with the cheap labor offered on the Texas side by undocumented workers. And by way of maintaining this profitable situation, criminalization of workers along the border makes them more vulnerable and exploitable, just as criminalizing them in the 1930s and 40s made it easier to channel them to certain places at harvest time. Likewise, in the current conditions more work for less money can be gotten out of the illegal work force as they are effectively made to compete for jobs, goods, and services with their compatriots across the border (see Dunn 157). To make matters worse, the same mechanisms are at play in the prevention of labor solidarity and the creation of unions that would unite immigration labor and U.S. citizens in similar labor conditions (159).

These are the circumstances that are evoked by Hinojosa through scenes depicting Mexicans "swarming across" the border to spend their dollars and pesos, most likely earned in economically precarious and politically vulnerable circumstances, in businesses in Texas. To expose the facile scapegoating of border crossers even further, other nutshell portraits of cross border existences, much in the vein of Hinojosa's *estampas* in earlier books, populate the novel. There is Daniel Varela, who is described as a clean kid, a hard worker, resident in Barrones and fry cook in Klail, who gets corrupted by the Gómez twins and pays with his life (*Ask a Policeman* 21-22, 25-27, 37-40). Lu Cetina, *la directo-*

ra del orden público, schooled in Klail City, married to a Texas Mexican, actually resides in Texas (23). Israel Buenrostro, Rafe's brother, farms in Soliseño, Mexico (35, see also *Becky and Her Friends*, 152). And then there is perhaps the most sobering, ominous type of border crossing, the steadily increasing number of bodies that are washed up on the Texas side of the river, and who end up in Henry Dietz's morgue, thus generating more "real police work" (10).

A different aspect of the social control wielded over the Mexican-origin population comes into play when scrutinizing Lu Cetina's deceptively cursory remarks concerning the Napoleonic Code (see 25-27). The *directora,* who like Rafe has gone to law school (albeit in Mexico City), points out that the Code Napoleon, the precursor of the Civil Code, is a legacy of the French occupation of Mexico, which provides the foundation of today's legal system. In terms of the provenance of legal systems, large parts of the world today can be divided into countries that either base their jurisprudence on the Civil Code or on the British Common Law tradition. It is well outside my expertise to go into the legal intricacies, so for our purposes suffice it to say that countries following Common Law traditionally entertain a hearty skepticism toward too much government and too much administration and control on the part of a country's executive. Countries following the Civil Code, though, tend to be less squeamish in this respect and focus more on the legal aspects that are conducive to a functioning administrative infrastructure.

Anybody who has ever changed residence from a Civil Code country to a Common Law one will have noticed the differences. For example, in Spain, Germany, and Mexico (within limits),[4] citizens and residents are obligated by law to carry a valid citizenship or residency card at all times, to have it periodically updated, and to register with the local authorities when changing residence for longer periods of time. For U.S. citizens,[5] who are accustomed to the Common Law tradition, this kind of overt, institutionalized control by the state arouses suspicions of right to privacy infringements and civil liberties abuse. Lu Cetina is aware of these differences, as a Mexican lawyer, an officer of the law, and a U.S. resident, and is not surprised when Sam Dorson asks her incredulously "You mean, you've got everybody in Barrones on computer?" (25). Lu Cetina explains that "that wiz kid who just left" computerized the entire population, and adds, by way of explanation: "The Napoleonic Code gives us some leeway, Sam." And yet, it would be extremely naïve to think that U.S. law enforcement agencies today do not avail themselves of the same methods. Whether they would do is as unabashedly as the *directora*, though, is another question altogether.

Ironically, in the context of immigration enforcement, the obligation to carry ID, for all citizens and legal aliens, might facilitate and lessen the immigration service bureaucracy, and would certainly obviate debates like the one surrounding SB Arizona. And while the following remark is purely based on personal observation (though amply corroborated by others who have shared their experiences with me), I would wager that few citizens of Spain, France or Germany will forget their puzzlement and uneasiness upon taking up residence in the U.S. and discovering that they are "carded" more times within the first week of their arrival in the U.S. than in their entire previous lives in their countries of origin. Bankers, bouncers, waiters, store clerks, officials of all types, all ask "to see some ID," but nowhere is this more notorious than in what Leslie Marmon Silko has called the "Border Patrol State." The Native American novelist relies on her personal testimony as a "powerful evidentiary form" to bear witness to the way in which the INS and the Border Patrol infringe "the rights of U.S. citizens to travel freely within the U.S." (Saldívar xi).[6]

In his 1997 *Border Matters: Remapping American Cultural Studies*, José David Saldívar discusses different theoretical approaches to border culture by scrutinizing a variety of cultural expressions along or about the border. Among them are the *corridos* composed and performed by Los Tigres del Norte, and in particular one song entitled "Jaula de oro" (Saldívar 4-5). Saldívar uses this song, "a shattering portrait of an undocumented Mexican father and his family," as a sounding board for his cogitations on the Border Patrol State's "nightmarish culture of surveillance, a profound sense of fear and anxiety," which illegal immigrants in the Southwest are faced with on a daily basis, and, oftentimes in the presence of their U.S.-born children. In his discussion of post-modern California, and the "panopticon barrioscape," Saldívar quotes urban historian Mike Davis, who diagnoses this phenomenon as the "proliferation of 'new repressions in space and movements,'" a condition that according to Saldívar is "doubly felt by the undocumented Mexican worker and his family" (6). It is therefore more than a little ironical that Lu Cetina feels she owes Sam Dorson an explanation for her country's legislature and law enforcement systems: "We're not a police state, Sam, we're just different from you, that's all. The French invade us, and they leave the Napoleonic Code. Tit for tat" (*Ask a Policeman* 27).

"It's a regular Panama"

The notion of LIC doctrine "coming home," as the title of Timothy Dunn's book has it, evokes the general perception in industrial nations that certain socio-political and economic conditions, as well as warfare and armed conflict, are only ever to be found in places at a considerable remove from one's own borders. And yet, Dunn demonstrates compellingly how a doctrine such as LIC is put into operation much closer to home. Accordingly, in the context of militarization and economic disparity, *Ask a Policeman* briefly alludes to the original, and primary, theater of LIC, namely the Central American countries and their one-time U.S.-sponsored dictatorships. Indeed, the D.A. Valencia's displaying his ignorance of Costa Rica's military status is not the only occasion that warrants mentioning a Central American country in *Ask a Policeman*. Costa Rica's neighbor to the south, Panama, surfaces when the homicide squad is investigating the Gómezes' banking activities and active accounts in Belken County. Along the way, they discover that in the original inquiry into Lisandro Gómez' assets, some twenty years earlier, Treasury had neglected to check if Lee had any accounts in the Valley. "The money was so close to home someone reasoned that Lee would never be so stupid as to leave money in the local banks," Rafe ventures (60). In the absence of a computerized database, the detectives make do with the *Valley-wide Yellow Pages* in order to canvass all the Valley banks. Sam Dorson can't suppress a whistle when he discovers that "For a place that ranks as one of the poorest in the U.S., the Valley has fifty-two banks. It's a regular Panama" (51).

Similar to some Central American or Caribbean tax and banking havens, the Valley region has generated enormous profits on both sides of the border but the wealth has not been passed on to the general population. Especially at the time the novel is set, as Dunn elaborates:

> Although the border was a dividing line between first—and third—world nations, social infrastructure (e.g. education, housing, water services, and environmental cleanup and protection) on both sides of the river was notoriously lacking. On the Mexican side, the vast working-class population in the northern cities received public services that were noticeably inferior to services received by their counterparts in the major interior cities of Mexico, despite the general economic dynamism and relatively higher income level of the northern cities. Furthermore, for most people in this group, their relatively superior income was insufficient to meet their basic consumption and housing needs. Meanwhile, although communities on the U.S. side of the border were far wealthier than Mexican border cities, poverty (as per U.S. federal guidelines) was nonetheless extensive, and particularly concentrated among the Mexican-origin population. For example, the *Lower Rio Grande Valley of Texas, which is overwhelmingly Mexican American, has consistently had some of the highest rates of poverty in the United States*. (161; my emphasis)

The allusion to Panama is not gratuitous. Rather, Panama was regarded the "western hemisphere's primary tax haven for many years," until its dictator Noriega was removed from power by President Bush because of his drug trafficking ties (Atherton). In the six years prior to his removal, though, his totalitarian regime was tolerated and even abetted by the U.S. precisely in exchange for services rendered to the U.S. in the pursuit of LIC doctrine in the region (see also Dunn 65). In his typical, roundabout fashion, Hinojosa sprinkles snippets of information throughout his text which, when assembled and put into the geopolitical context by the perceptive reader, amount to a crushing verdict: the Valley is among the poorest places in the U.S., though with the richest crooks, with a profusion of banks like Panama, and in need of an army the size of Costa Rica—if Costa Rica had an army, that is, and Chip Valencia had his way.

Mexico's War?

Perhaps the most uncomfortable query into simplistic, commonly accepted, border topoi deals with those passages in *Ask a Policeman* that point to the unfortunate mechanism that has the border region locked in a downward spiral. I am aided in my reflection by another *60 Minutes* report, "The War Next Door: Mexico's Drug War," which aired on March 1, 2009. The feature persistently refers to the conflict, that has long since crossed the border, as "Mexico's war," even though Janet Napolitano tells *60 Minutes'* Anderson Cooper right at the beginning that "the stakes are high" for both Mexican and U.S. citizens in this "war." The investigating journalists actually stress that the drug cartels have expanded into the U.S. for some time now. And while in 2009 the 700 drug-related U.S. arrests seem few compared to the 46,000 made in Mexico, it appears that Janet Napolitano is a little behind the times when she says that U.S. law enforcement has "contingency plans *should it* [the war] actually escalate and spill over" (*my emphasis*). However, consistent with Low Intensity Conflict doctrine, the really decisive stakes the U.S. has in this war are not arrests and casualties. According to Eduardo Medina-Mora, Mexico's Attorney General, the fundamental contributions the U.S. is making to the war are: demand for drugs, cash in abundance, and

90% of all weapons used in drug-related crimes in Mexico. "It's a service possibility," he adds.

The lengths Mexican and U.S. criminals are willing to go to in order to get their hands on assault weapons is vividly depicted in *Ask a Policeman* when a gang made up of thugs from both sides of the border crashes a truck into the front of a Flora pawn shop during business hours, hitting several customers, then backing up and running over the victims repeatedly to get deeper into the store room (127). What they are after are not, as one might perhaps expect, pawned objects that can be turned into cash. To the detectives' consternation it emerges that the pawn shop sells brand new automatic assault weapons by the crate-full, and the crooks drove their truck far into the store so that they could load the crates directly inside and drive off with their haul (132-34). Readers familiar with previous novels in Hinojosa's *KCDTS* are unlikely to miss the fine irony with which the incident is laced, compounded by the fact that it occurs in Flora of all places. In Belken County lore, Flora is the town where things are always done slightly differently. Flora is a town of rogues and rascals who habitually set themselves up in their attempt to be smarter than everyone else. The pawn shop incident is a case in point. If one sells military hardware in a border town, one cannot be too fussy about the clientele, and it is only a matter of time until the clients start asking themselves why they are spending their hard-earned drug dollars on the weaponry if they can simply steal it.

Eduardo Medina-Mora is loathe to utter the word "blame" in front of the CBS cameras, but it is the reporters who conclude that the drug cartels "have the police outgunned" with grenade launchers, hand-grenades, automatic assault rifles and sniper rifles, overwhelmingly acquired from the U.S. And when asked about the reasons for the rampant corruption in Mexico, the Attorney General seizes the opportunity to point out, again without leveling any direct criticism, that it is largely made possible through the drug cartels' "tremendous economic power and power of intimidation," both directly attributable to the drug demand in the U.S. and the weaponry procured from U.S. arms dealers.

"The second amendment was never designed to arm foreign criminal groups," Medina-Mora says, and given the scope of U.S. involvement, Napolitano risks appearing callous when she replies "I haven't thought that far," to Anderson Cooper's question whether the U.S. government has considered renewing the assault weapons ban that expired in 2004. Instead, in a veiled endorsement of the National Rifle Association's slogan "It's not guns that kill people . . . ," Napolitano declares that she is working with U.S. customs and the ATF (Bureau of Tobacco, Alcohol, and Firearms) to find out "*who* is putting these unlawful guns into the hands of the traffickers who are using them to murder people" (*my emphasis*).

Tragedy averted?

If in my foregoing analysis *Ask a Policeman* has emerged as a scathing rebuttal of recent ideological constructions of a border-crisis narrative, this is to large degree attributable to reading the mystery novel jointly with studies that explore the geopolitical circumstances in the border region during the late 1980s and early 90s. The border conflict is usually framed in sensationalist media coverage that has us believe that this is a national Mexican conflict that threatens to spill over the border both in the shape of drugs, crime, or humans desperately seeking to secure their livelihood. The creeping militarization of the border, compellingly explored and denounced by Timothy Dunn as an integral aspect of Low Intensity Conflict doctrine, is opposed in *Ask a Policeman* consistently and convincingly to "real police work": the daily grind and unglamorous grunt work in the squad room, the detectives barely staying awake, drinking coffee, leaning against filing cabinets, poring over case files, and thumbing through telephone directories when they are not compiling evidence lists on word processors. All-too-readily accepted border platitudes are expertly and incisively demolished one by one. Border crossing in Belken County and Tamaulipas is a two-way street and people travel in either direction to go to work, to shop, to visit, to farm, to do police work, to take revenge, to ask forgiveness, and, yes, to commit crimes and smuggle drugs, too. Tamaulipas law enforcement boasts a modern police force with crime labs, European-style centralized computer databases, and an incorruptible female police chief who is cleaning house knowing she has the backing of stakeholders on both sides of the border.

On the Texas side, the Belken County Homicide Squad doggedly pursue their perps while other competing law enforcement agencies vie for a spot at the "federal trough," which is "longer than the Rio Grande," though apparently, like the river it all but dries up before reaching the Gulf (33). Thus, the platitude of the U.S. as the "home of the free" is seriously questioned by drawing a picture of a Border Patrol State that engages in surveillance of illegal immigrants and legal Mexican-origin people alike. And finally, *Ask a Policeman* leaves no doubt as to where the drug lords' military-style weaponry comes from, and which are the channels and methods of procuring them. And so the dynamics of cash flow, violence, corruption, intimidation, bribery and militarization come full circle.

In the face of this bleak picture, it comes as a relief that at the end of the day Hinojosa invokes poetic license to issue a hopeful message appropriately couched in imagery of tropical storms to be weathered. From the first line of the novel, and throughout the rest of the narrative, a consistent climate of hot, humid, hurricane-season atmosphere prevails. And indeed, (almost like LIC doctrine) hurricane Ella gathers force south of Mexico, makes landfall on the coast of Texas and floods areas "south of Houston and Corpus Christi" (53). But then, about three quarters into the story, Sammie Jo reports to Rafe: "Tragedy was averted . . . It's moved up the coast toward Galveston" (159). Only two weeks later, "the third hurricane of the season stalled in the Gulf, and the Valley sweltered under the heat and humidity" (192). It is the morning of the day José Antonio, one of the wanted Gómez brothers, is cornered by the police in a Barrones brothel. And again, "tragedy is averted" although the collar goes awry, and Lu Cetina is held by the crazed José Antonio at point blank range before turning the gun on himself. As with an earlier, related collar at the Flamingo hotel, the vengeance by the son of the betrayed gangster Salinas, and Chip Valencia's armament project, tragedy is eventually averted owing to the police officers' efforts to de-escalate, to forgo revenge, to exercise patience and moderation in law enforcement. The momentary calm notwithstanding, other hurricanes will have to be weathered, and Judge Garza, after shelving Chip Valencia's armament budget, battens down the hatches against the next storm (179).

Notes

[1] Subsequently, page numbers in parentheses with no additional information refer to citations from the most recently identified creative or critical work. In this case the reference is taken from *Ask a Policeman*.

[2] The writers of the cult fantasy TV series *Lost* must have been thinking of SBInet when they created the sonar fence built by the Dharma Corporation to keep out the smoke monster.

[3] See also my discussion of the novel's title, the English music hall song, and its significance in that British bobbies patrol with a watch, a whistle, but without firearms (Zilles 71-72).

[4] At present, in Mexico a legal document with the CURP ("clave única de registro de población") is not strictly mandatory, though practically indispensable. See this official Mexican web site designed for the Mexican citizens to easily familiarize with their CURP number: http://www.emexico.gob.mx/index.php?option=com_flexicontent&view=items&cid=3575&id=8346. Interestingly, it's precisely Lu Cetina's State of Tamaulipas that has started a pilot program to introduce a national Mexican ID card (https://www.tractis.com/contracts/104841083/compare/29/28).

[5] Laws are different for U.S. citizens residing in Louisiana, for obvious reasons, as Kowalski points out to Blanche in *A Streetcar Named Desire*.

[6] I have the questionable privilege to share Leslie Marmon Silko's experience. During my stays in the borderlands, both as an exchange student in New Mexico and traveling in Texas on a research grant, I have been stopped and "carded" by the Border Patrol checking passengers of motor coaches and cars.

Works Cited

Atherton, Mark. "Q&A: Why Panama Attracts Wealthy Foreigners." *The Times Online.* Dec. 5, 2007. Web. Oct. 3, 2010.

Davis, Mike. *City of Quartz: Excavating the Future in Los Angeles*. London: Verso, 1990. Print.

Dunn, Timothy. *The Militarization of the U.S.-Mexico Border, 1978-1992: Low-Intensity Conflict Doctrine Comes Home*. Austin: Center for Mexican American Studies, 1996. Print.

González-Berry, Erlinda. Introduction. *El condado de Belken: Klail City.* By Rolando Hinojosa. Tempe: Bilingual Press/ Editorial Bilingüe, 1994. 1-20. Print.

Hinojosa, Rolando. *Ask a Policeman: A Rafe Buenrostro Mystery*. Houston: Arte Público Press, 1998. Print.

___. *Becky and Her Friends*. Houston: Arte Público Press, 1990. Print.

___. *Claros varones de Belken: Fair Gentlemen of Belken County*. Trans. by Julia Cruz. Tempe: Bilingual Press/Editorial Bilingüe, 1986. Print.

___. *El condado de Belken: Klail City*. Clásicos Chicanos/Chicano Classics 8. Tempe: Bilingual Press/Editorial Bilingüe, 1994. Print.

___. *Estampas del Valle.* Tempe: Bilingual Press/Editorial Bilingüe, 1994. Print.

___. *Partners in Crime: A Rafe Buenrostro Mystery*. Houston: Arte Público Press, 1985. Print.

Lloyd, David. "Adulteration and the Nation." *An Other Tongue: Nation and Ethnicity in the Linguistic Borderlands*. Ed. Alfred Arteaga. Durham: Duke University Press, 1994. 53-92. Print.

"Montejano, David. *Anglos and Mexicans in the Making of Texas: 1836-1986*. Austin: University of Texas Press, 1987. Print.

Pilkington, Ed. "Arizona Immigration Law Blocked by Judge in Temporary Victory for Obama." *The Guardian*. July 28, 2010. Web. Oct. 3, 2010.

Saldívar, José David. *Border Matters: Remapping American Cultural Studies*. Berkeley: University of California Press, 1997. Print.

"The War Next Door: Mexico's Drug War." *60 Minutes*. CBS, Mar. 1, 2009. Television.

"Watching the Border." *60 Minutes*. CBS, Jan. 10, 2010. Television.

Zilles, Klaus. *Rolando Hinojosa: A Reader's Guide*. Albuquerque: University of New Mexico Press, 2001. Print.

Interview with Rolando Hinojosa: His Doctoral-Study Years (1963-69) at the University of Illinois

Stephen Miller
Texas A&M University

The following interview with Rolando Hinojosa took place in September 2010. The main topic addressed: his doctoral-study years (1963-69) at the University of Illinois.

1. *SM: Why did you decide to do Ph.D. studies in Spanish?*

   RHS: I'd majored in Spanish literature for my baccalaureate degree and worked for some nine years before starting graduate work. The intent, then, was to earn the doctorate degree, to teach and to write, something I'd been doing since high school. I thought I'd teach in some small college and concentrate on my writing. Of course, Burn's words on the best laid plans of mice and men came into play.

2. *SM: Why the University of Illinois after the University of Texas at Austin and New Mexico Highlands University?*

   RHS: Why Illinois for graduate work? The head of Modern Languages at Highlands was a U of I graduate, and he thought I would do well there. I'd also written to Ohio State, which offered a teaching assistantship, and interviewed at the Rackham School of Graduate Studies at Ann Arbor, and so on, but Illinois was my first choice and I went to Urbana.

3. *SM: During the period of the war in Vietnam, many combat vets who began graduate study in language and literature found it difficult to focus on such study and dropped out from their doctoral studies. Did you, as a combat vet of Korea, have any similar situation?*

RHS: I have a very good friend and former colleague, a West Point graduate, who served in Vietnam; disillusioned, he resigned his commission and eventually earned his degree at Tulane. With him it was a matter of dedication. Graduate school is not for everyone, and those who dropped did so because they may have wanted to do something else with their lives.

In 1963, when I had finished my M.A. and a teaching stint at Highlands, jobs were plentiful as they were in the late sixties up to 1974. When I was finishing my thesis and during my MLA meetings with various chairs and heads of department, I, along with those who received their degrees in '68 or '69, had a wide choice. I was offered a position at Clemson, The Citadel, SMU, Syracuse, and so on. I chose Trinity University in San Antonio.

4. *SM: Returning to the University of Illinois. Was the department then called the "Department of Spanish, Italian and Portuguese" when you were there?*

RHS: It was called that and remains so.

5. *SM: Would you talk about your experience in the Department?*

RHS: Starting with Portuguese. I'd taken a year of Portuguese at UT and then roomed a semester with two Brazilians from São Paulo. The deal was I'd teach them English and they, in turn, would teach me Portuguese; no such thing, we spoke Portuguese all the time. When they left, after a year or so, they gave me some ten albums of Brazilian sambas, marchas, and country music. I kept up my reading of Brazilian as well as Continental Portuguese and have done so since. I was also assigned a course in beginning Portuguese during my third year at Illinois. Latin was a requirement as were the old standbys: French and German or French and Russian. Instead of taking an exam in German, I decided to take the two semester course. As for French, after a six-week study, I took the exam and thus completed the language requirements. No credit was given for any of the languages; they were requirements and that was that. The focus was on study and research. Doctorate students were allowed to take only two courses per semester; the teaching requirements were these: teaching two courses in the fall and one in the spring for half-time work, or, two courses each term for a full-time assistantship. I majored in Peninsular literature and minored in Latin American history, something I'd done in the two previous degrees. I was lucky to have taken a course with Charles Newton, a renowned Latin American historian; he sat in the sixteen-hour written examination as well as in my defense of the thesis.

6. *SM: Would you talk more about your time of course work at Illinois, especially your experience with Luis Leal and William Shoemaker?*

RHS: At Highlands I had read Leal's work on the theory of the short story and wanted to work under him. The head, William Shoemaker, called me in and assigned me a second course; the time coincided with Leal's class and I transferred to Merlin Forster's course in Portuguese. Merlin had worked with Leal during his graduate career. That was the first semester. Once again I enrolled in Leal's class and again Shoemaker called me in. As a result, I was a two-thirds assistant; more money, but again I had to drop Leal's course. During my second year, Shoemaker said I was to sponsor the Sigma Delta Pi Society which I did. As we talked in the hallway, Luis overheard us—Shoemaker had said he needed for me to be close by, and Leal said I could share his office. And that was it; we were office mates where, when he was absent, I would answer the calls; he was much in demand. This brought us closer and from then on, the two of us and Don Marcos Morínigo, a first-class linguist, would go for coffee at the Vatican, our name for the Newman Club. The chats included national politics, jokes, and literature and linguistics. Talk about luck!

With Galdós as my favorite writer and with Shoemaker as a renowned Galdosista, I had to study with him. Old Bill would assign the thesis subjects; I didn't care, but luck was with me since he wanted me to write on money in Galdós and, more importantly, I had always wanted to study Galdós's use of it in the plot, the characterization, and the setting. I'd read *La Fontana de Oro*, *El audaz*, *Gloria* and *Doña Perfecta* and some *Episodios nacionales*: *Gerona*, *Trafalgar*, etc. The latter [historical] novels served to widen my knowledge of the history of the Peninsula. I taught two classes, directed nineteen sections of third semester Spanish, and read the *Novelas contemporáneas* and all manner of critical work on Galdós. In the fifth year, I continued to teach two classes and to direct the nineteen sections, and I began to write the thesis.

I consulted with Shoemaker once, and that was it. I finished it in the Spring of 1968; Shoemaker was in Spain that semester, so I left the thesis on his desk. Upon his return, I made some changes, turned it into the College of Liberal Arts which then sent it to the Graduate School. And that was it.

7. *SM: Were there any tensions among the faculty rooted in hierarchical jousting among specialists in Peninsular, Latin American, Mexican and U.S. Hispanic fields?*

RHS: There were not tensions in regard to the many fields. Jim Crosby, the world-wide expert on Quevedo headed the Golden Age with aid of an assistant professor and two associate professors. Luis and Merlin headed the Latin American field with Merlin doing double-duty with Mexican and Portuguese literatures. Angelina Pietringeli was in charge of the Italian section and everyone—everyone—spoke Spanish, Portuguese, or Italian in Lincoln Hall. The only times we heard or spoke English would be at parties. Twentieth-century Mexican-American literature was in its infancy, and I was 1) away from the Southwest, 2) finishing my work on Galdós. Added to which I had no time to write fiction, but that didn't matter; I was reading like mad and that's what writers do.

8. *SM: Anything else about faculty, fellow students, visiting speakers and writers who helped create the atmosphere of the Department?*

RHS: At the beginning of my third year, when I became an Instructor, I was invited to eat with the senior faculty whenever we had writers and scholars on campus, such as Ana María Matute and Ignacio Aldecoa who were in Indiana that year, or Díaz Plaja, Cela, and so on, as well as Mexican and Argentine writers of note. Shoemaker made sure as head, not chairman, he met with Dean Rogers frequently and hence our ample funding.

By the bye, Shoemaker said he forgot to give me a raise my fifth year. It didn't matter, I had strong letters from him, from Luis, from Don Marcos, and so on. Those letters were worth more than the raise. No complaints from me; Shoemaker's secretary, however, was embarrassed, but I told her to forget it. She had nothing to do with it, poor thing. Too, I'd reccived offers from chairmen before MLA; this, I'm sure, upon the recommendation of Bill Shoemaker. I thanked them, but we were not leaving Illinois until the dissertation was finished.

About the Editors

STEPHEN MILLER is a full professor of Spanish and Hispanic Studies at Texas A&M University in College Station, Texas. He is the author of *El mundo de Galdós* (1983), *Del realismo/naturalismo al modernismo* (1993) and *Galdós gráfico (1861-1907) (2001).* In 2001, he edited facsimile editions of the five Galdosian sketchbooks, including the satiric graphic narratives *Gran teatro de la pescadería, Las Canarias* and *Atlas zoológico.* Miller co-edited two previous collections of essays: *Critical Studies on Gonzalo Torrente Ballester* (1988) and *Critical Studies on Armando Palacio Valdés* (1993). In addition to editing special numbers of journals on Hispanic Nobel Prize winners, "*materia novelable*" in contemporary Spanish narrative, the last decade of Torrente's Ballester's production (the "*novelas esquemáticas*"), and on Galdós, Pérez-Reverte and the Spanish War of Independence from the French, Miller is presently preparing books on a theory of illustrated narrative and on Hinojosa's practice of bilingual biculturalism.

JOSÉ PABLO VILLALOBOS is an associate professor of Spanish in the Department of Hispanic Studies at Texas A&M University in College Station, Texas. His research and teaching interests encompass U.S./Mexico Border Studies, Latin American Literature and Latino Studies. He is the author of *La imaginación genealógica: Herencia y escritura en México* (2006) and numerous articles on Mexican literature and Mexico/U.S. border literature and culture.

Contributors

Joan Parmer Barrett is a Senior Lecturer of Spanish at Baylor University in Waco, Texas. Her recent presentations include: "La voz minoritaria como conservadora de la cultura: La resistencia por medio de los ritos pasivos en los testimonios de Rigoberta Menchú, Juan Francisco Manzano y Erasmo Palma" at OSU (2012); "De Lumholtz 1890-98 hacia el siglo XX: Perfil de los Tarahumara" at UMHB (2012); and, "Don Erasmo Palma: Hombre del tercer espacio" at UT Austin (2011). She has networked for decades with U.S. and Mexican medical professionals to aid the indigenous Tarahumara of the Sierra Madre. She is currently a Doctoral Candidate at Texas A&M University.

Eduardo Espina is Professor of Hispanic Studies at Texas A&M University. Among his many local, national and international honors figure the Uruguayan Premio Nacional de Ensayo (1996, 2000), the Texas A&M University Association of Former Students Distinguished Teaching Award (2007), and a Guggenheim Fellowship (2010-11). He is the author of eight volumes of literary and cultural criticism, editor of two volumes of scholarly essays, and author of eleven volumes of his poetry. Two of these volumes, *La caza nupcial* (Buenos Aires, 1993) and *El cutis patrio* (Mexico City, 2006), have been re-edited respectively in Jalapa (1997) and Buenos Aires (2009). An anthology of his poetry, *Quiero escribir pero me sale Espina*, will be published in 2013. He is co-founding editor of *HPR* (*Hispanic Poetry Review*).

At the University of California, Santa Barbara **María Herrera-Sobek** is Associate Vice Chancellor for Diversity, Equity and Academic Policy, Luis Leal Endowed Chair (1997-2009) and Professor of Chicana/o Studies. She has taught at UC Irvine, Harvard and Stanford. Among her books figure: *The Bracero Experience: Elitelore Versus Folklore* (1979); *The Mexican Corrido*; *Northward Bound: The Mexican Immigrant Experi-*

ence in Ballad and Song (1993); *Chicano Folklore: A Handbook* (2006); and, *Celebrating Latino Folklore: An Encyclopedia of Cultural Traditions* (2012). In addition to a volume containing her own poetry, *Three Times a Woman* (1989), she has edited or co-edited fourteen books, published over 130 articles and book chapters, been guest editor for journals based in the Canary Islands, Germany, Taiwan and Turkey.

Nicolás Kanellos is the Brown Foundation Professor of Hispanic Studies at the University of Houston. He is founder and editor of *The Americas Review* (formerly *Revista Chicano-Riqueña*), and is founder and Director of Arte Público Press as well as of the national research program Recovering the U.S. Hispanic Literary Project. He is the author or editor of twenty-five volumes on U.S. Hispanic literature and culture, as well as the author of more than 100 scholarly articles and chapters. His most recent book is *Hispanic Immigrant Literature: El Sueño de Retorno* (2011) which won the PEN Southwest Award for Non-Fiction.

José E. Limón is a native of Rolando Hinojosa's south Texas. He is currently the Director of the Institute for Latino Studies and holds the Julian Samora Endowed Chair in Latino Studies at the University of Notre Dame where he also serves as Professor of American Literature. His most recent book is *Américo Paredes: Culture and Critique* (2012). He is currently at work on another book manuscript, *Neither Friends, Nor Strangers: Mexicans and Anglos in the Literary Making of Texas,* from which his contribution to this volume is derived.

After a career as a Marine Corps infantry officer which spanned twenty years and thirty-six countries, **Mark David McGraw** entered the doctoral program in Hispanic Studies at Texas A&M University in 2008. He is the translator of Joseph Avski s novel *Heart of Scorpio* and has published wartime memoirs, creative non-fiction pieces, short stories, poetry, translations and scholarly articles in English and Spanish. Beginning in the fall of 2013, he will be an Assistant Professor of Spanish at Ouachita Baptist University in Arkadelphia, Arkansas.

Stephen Miller is Professor of Hispanic Studies at Texas A&M University. His research centers on Spanish realist narrative since the 19th century. He is author of *El mundo de Galdós* (1983), *Del realismo/naturalismo al modernismo* (1993), and *Galdós gráfico (1861-1907)* (2001). He is editor of the five Galdosian sketchbooks, including three graphic narratives, in 2001 facsimile volumes. He is co-editor of two previous volumes of scholarly essays on Torrente Ballester and Armando Palacio Valdés. Presently he is preparing books on a theory of illustrated narrative and on Hinojosa's practice of Spanish-English bilingual biculturalism.

Alejandro Morales, the son of Mexican immigrants, was born in Montebello, California. He grew up in the bordering Simons, the company town of the Simons Brick Yard #3, which is the setting of his novel *The Brick People* (1988). This novel inspired the eponymous documentary film of 2012. Morales' B.A. is from California State University, Los Angeles, and his M.A. and Ph.D. from Rutgers University. He is currently a professor in the Department of Chicano/Latino Studies at the University of California, Irvine, and was awarded the Luis Leal Award for Distinction in Chicano/Latino Literature in 2007 from UC Santa Barbara. Other literary works by him include: *Caras Viejas y Vino Nuevo* (1975); *La Verdad sin Voz* (1979); *Reto in Paraíso* (1983); *The Rag Doll Plagues* (1992); *Barrio on the Edge* (1997); *Waiting to Happen* (2001); *Pequeña Nación* (2005); and *The Captain of All These Men of Death* (2008). He is currently working on a new novel titled *River of Angels.*

María Esther Quintana Millamoto is an Assistant Professor of Hispanic Studies at Texas A&M University. She is author of *Los pícaros, bufones y cronistas de "Maluco: la novela de los descubridores*" (2008). Her second book, *Madres e hijas melancólicas en las novelas de crecimiento de autoras latinas*, is currently in press. She has also published critical essays in refereed journals in Mexico, Cuba, Spain and the U.S. Her teaching fields are Hispanic Literatures, U.S. Latino Literature, Women's Studies, Latin American culture and Spanish language.

Rogelio Sáenz is Dean of the College of Public Policy and Peter Flawn Professor of Demography at the University of Texas at San Antonio. A native of Mercedes, Texas, Sáenz received his Ph.D. in sociology from Iowa State University. He has written extensively in the areas of demography, Latina/os, race/ethnic relations, inequality, and immigration. Sáenz is co-editor of *Latina/os in the United States: Changing the Face of América*, co-author of *Latino Issues: A Reference Handbook*, and author of a population bulletin titled *Latinos in the United States 2010.* Sáenz is currently the President-Elect of the Southwestern Social Science Association and is also Chair of the Council of the Inter-University Consortium for Political and Social Research (ICPSR).

Travis Sorenson, translator of the Espina chapter in this volume, is an assistant professor of Spanish at the University of Central Arkansas. He received his BA in Spanish from Utah State University, his MA in Translation from the Monterey Institute of International Studies, and his PhD in Hispanic Studies/Spanish Linguistics from Texas A&M University. He has worked as a translator for fifteen years, both full-time for the U.S. Government and as a freelancer. In addition to translation, his teaching and research interests include dialectology and sociolinguistics.

José Pablo Villalobos is Associate Professor of Hispanic Studies at Texas A&M University. His research and teaching interests encompass U.S./Mexico Border Studies, Latin American Literature and Latino Studies. He is the author of *La imaginación genealógica: Herencia y escritura en México* (2006), and numerous articles on Mexican literature and U.S./Mexico border literature and culture. Currently, he is Book Review Editor for the journal *Camino Real. Estudios de las hispanidades norteamericanas*, published at the Universidad de Alacalá in Spain.

The multi-lingual **Klaus Zilles** is a graduate of Heidelberg University, and teaches at the Ramon Llull University in Barcelona. His research is in border studies, media studies, critical theory, and English as a second language for speakers of Spanish and Catalonian. He is the author of *Rolando Hinojosa. A Reader's Guide* (2001), and co-editor of the anthology "*En la frontera*"*: i migliori raconti della narrativa chicana* (2008).